ACTRESSES AND WHORES

The image of the actress as prostitute has haunted the theatrical profession since women first went on the stage. Kirsten Pullen explores the history of this connection both in the cultural imagination and in real life. She shows, through case studies of women working in Britain and the United States between the seventeenth and twentieth centuries, that some women have drawn on the dual tradition of "whore" as radical and victim to carve out a space for female sexual agency. Female performers from Elizabeth Boutell and Charlotte Charke to Mae West redefined gender identity and appropriate female sexuality. Pullen integrates substantial archival research and interviews with working prostitutes with a consideration of feminist and cultural perspectives on the myth and reality of the actress/whore. This highly original study offers many new insights to theatre historians and scholars of cultural, social, and gender studies.

KIRSTEN PULLEN is Assistant Professor of English Studies at the University of Calgary.

ACTRESSES AND WHORES: ON STAGE AND IN SOCIETY

KIRSTEN PULLEN

CAMBRIDGE
UNIVERSITY PRESS

PUBLISHED BY THE PRESS SYNDICATE OF THE UNIVERSITY OF CAMBRIDGE
The Pitt Building, Trumpington Street, Cambridge CB2 1RP, United Kingdom

CAMBRIDGE UNIVERSITY PRESS
The Edinburgh Building, Cambridge, CB2 2RU, UK
40 West 20th Street, New York, NY 10011-4211, USA
477 Williamstown Road, Port Melbourne, VIC 3207, Australia
Ruiz de Alarcón 13, 28014 Madrid, Spain
Dock House, The Waterfront, Cape Town 8001, South Africa
http://www.cambridge.org

First published 2005

Printed in the United Kingdom at the University Press, Cambridge

Typeset in 11/12.5 pt Adobe Garamond [PND]

A Catalogue record for this book is available from the British Library

ISBN 0 521 83341 8 hardback
ISBN 0 521 54102 6 paperback

For Josh Heuman

Contents

List of Illustrations

Acknowledgments

Like all books, mine is the culmination of conversations with friends, colleagues, and mentors. I am grateful to all those who shared drinks, books, pound cake, and brunches where we wrote notes on napkins – the social and scholarly activities that make us academics. Henrik Borgstrom and Juliette Willis made important contributions to my early thinking and writing. The book began as a dissertation, and the brilliant members of my dissertation writing group, Jessica Berson, Ann Linden, Carrie Sandahl, Lisa Yaszek, and especially Jami Moss contributed a great deal; if there are sentences that sing, phrases that ring true, analyses that elegantly argue, they were probably worked through by one or more of these remarkable women. At the University of Wisconsin-Madison, Professors Julie D'Acci, Jack Kugelmass, Michele Hilmes, and Philip Zarrilli generously gave their time and energy to different phases of this project. My advisor Mike Vanden Heuvel and committee member Sally Banes provided examples of the kind of scholar and teacher I hope someday to become; their personal and academic support made this book possible. Though I bene-fited and borrowed from all these people, any mistakes and omissions are my own.

This book also owes an enormous debt to the sex workers whose stories I include. These women and men agreed to tell me their experiences working in prostitution, a decision often fraught with emotional and possibly physical peril. Because they lived, worked, and even studied in the same small city where I wrote my dissertation, their contributions were especially generous. My interview subjects were concerned with anonymity, and their names, agency names, and identifying details have been changed in order to preserve their privacy. I hope only they will recognize themselves in these pages.

As the dissertation became a book, editor Victoria Cooper was unfailing in her support and accommodation. She chose reviewers who made thoughtful and helpful comments. The book is much stronger because my anonymous reviewers indicated productive avenues of research, thinking, and theorizing. I am grateful for their otherwise unacknowledged help. I also thank Kristine Krueger at The Academy of Motion Picture Arts and Sciences, Erin Pauwels and Marcus Risdell at the New York and London offices of the David Garrick Club, Kathleen Coleman at The Harvard Theatre Collection, and Tim Bower for help locating and securing permission to use several of the illustrations included; Maartje Scheltens at Cambridge also deserves thanks for her help.

My sister, Heidi Pullen, and her partner, Clark Stroupe, provided citations and vacations. My parents, Carl and Norma Pullen, offered unwavering emotional, intellectual, and financial support. I owe them more than I can ever repay. Finally, Josh Heuman has lived and breathed this book with me. Though not always graciously accepted, his suggestions were always gratefully applied. I could never have written this book without him, and reward his dedication to my project by dedicating it to him.

CHAPTER I

Prostitution, performance, and Mae West: speaking from the whore position

> *There's a chance of rising to the top of every profession... Why not?*
> *Others do it, why can't I? Why can't you? When I think of the dames*
> *riding around in swell limousines, buying imported gowns, living at the*
> *swellest hotels, terrible looking janes, too... It's all a question of getting some*
> *guy to pay for the certain business, that's all.*
>
> (West *Sex* 40–41)

Poured into a sequined 1890s gown, pinwheel hat dipped over one eye,
diamonds glittering at her neck and wrists, Mae West beckons. Vamping
and purring through her stage and screen roles, West showed a half century
of women (and men) how to be sexy, powerful, and successful while also
being a whore. Dressed in beautiful gowns, surrounded by servants, and
inhabiting lush boudoirs, West made millions laugh, cry, and envy. In her
1920s and 1930s stage and screen roles, she played a prostitute entertainer
who always got her man. In addition, West exercised an enormous amount
of control over her career and image, writing dialogue for her films and
publishing her autobiography. West is the descendant of early female
performers who struggled to influence their reception; at the same time,
her version of prostitution foreshadows contemporary prostitutes' rights
activists who argue for the legitimization of sex work. She's simultaneously
a camp figure and hypersexual throwback too whorish for incorporation
into discourses of self-empowerment. Ultimately, West defies simple categorization: is she an agent of sexual expression, or is she a victim of a
patriarchal discourse that determines a woman's worth by her body? The
same question is posed by the prostitute: is she a feminist or a whore?

This book tries to reconcile those two competing discourses. On one hand,
the prostitute is a victim: denied sexual agency she is also denied a voice, a
place in history, an identity as an autonomous woman. On the other hand,
though vilified, the prostitute can speak for and from the margins. Though
these two positions are not easily reconciled, some women have drawn on this
dual tradition of victim and radical to carve a space for female sexual agency.

Historically as well as in the contemporary moment, the whore[1] has been silenced or ignored. This project attempts to recover whore stories, to bring these narratives into sharper focus. I argue here that particular women incorporate the tradition of transgression and marginalization in order to name their own experiences. Ultimately, the whore position may allow women a space for agency; performance is the strategy by which they expand that position to offer alternative narratives of female sexuality and experience.

The stories I tell are whore stories, but they are also the stories of female performers. Betty Boutell, Charlotte Charke, Lydia Thompson, and Mae West worked as actresses; as I demonstrate below, they used their perform-ances to engage questions of gender identity and appropriate female sexuality. The prostitutes included, whether the eighteenth-century madam Margaret Leeson or the 1990s escorts working in Madison, Wisconsin, are also perfor-mers, albeit in less standard ways. Their narratives indicate that they perform for their clients and their reading audiences, acting out a version of femininity that simultaneously masks and projects subjectivity. While acknowledging that conflating the prostitute and the actress risks flattening out important differences between their specific performance contexts, I want to insist on its polemic and analytic value. Occupying one identity without the other is impossible and indescribable for the women I consider here.

The enduring tie between prostitution and performance, between actresses and whores, tells a great deal about Western cultural myths of women and sexuality. Though this is not a comprehensive history of either prostitution or actresses, the case histories I've chosen crystallize moments when some of these myths were vigorously debated. At these moments, I argue, the whore stigma was used to limit female experience and expression. As prostitutes' rights activist Priscilla Alexander points out, women are kept from "freely exploring, experiencing, and naming their own sexuality lest they be called whore" ("Prostitution" 184), and the boundaries between women and whores are policed in order to constrain the activities of all women. At particular historical moments, the body of the actress (assumed to be an object onto which male desires were projected) and the body of the prostitute (assumed to be an object onto which male desires were enacted) slipped discursively into one: whore/actress. Though traditionally this "slip" is viewed as detrimental, I argue that Boutell, Leeson, Charke, Thompson, and West accepted the whore stigma precisely to construct their own narratives. By turning the accusation on its head, these women provided new images and new words to construct female sexuality.

The trope of the actress/whore pervades histories of prostitution. These histories, whether medical, social, or feminist, often take as their starting point the Greek *auletrides*, or flute girls, situating the association between actress and prostitute within the foundations of Western civilization. George Ryley Scott in *The History of Prostitution* characterizes "the female flute-players and dancing girls" as "accomplished professional musicians and entertainers" who also "had to satisfy other appetites . . . every form of sexual depravity was pandered to by these girls" (64). Thus, female performance is figured to include displaying a talent for an audience as well as catering to the sexual desires of that audience. Other prostitution histories link the prostitute and the actress throughout their narratives, highlighting sites where the actress/prostitute is particularly visible. For example, Vern Bullough and Bonnie Bullough's *Women and Prostitution* includes a lengthy section on Restoration actresses; Nickie Roberts' *Whores in History* highlights links between classical prostitution and theatre; and Shannon Bell's *Reading, Writing, and Rewriting the Prostitute Body* valorizes prostitutes turned performance artists such as Annie Sprinkle who highlight the theatrical origins of prostitution within their performances. Prostitution histories attempt to validate prostitution through reference to its theatrical foundations. Further, the contemporary prostitutes' rights movement has vigorously maintained that prostitution is "like" acting and that prostitutes should be considered actresses, a rhetorical strategy that highlights the legitimate labor involved in sex work. As the stories of the Madison escorts suggest, performance also mitigates the whore stigma, offering some prostitutes ways to distance themselves from traditional, oppressive descriptions of prostitution.

Acting histories tend to salvage the actress from her association with the prostitute by focusing on her incipient professionalization. Further, recent feminist historiography stresses the importance of untangling historicized assumptions about the sexual availability of actresses from their actual experiences. For example, Katharine Eisaman Maus and Elizabeth Howe reconsider the Restoration actress from a feminist perspective, and Tracy C. Davis' *Actresses as Working Women* attempts to dispel notions that Victorian actresses always supplemented their theatrical income with prostitution. In the contemporary period, although the sex lives of actresses (and actors) is frequent tabloid fodder, and conservative America is assumed to consider Hollywood a hotbed of sexual activity both on- and off-screen, the explicit link between actress and prostitute has all but disappeared.[2]

Prostitution has been variously defined to include women who are merely promiscuous, to women who marry for financial security, to women who receive cash or gifts for sexual acts. For example, in 1936, sociologist Gladys Mary Hall defined prostitution as "promiscuous sex relations paid or unpaid" with "the main emphasis being laid upon the fact of promiscuity" (*Prostitution in the Modern World* 21). Many second-wave feminists, especially those influenced by Marxist theory, have included marriage under prostitution's umbrella. Andrea Dworkin, Carol Pateman, Gayle Rubin, and Kathleen Barry place marriage on a continuum with prostitution, labeling all heterosexual relations "female sexual slavery," in Barry's signature phrase. Most contemporary definitions of prostitution discard promiscuity and its accompanying double standards and value judgments, and most prostitutes' rights activists and pro-sex feminists separate marriage from prostitution, if only to insist on prostitution's specificity as paid labor. The definition I use when considering contemporary prostitution is drawn from pro-sex feminists: prostitution is the exchange of sexual relations between two or sometimes more people for money or gifts, where the financial reward is received immediately before or after the service is rendered. In the seventeenth, eighteenth, and nineteenth centuries, however, definitions of prostitution are based on assumptions of morality and promiscuity as much as behavior; Boutell, Charke, and Thompson were not prostitutes in a modern sense, though they were labeled "whores."

My study is limited to women working in Great Britain and the United States during the seventeenth through the twentieth centuries. Though male actors were also subject to sexual scrutiny and male prostitutes undoubtedly perform prostitution in ways similar to their female counterparts, an examination of their experiences was beyond the scope of this project.[3] Similarly, though the association between actresses and prostitutes is cross-cultural – Binodini, the "most celebrated actress on the [nineteenth-century] Calcutta stage" was, like all nineteenth-century Indian actresses, also a concubine (Chatterjee *Nation and its Fragments* 151–54) – I limit my study of actress/ whores to the West.[4] Confining my inquiry to case histories of British and US-American actress/whores provides a close examination of how the whore position might be used to voice women's experiences within a specific context. Further, I suggest that these specific narratives build on each other. That is, contemporary prostitutes' rights activists claim affinities with historical actresses, West challenges conventional theatrical representations of the prostitute, and Thompson draws on Boutell's and Charke's experiences as cross-dressed performers stigmatized as whores.

NODAL MOMENTS: A METHODOLOGY

Though my approach to the trope of the actress/whore places transformations in the discourse into a historical context, I am not attempting to write a definitive or unitary history of prostitution or even the history of the actress/whore. Rather, I am writing what Mark Cousins and Athar Hussain term "case histories." Explicating Foucault, they describe case histories as producing tentative, incomplete, revisable conclusions. Rather than "History," a case history focuses on the micro-narrative,[5] examining how power works through retellings of the past. "Nodal moments" offer an opportunity to examine the notion of the actress/prostitute at a particularly contested point, when a new performance engendered new terms within discourse. What their contemporaries and modern historians have made of these nodal moments suggests that stories of female sexual agency carry precise meanings that vary according to context. Further, as Michel-Rolph Trouillot reminds us, such histories do not "[entail] an absence of purpose. They certainly do not entail an abandonment of the search and defense of values. . . . Positions need not be eternal to justify a legitimate defense" (*Silencing the Past* 153). The case histories I use here suggest particular understandings of how the whore stigma serves power, both in terms of dominant discourse and in the power of the margin. Thus, each nodal moment signals the rearticulation of tendencies within dominant ideology.

Obviously, this study draws heavily on Michel Foucault's theory of discursive formations, defined as a group of statements, objects, and concepts that function and exist in relation to each other (*Archaeology* 38). In the specific case of prostitution, the whore is constructed through often contradictory terms: she is simultaneously dangerous and pathetic. The whore is relegated to the fringes of society but always threatens to infect the middle class; she is free from moral constraints but is always a criminal; she is young and attractive, but is always diseased or addicted; she has the accoutrements of wealth and luxury, but is always lower class; she freely enjoys sexual activity, but is always at the mercy of demanding customers and pimps. These implicit contradictions suggest that ambivalence inheres in definitions of prostitution.

Despite contradictory definitions of prostitution, most histories posit a "real" prostitute who structures understandings of female sexuality and is the extreme to which all women are compared. Even feminist historians may deploy the figure of the "real" prostitute when recovering women's history. For example, Anna Clark writes about how gossip, specifically gossip that addressed a woman's sexual habits, was used in Regency London to regulate and control women's political and economic activities outside the home. Her study examines working- and lower-middle-class women's reactions to both actual prostitution and accusations of prostitution and promiscuity. Clark disproves that women working outside the home were more likely to be promiscuous or to work as prostitutes than women who stayed at home, and suggests that women resisted accusations of prostitution and promiscuity by seeking legal redress from their accusers. In general, Clark's essay untangles the everyday lives of working-class women from traditional stereotypes about their sexual licentiousness. Halfway through her essay, however, Clark states "[t]he drunken streetwalker clothed only in rags, grabbing and swearing at male passers-by on a freezing winter night was a familiar and chilling sight to London women" (235). This statement is remarkable because it points to Clark's reliance on dominant discourses of prostitution. Her representation of the "real" prostitute (as differentiated from those working- and lower-middle-class women who were called whores) as drunken, rude, and desperately poor demonstrates the difficulty separating the material conditions of prostitution from its discursive construction. Despite academic acknowledgment that prostitution was a complicated economic and social system, Clark's study demonstrates how dominant discourse structures historical inquiry. Her drunken streetwalker remains stranded in discourse, bereft of the agency Clark carefully explicates for the "legitimate" objects of her study.

The metaphor of contagion further illuminates how discourse has material effects for working prostitutes. In the Victorian era, the prostitute was a contaminant, spreading venereal disease and sexual immorality to middle-class women. In the contemporary period, the association between prostitution and AIDS has continued to cast the whore as an agent of destruction. The contamination metaphor pervades debates about prostitution and limits prostitutes' discursive agency. Further, fear of contagion limits the options prostitutes have when and if they choose to leave prostitution. For the Victorians, repentant prostitutes had to be immediately quarantined and then kept from middle-class households, severely limiting their employment options; now, former prostitutes are unable to acknowledge their previous career for fear of AIDS stigmatization.

As the above examples demonstrate, discourse is a mode of power, one that acts as a constraint on the material actions of real men and women and the representations of those actions. As Alan Sinfield points out, however,

dissident potential derives ultimately not from essential qualities in individuals (though they have qualities) but from conflict and contradiction that the social order inevitably produces within itself, even as it attempts to sustain itself. Despite their power, dominant ideological formations are always, in practice, under pressure, striving to substantiate their claim to superior plausibility in the face of diverse disturbances. (*Faultlines* 41)

Taking Sinfield's observation as a corrective to Foucault, discourse is not seamless, but rather riven by internal contradiction: that contradiction provides for the negotiation of agency. The discourses of prostitution are multiple and fluid, deployed and inflected differently by different women at different historical periods. I argue that agency has always been a part of the discourses of prostitution; the tension between the prostitute as exploited victim and sexual predator in dominant discourse is just one example of the dissident potential inherent in discursive representations of prostitution. The way a prostitute performs discourse determines the amount and kind of agency she is able to negotiate.

Though performances do not easily lend themselves to historical empiricism, theories of performance and performativity suggest historical events are understood as enactments of specific discourses. In this framework, performance draws from the models of human interaction suggested by Erving Goffman in *The Presentation of Self in Everyday Life*. For Goffman and those who have developed his models, performance refers to the conscious actions of people to convince others of their competence, trustworthiness, character, and purpose (14). In daily life, people attempt to create the illusion that they are something better than they are. Through this performance and its acceptance, the illusion is made real and the practice it represents is legitimated.

New historicists have also deployed a meta-theatrical framework in order to explain cultural shifts. Steven Mullaney reads the creation of an "authentic" Brazilian rain forest and the staged battle between members of the Brazilian Tabbagerres and Toupinaboux Indians imported for the occasion of Henri II's 1551 royal entry into Rouen as a "*rehearsal* of culture" ("Strange Things"48). This kind of performance "allows, invites, and even demands a full and potentially self-consuming . . . consummation, colonization, or less clearly defined negotiation between a dominant culture and its Others"(49). Following from Mullaney, the performances of the first generation of English actresses, eighteenth-century female memoirists, and early female burlesquers are a "rehearsal" of anxieties over shifting ideologies of gender. What happens onstage and in print is not merely a reflection of life, but also a site for contesting and legitimating dominant culture.

"Performativity" is used to describe the relations between individuals and society, and between individuals and other individuals. Judith Butler defines this kind of performativity as "not as a singular or deliberate 'act,' but, rather, as the reiterative and citational practice by which discourse produces the effects that it names" (*Bodies* 2). Thus, Butlerian performativity depends on a collective knowledge of gendered behavior. For example, when actresses and prostitutes perform a version of femininity for their audiences and clients, they are citing established and historicized behaviors. The historical background of these behaviors insures that they will be read as specifically female and sexual. This history, however, does not completely limit the dissident potential of enacting discourse: "'[P]erformance' is . . . a ritualized production, a ritual reiterated under and through constraint . . . controlling and compelling the shape of the production, though not, I will insist, determining it fully in advance"(95). Following from Butler, I read the self-conscious performance of femininity by early actresses, memoirists, burlesquers, and contemporary prostitutes as drawing on a history of feminine behaviors. Importantly, their performances rely on dominant codes as well as dissident traditions. These women occupy the whore position and behave within its historicized constraints; as Butler promises, however, this constraint is not absolute. Thus, Mae West performs female sexuality more candidly than Betty Boutell, and contemporary prostitutes tell more complex stories than Margaret Leeson. Whore performances, embedded in discursive practice, expose contradictions within discourse and offer an opportunity to inflect dominant ideology with new perspectives.

The story of Elizabeth (or Betty) Boutell, a middle-range actress known primarily for her breeches roles and her sexual availability, demonstrates again that Restoration commentators were preoccupied by actresses' sexuality: dozens of lampoons, memoirs, critical reviews, and even play texts themselves record the specific sexual peccadilloes of most of these women. Historians have used this primarily anecdotal record in order to continually link Restoration actresses with prostitution, building a nearly seamless narrative of the Restoration actress as a prostitute. Boutell provides a case study of the average Restoration actress and her construction as a prostitute. Though little "evidence" supports the assumption that Boutell worked as a prostitute, her contemporaries called her a whore, a designation historians have continued to use. This chapter investigates history's complicity with dominant ideology, determining that historical narratives elide the potential agency of the Restoration actress. Further, alternative narratives of Boutell's life suggest that rather than being stigmatized by her sexual notoriety, she used it to further her theatrical career.

Masquerade and memoir are two eighteenth-century technologies of self. Charlotte Charke and Margaret Leeson extended both forms to fashion a self outside polite society. Charke, daughter of playwright, actor, and fellow memoirist Colley Cibber, is perhaps best known through her published narrative detailing her adventures as a cross-dressed strolling player. Her memoirs, the first by an English actress, use performance metaphors throughout: Charke is not so much living her life as performing (both in print and everyday) for an audience who delights in her exploits. Leeson, a brothel-keeper who wrote one of the earliest English first-person prostitute narratives, masquerades in her narrative as in life. In her memoirs, Leeson performs remorse, praying to be redeemed and made as chaste as the goddess Diana she once portrayed at masquerade balls. Leeson offers first-hand testimony to the agency offered by performing inside and out of the whore position. Both Charke and Leeson constructed an other world, one that drew on eighteenth-century feminist philosophies as well as traditional discourses of femininity to privilege female experience and community.

Lydia Thompson struggled to participate in her own discursive representation. Like the first generation of English actresses, the first generation of female burlesque performers instigated public debate on the proper display of female sexuality and forever changed the face of (US-American) theatre. Female burlesque performers reinterpreted what had previously been an all-male variety entertainment, and the inclusion of women into an all-male form illuminated tensions about the kinds of theatrical entertainments in which women could participate. The Blondes occupy the gap between the ideal, as personified in the Cult of True Womanhood, and the real, as marked by nineteenth-century women's attempts to participate in the public sphere at greater levels than before. The Cult of True Womanhood "prescribed a female role bounded by kitchen and nursery, overlaid with piety and purity, and crowned with subservience" (Smith-Rosenberg *Disorderly Conduct* 13); feminists, prostitutes, and female burlesquers challenged this domestic ideology, suggesting that women could successfully engage in masculine activities and that female sexuality was not necessarily determined by masculine desire. The British Blondes, whose stage performances featured barely dressed women joking about romance, vigorous and suggestive dancing, and sexually aggressive, cross-dressed characters, triggered existing Victorian debates over gender and sexuality. Thompson struggled to influence and control her own discursive representation; recovering this labor reflects feminist historian Carroll Smith-Rosenberg's warning that historians must be careful to "hear women's words" as embedded in other powerful discourses (25–26).

Late twentieth-century feminism is divided by debates over prostitution and pornography. Theoretical models of performance and performativity open up analytic space between the poles. The narratives of Madison, Wisconsin escorts indicate how performance is a strategy to mitigate the whore stigma. Further, the trope of the actress/whore offers working prostitutes an opportunity to both legitimate their work and claim kinship with a sisterhood of historical women who transgressed gender norms by using their sexuality to reap economic and (sometimes) political and social rewards. Placing the work prostitutes do with their clients into a framework of acting theory and technique, some prostitutes may negotiate agency by thinking of sex work as a performance. These escorts occupy the whore position, and use performance to account for their experience.

MAE WEST: THE PERFORMER AS PROSTITUTE

Before turning to the extended case histories of the following chapters, I want to focus on Mae West, whose career and image bridge historical performers and contemporary whores. Mae West's 1926 production of *Sex* offers a potent site for examining shifts within the discursive formation of the actress/whore and the resistance with which such shifts were met. As Margy LaMont, West laid the foundation for her iconic status as an unrepentant, social climbing prostitute/entertainer who liked men nearly as much and as often as they liked her. Frustrated by a lack of Broadway roles appropriate to her style, West wrote *Sex* under the pseudonym Jane Mast to spotlight her particular talents and persona. As Margy LaMont, as in all of her stage and screen star turns, West played a prostitute or "kept woman" who rose through society by rejecting one lover when a richer one came along. Further, Margy, like all West's roles, was also an entertainer who used the stage to advertise her sexual charms and availability. West's prostitutes/entertainers exhibit a remarkable amount of textual agency; these characters drive the action, focus the narrative, and provide West with a showcase for her musical talents and comic patter. Capitalizing on her sexuality, West climbed the ladder of success in unconventional and even dangerous ways. Her representation of the prostitute, then, stressed the possibility of upward mobility through sexual liaisons.

West troped the familiar conflation of the actress and the whore in order to depict women who successfully traded their theatrical and sexual talents for both financial and personal power, a depiction very different from conventional representations. The prostitute in most canonical plays is usually a peripheral figure who displaces tension over correct female behavior alluded to in the main plot or serves as a vehicle for the playwright and his society's deep-rooted misogyny. Before the nineteenth century, few plays featured prostitutes as the central dramatic focus. However, nineteenth-century stages fully exploited the dramatic potential of prostitute narratives: "courtesan plays" were among the most popular theatrical offerings. The stage prostitute was generally a young, beautiful woman, full of love and life. She adored pleasure and adored pleasing people. In many cases, she was the centerpiece of the drama and, except for her sexual taint, was the kind of carefree, lovely creature many women supposedly aspired to be. These plays also presented a consistent representation of the inevitable death and destruction that awaited the prostitute, offering her little opportunity to exercise textual agency.

Alexandre Dumas *fil*'s *La Dame aux Camelias* (*Camille*) exemplifies the fallen-woman narratives of the nineteenth century: the prostitute heroine sacrifices herself for another's happiness and dies tragically. *Camille*, first produced in Paris in 1849, tells the story of beautiful, desirable Marguerite, a courtesan available to both the characters in the play and the gaze of the audience. Marguerite dances about her Parisian apartments, bosom heaving; wears lingerie or low-cut ball gowns; cries prettily and constantly; is kissed and fondled by the male characters; and finally dies for the entirety of the final act, falling across couches and beds, onto the floor, and into the arms of her maid Nanine, her friend Gaston, and her lover Armand. Marguerite is utterly helpless, unable to do anything but sacrifice herself, and totally dependent on men for financial support, emotional fulfillment, and moral guidance. *Camille*'s importance is supported by its theatrical longevity. Actresses throughout the nineteenth and twentieth centuries have vied for the most convincing, erotic, and romantic death scene in the theatrical canon: Marguerite has been played by Sarah Bernhardt, Greta Garbo, and Vanessa Redgrave to critical and popular acclaim. This enduring story of sacrifice and sensuality has solidified into a pervasive popular-culture representation of the prostitute: she is initially shallow and greedy, but true love brings out her best instincts and she dies rather than continue to pollute her family, friends, and lovers.

Throughout the nineteenth century, courtesan plays ended with the tragic, sacrificial death of the heroine. Arthur Wing Pinero's *The Second Mrs. Tanqueray* adopted Dumas' formula to enormous popular success in the late nineteenth century, and he followed its production with the similarly themed *Iris, Letty*, and *The Notorious Mrs. Ebbsmith*. *Camille* and its numerous imitations present an image of the doomed and morally flawed woman. In the traditional courtesan play, the passive protagonist merely reacts to outside provocations rather than furthering the narrative on her own terms. Because she is morally weak and overly sexual, her influence on the "good" women in the play must be narratively contained.[6]

George Bernard Shaw's *Mrs. Warren's Profession* (1894, first produced 1902) presents, in the words of critic Martin Meisel, a "genre anti-type . . . designed to make the conventional uses of the materials [of the courtesan play] artistically unacceptable to men of intellectual conscience" (*Shaw* 141). Kitty Warren is Shaw's corrective to the typical representation of the prostitute. She is not young and beautiful; she is not loved by all who know her; she is not dead or dying. In addition, Kitty entered into prostitution because she was a working-class woman with no other option than the "killing" factories, not because she loved pleasure and pretty clothes. Shaw, in the lengthy "Author's Apology" that prefaces all print editions of the play, suggests that *Mrs. Warren's Profession* is not a sensational or melodramatic treatment of prostitution intended to titillate, but is instead a consideration of the causes of prostitution and a condemnation, not of whores, but of the capitalistic, bourgeois society which supports them.

Explaining *Mrs. Warren's Profession* is complicated by Shaw's socialist/ Fabian ideological stance. Prostitution functions as a synecdoche for capitalism in the play, and though Shaw allows Kitty Warren to defend prostitution, his narrative ultimately sides against her. *Mrs. Warren's Profession* is an important representation of prostitution, as it introduces the economic circumstances that lead many women to choose sex work. This more sympathetic portrayal of prostitution, however, is ambivalent. In this representation of prostitution, the whore is a victim of society; desperately poor, she willingly trades even her body for her daily bread. In this marxian interpretation of the causes of prostitution, which has enormous currency in its histories and theories, the prostitute is still without agency, subject to economic forces beyond her control. This portrayal ultimately condemns the prostitute. If she entered prostitution because the economic system under which she was living offered no other opportunities, she should leave prostitution once she is financially secure, an assumption that dogs even the most politically powerful and well-respected contemporary prostitution advocates, such as Tracy Quan and Carol Leigh. Thus, the assumptions about prostitution inherent in nineteenth-century plays still circulate throughout contemporary US-American culture. They leave the prostitute with little agency, suggesting that she has no power to control her actions or influence her own representation.

In the early twentieth century, primarily through Mae West's theatrical and film roles, conventional representations of prostitution met serious challenge. In the 1930s, West was a major movie star; her first two films,

She Done Him Wrong (1933) and *I'm No Angel* (1933), "temporarily helped revive the film industry" hit hard by the Depression, and the "unexpectedly high profits" from those films helped Paramount, which had gone into receivership, "reorganize and recover as an intact corporation" (Curry *Too Much of a Good Thing* 48). West had enormous box office clout and her films were major events. In the stage productions *Sex, The Wicked Age* (1927), *Diamond Lil* (1928), *The Constant Sinner* (1931), and *Catherine Was Great* (1944), as well as her wildly successful films *She Done Him Wrong, I'm No Angel, Belle of the Nineties* (1934), *Goin' to Town* (1935), *Klondike Annie, Go West, Young Man* (1936), *Every Day's a Holiday* (1938), *My Little Chickadee* (1940), and *The Heat's On* (1943), West always played a prostitute/kept woman who displayed her theatrical talents and sexual availability in order to rise financially and socially through liaisons with rich, attractive men. Except for *Sextette* (1977), when the eighty-four year old West married a very young Timothy Dalton as her sixth husband, West's characters never marry, or even promise sexual fidelity to the man they are with at the drama's end. Thus, West's characters are always free to accept a better offer when it comes along; the end of her plays and films deny the narrative closure promised by the traditional marriage finale of most Hollywood romantic comedies and suggest that West's characters continue to move from one man to another.

Sex was West's first attempt to offer an alternate representation of prostitution; the critical and legal response indicates how forcefully that project was resisted. Though Broadway in the 1920s featured several plays about prostitutes, all followed the conventions of the nineteenth-century courtesan play, "obedient to the unwritten rule that prescribed ruin for fallen women" (Schissel *Three Plays* 7). *Sex*, on the other hand, told the story of Margy LaMont, a Montreal prostitute who rescues a society woman, Clara Stanton, from a pimp's clutches; follows the Royal Navy to Trinidad; falls in love with Clara's son and returns to Connecticut to marry him; but leaves with another of her lovers, Lieutenant Gregg, to start a new life in Australia. The convoluted narrative, which also featured a nightclub act with full jazz band and West performing several musical numbers, offered a different theatrical representation of the prostitute. The whore was the heroine of the story. She was not punished at the end, nor did she accept a conventional marriage arrangement. Instead, Margy left the socially stratified suburban United States for further adventure as the sexual and financial partner of a former client.

Setting *Sex* primarily in Montreal and Connecticut rather than exotic Asian, European, or South American locales – even Trinidad was represented as an Americanized saloon and dance hall, with the focus on US and

British soldiers rather than "natives" – West put prostitution into a familiar setting, implying that women like Margy were everywhere. Her language was the speakeasy slang of the 1920s, recognizable to her audiences as the patois of New York nightlife, and the songs included standards like "Home Sweet Home" and "Shake that Thing." Margy LaMont was both familiar and frighteningly new (Schissel *Three Plays* 8). Though the language, setting, and subject matter were common to sophisticated New York audiences, West's representation starkly contrasted theatrical conventions because of its depiction of an autonomous and successful prostitute.

West's characters drive the action of her plays. Unlike Kitty Warren and Marguerite, Margy LaMont is neither reactionary nor passive. She chooses to follow the Royal Navy in order to increase her financial prospects and expand her horizons, and she chooses to leave with Lieutenant Gregg rather than remain in suburban Connecticut. Consistently, she opts for adventure over security and is unconcerned about respectability or her reputation. More importantly, she takes the lead in all her sexual relationships. In the first act in Montreal, she refuses to sleep with four separate men, including her good friend Lieutenant Gregg. Gregg is particularly distressed over her refusal: "I'd hate to be disappointed. I put myself out a lot to come and see you, I don't mind telling you." Margy responds that he's "out of luck," and Gregg finally agrees to take her to "the Black Cat Café and spend the money I was going to spend here." Margy agrees to go out with him, but only if they go to her favorite café, the Tremaine (West *Sex* 46). When the audience sees Margy conducting business, they see a prostitute in control of her clients, refusing their demands in order to do what she wants.

Margy's relationship with Jimmy Stanton, the Connecticut business scion, is also conducted on her terms. Though she claims to love him, it is clear she also loves his money. In the first act she tells her prostitute friend Alice that she plans to "rise to the top of her profession" and marry a rich man. Visiting Jimmy in his Connecticut home, Margy seduces him in order to be sure their connection is not based on unsatisfied lust and that he will remain with her after they have consummated their marriage. In fact, the morning after their illicit lovemaking, Jimmy hovers around Margy, promising to marry her. She is clearly thrilled they are still going to marry but sends Jimmy, who wanted to spend the day with her, to the office. Margy wants to be sure that the money keeps coming in.

In the final scenes of the play, Margy's pimp, who seduced Jimmy's mother Clara, also visits the Stanton home to blackmail Clara. Margy calls the police to arrest him but lets him go before they arrive. She recognizes one of the police officers and goes upstairs to pack her bags. She returns to tell Jimmy that she is leaving him because she does not fit into Connecticut society. Lieutenant Gregg, who is conveniently also visiting the Stantons, "appeals to her mutely to remember his feeling for her" (West *Sex* 92) and she leaves with him. When a horrified Clara asks whether Margy is "going back to that life," Margy responds that she is "going straight – to Australia" (West *Sex* 92). This curtain line, with its clarifying pause, suggests that Margy is not sacrificing anything, but rather choosing to abandon the Stantons and the respectability they represent.[7]

Mae West, of course, is a twentieth-century icon of female sexuality, generally understood to have had unique control over her career, her love life, and her own representation.[8] West wrote *Sex* as her breakout role and continued to write her own theatrical vehicles. She is credited with writing or contributing dialogue to all her Hollywood films. West was closely associated with her roles: according to biographer Ramona Curry, West's publicity "fostered audience conviction that West's characters extended the actor's private persona" (*Too Much of a Good Thing* 101), a claim that echoes representations of Restoration actresses. West typecast herself as a beautiful, desirable entertainer who readily used her sexual charms to entice men and take their money. Even in her earliest play, West's signature comic patter and risqué stage business establish her as the fulcrum of the drama's action. For example, when Lieutenant Gregg visits Margy in Montreal, he brings her a present.

GREGG: . . . Oh, I've got something for you, wait until you see this, wait until you see this.
MARGY: Well, come on and let's see it.
GREGG: You'll get it, you'll get it. I don't mind telling you I had an awful time saving it for you. Why all the women were fighting for it.
MARGY: It better be good.
GREGG: It's good alright. It's the best you could get, but you've got to be very careful not to bend it.   (*Sex* 44)

Despite the sexual innuendo of the dialogue and accompanying stage business, Gregg gives Margy a bird of paradise feather. Margy is delighted by the gift and clearly values Gregg more for his exotic present than his sexual company. Curry suggests that "[i]n delivering almost all of the visual as well as the verbal jokes in her films, West in effect narrates her comedies" (*Too Much of a Good Thing* 85), making her character's perspective the one with whom the audience identifies. Unlike traditional prostitution narratives, West's vehicles place her characters in a position to be admired rather than pitied and the narrative structure suggests that she is the dominant protagonist.

Not only did West structure her theatrical and film vehicles in order to place her promiscuous characters at the center of the drama, the mise-en-scène itself contributed to West's self-promotion as a sexually desirable woman. The majority of West's vehicles are set in the 1890s, which allowed West to costume herself in daring décolletage, tight corsets, and spreading skirts that trailed behind her and pooled at her feet. These period pieces are an important component in West's image as a glamorous and sexually desirable woman. At only 5′″ tall and definitely heavier than most Hollywood and Broadway glamour queens,[9] this period costuming highlighted the strengths of West's figure and disguised its considerable flaws. As she controlled the dialogue and narrative in order to present herself in the best possible light, West set most of her plays at the turn of the century in order to control her costuming and physical appearance.

Though West did have considerable influence over her own representation and structured her productions in order to maintain her characters' sexual freedom and financial success, her efforts were frequently resisted. *Sex*, which opened in April 1926, was criticized as "nasty, infantile, [and] amateurish" by *Variety*, the *New York Times* called it "crude and inept," and *Billboard* complained that it was "the cheapest, most vulgar, low show to have dared to open in New York this year." West in particular was criticized for her aggressive onstage sexuality. For example, the December 31, 1926 *New York Daily Mirror* review charged that "West cavorts her own sex about the stage in one of the most reviling exhibits allowed public display. She undresses before the public, and appears to enjoy doing so" (quoted in Schissel *Three Plays* 10). Though *Sex* was a popular success, West's play was condemned for its sympathetic portrayal of the criminal underworld and the unmediated sexuality of Margy LaMont was singled out.[10]

The New York Herald Tribune review of April 27, 1926 expressed the general horror West's production engendered: "All the barriers of conventional word and act that the last few seasons of the theater have shown us were swept away and we were shown not sex but lust – stark, naked lust." The conventions with which *Sex* broke included style as well as subject matter; West presented prostitution too "realistically" for its Broadway venue. Marybeth Hamilton suggests that *Sex* was deemed realistic because its "style of representation . . . presented sexuality in a style that legitimate theatre scorned" (Hamilton *Queen* 43). For example, West foregrounded the cash exchange fundamental to prostitution, rather than euphemistically presenting Margy and her cohorts as "kept women" who relied on the gifts of admirers. Further, West's particular body language and vocal style – "raw, "crude," and "unvarnished" (in Hamilton *Queen* 43) in the words of several critics – offered a portrait that was too close to audiences' idea of a "real prostitute" for comfort. In the eyes of theatre critics, *Sex* was not a theatrical representation, but rather a literal presentation of commercial sexuality that highlighted its brutality and overt sexuality rather than glossing over these unseemly aspects.

Efforts to regulate West's representation of prostitution ultimately included police intervention. On February 9, 1927, after approximately 350 performances,[11] *Sex* was raided. West, producers John Timony and C. W. Morgenstern, theatre owner John Cort, and the entire cast were arrested for corrupting the morals of youth through *Sex*'s "wicked, lewd, scandalous, bawdy, obscene, indecent, infamous, immoral, and impure" content, according to the grand jury indictment.[12] Timony and Morgenstern filed an indictment against further police interference before the trial and *Sex* continued until May 1927. West was ultimately sentenced to ten days in jail and a $500 fine. The arrest, trial, and resulting play closing thus suggest that West's representation of a powerful prostitute was resisted by the enforcers of a bourgeois moral code.

West herself framed the raid and arrest in terms of censorship. In June 1927, she served her sentence at the New York City Women's Penitentiary. When she was released, she compared her incarceration to other state censorship attempts and aligned her cause with crusading women such as the suffragettes and Margaret Sanger. She used the $1,000 fee she received for an exclusive interview to *Liberty* magazine to found the Mae West Memorial Library at the Women's Penitentiary. By comparing her efforts with other censored feminists and supporting women's education, West's actions suggest that she understood her arrest as part of official discourse's attempts to suppress the expression of female sexuality. Like Boutell, Charke, and Thompson, West used the stage and press to present her own version of events; when official channels were closed to her, she used alternate modes of communication.

Mae West's experience with *Sex* concretizes many of the issues addressed below. Like many early performers, West displayed her sexuality on stage, making her body – not her talent – the spectacle audiences paid to see. Like the other women I consider, West had to contend with dominant ideology that insisted women were not supposed to enjoy sex, much less talk about it. However, unlike those women, West specifically deployed her physical attractiveness and capitalized on her sexual appeal; she never rejected the label whore nor denied her promiscuity. In this way, she echoes Margaret Leeson and members of the prostitutes' rights movement. She controlled

Figure 1.1 "Crusading" Mae West, surrounded by male supporters, after her arrest for *Sex* (Courtesy of the Academy of Motion Picture Arts and Sciences)

her image and aggressively marketed herself as an eager participant in sexual relationships. Her body and her narratives exceeded good taste and challenged assumptions about female sexual desire; not surprisingly, she was subject to contempt.

West's arrest for *Sex* demonstrates the seriousness of her threat to traditional understandings of appropriate female sexuality. Throughout her career, she struggled with attempts to silence her voice and control her representation. For example, West's Hollywood films were cut by censors as she warred with the Motion Pictures Producers and Distributors Association over the content of her films.[13] Thus, West's experience in the early part of the twentieth century demonstrates how dominant discourses of female sexuality worked to contain transgressive representations, an observation I draw out in subsequent portions of this book.

West is also important for understanding how some women are able to negotiate agency through the performance of female sexuality. West is famously known as "the greatest *female* female impersonator" and her performances are often understood as a kind of drag. West put on the accessories – furs, jewels, lavishly feminine clothing – and behaviors – sinewy hips, breathy speech, rolling eyes – of hyperfemininity, illuminating how women are able to manipulate men with their bodies, and pointing to the constructed nature of gender categories. In her stage and screen vehicles, West seems to portray sexuality as a role women adopt in order to manipulate men. Further, she exploits the connection between acting and prostitution. In this way, she prefigures the arguments of late-twentieth-century prostitutes' rights activists who argue that sex (and sex work) is necessarily theatrical and performative.

Despite West's status as an icon of performed femininity, her later career suggests the limits to sexual agency offered by performative strategies. Here too she echoes the struggles faced by early female performers. In the 1990s, several critical biographies of Mae West were published: Ramona Curry's *Too Much of a Good Thing: Mae West as Cultural Icon* (1996); Marybeth Hamilton's *The Queen of Camp: Mae West, Sex, and Popular Culture* (1996); Emily Wortis Leider's *Becoming Mae West* (2000); Maurice Leonard's *Mae West, Empress of Sex* (1991); and Pamela Robertson's *Guilty Pleasures: Feminist Camp from Mae West to Madonna* (1996). These biographies explain West's status as American cultural icon, arguing that West crafted a specifically sexual feminist persona that transgressed traditional class and gender boundaries. Most championed West's position within gay subcultures and academic queer studies, suggesting that West's self-conscious performance of femininity pointed toward theoretically complex explorations of the construction of gender. For feminists and queer theorists in particular, as well as her legions of gay male fans, West's version of mercenary, aggressive sexuality offered an alternative to the domestic, feminine, reproductive sexual economy determined in heterosexual and patriarchal definitions of feminine (or non-masculine) sexuality. In addition, West's control over her career is cited by most biographers as proof of her feminist politics.[14] These critical biographies insist on West's iconic status, immortalizing her early stage and film performances and extrapolating their theories of gender performativity from such memorable roles as Diamond Lil and Klondike Annie.

For the most part, these biographies omit West's final decades (Lieder and Curry, for example, end their narratives after West's association with Paramount in the 1940s) or downplay its significance. In the 1960s and 1970s, West attempted to hold on to her fame and status by performing in Las Vegas revues and accepting roles in *Myra Breckenridge* (1974) and *Sextette* (1977). For feminist scholars who want to see West as a powerfully sexual woman – myself included – the last twenty years of her career are hard to explain. Why couldn't West age gracefully, or, better yet, not age at all? The octogenarian Mae West has no place in these biographies. Rather, the persona of Mae West as defined by her early roles fixes the limits of these biographies. The powerful, sexy, wisecracking Mae West – the icon – is the only West rendered visible.

In biographies that do include West's last decades, her final roles are critically dismissed; this reaction demonstrates the limits of transgressive female performance. At eighty-four, West produced and starred in her final film, *Sextette*. She played a much-married screen legend who commanded a legion of male admirers despite her advanced age, re-presenting the persona that brought her fame and admiration in the first half of the twentieth century. *Sextette* recycled familiar ripostes from other West vehicles, presented West corseted into pooling gowns replete with décolletage and wearing enormous blond wigs styled to resemble her 1930s appearance, and played out the familiar Westian plot. Film critics, biographers, and feminist scholars are particularly harsh when commenting on this final foray into cinematic excess: in the words of critic Rex Reed, West looked like "something they found in the basement of a pyramid" (quoted in Hamilton *Queen* 225). Marybeth Hamilton castigates West for being an "elderly woman who persisted in playing her much younger persona, saying those same ribald lines, making those same overblown gestures, seemingly oblivious to the passage of time" (*Queen* 225). At the end of her life and career, West was a pathetic joke, a source of embarrassment for fans and critics alike.

Sextette failed precisely because it resurrected the iconic West in an aged and failing body. West's final performance of femininity no longer seemed authentic, an irony in light of earlier critiques. The Mae West of *Sex* was condemned for being too realistic, for moving her "buttocks and other parts of her body in such a way as to suggest an act of sexual intercourse" (quoted in Hamilton *ibid.* 47); the Mae West of *Sextette* was condemned for being too obviously a performance. West could not, in the minds of her audience at least, convincingly portray feminine sexuality. As a young and even middle-aged woman, West was believable as a sexual dynamo. As an octogenarian, she was not. Though her early film and stage work certainly broke with conventional representations of prostitution and female sexuality, it remained recognizable as a specific feminine type. West's energy, eroticism, and humor were appropriate for the working women she portrayed even as they exceeded the bounds of good taste and proper decorum. However, her Las Vegas shows and final films depicted inappropriate femininity. West was too old and unattractive to hold audiences' sexual attention. She no longer embodied her persona. The raw sexuality that she had seemed to self-consciously craft into a transgressive portrayal of the actress/whore in her early stage and film work was now mere grotesquerie.

West's centrality as female icon was challenged by her "real" self; her two later films undermined the performance of femininity hailed by critics and fans alike. In feminist accounts, biographies, and film critics' eyes, the West of *Sextette* had to be discounted and mocked in order that the iconic West could retain her centrality. As a site of discursive production, Mae West biographies limit definitions of appropriate female sexuality while championing West's seeming transgression of such limits. The early Mae West is a camp icon; the later Mae West is a (not camp) joke, rendered unimportant and invisible in narratives of her life, career, and impact.

The following chapters explicate the history that informs West's persona and the varied critical response it engenders. Betty Boutell, Charlotte Charke, Margaret Leeson, Lydia Thompson, and working prostitutes struggle to intervene in the construction of female sexuality. Though the whore stigma is used to police the boundaries of their narratives, these women claimed the whore position and spoke to the center, influencing normative understandings of female agency. As West aptly demonstrates, theatrical performance, performance in everyday life, and Butlerian performativity suggest how both actresses and prostitutes employ a variety of strategies to intervene in their discursive representations.

CHAPTER 2

Betty Boutell, "Whom all the Town Fucks": constructing the actress/whore

*[Y]oung women without dowries had discovered the possibility of a thea-
trical career as a springboard to matrimony or "keeping." Husbands were
scarce, but "keepers" swarmed. There were hundreds of lecherous gentlemen
eager to seduce an actress as cheaply as possible. The foolish virgins suc-
cumbed to their blandishments and paid the usual penalty of folly. The wise
ones teased their admirers into some kind of settlement, hoping to live in
clover for the rest of their lives.*

(Wilson *All the King's Ladies* 11)

This chapter takes its title from the 1688 lampoon *Session of the Ladies*.
Suggesting that Elizabeth (Betty) Boutell, a mid-range actress who specialized in breeches roles from the 1660s to the 1690s, was a whore, the lampoon
seems to confirm a commonplace link between first-generation English
actresses and prostitutes within theatre studies. The first women on the
English public stage, such narratives maintain, were subject to the sexual
demands of male audience members. Boutell was repeatedly named a whore
in popular satires and play epilogues of the period, and current histories
have preserved this convention. Though Nell Gwyn is perhaps a more
familiar figure for drawing out the discourse of the actress/whore during
Restoration England, Boutell's biography suggests that this discourse
affected actresses at all levels. Further, Boutell's case history suggests that
current assumptions about the effect of the whore stigma elides its transgressive potential. As a "whore," Boutell enjoyed a long career, financial
security, and personal freedom: the effects of the assumed link between the
first generation of English actresses and prostitutes need to be reexamined.

First, it is important to note that "whore" seems to have meant differently in the seventeenth century. Though the word seems particularly
derogatory now, during the Restoration it seems to have been used more
frequently and with less force than it is currently applied. During the
Restoration, the word "whore" was as an insult, certainly, but one along
the lines of the contemporary "bitch," designating an unruly woman rather

than one who engaged in commercial sex. For example, Samuel Johnson's dictionary offered "a woman who converses unlawfully with men; a fornicator; an adulteress; a strumpet" as the primary meaning for "whore"; only the secondary meaning defined the whore as a prostitute who traded sex for money (quoted in Trumbach "London's Sapphists" 73). In Restoration England, "whore" (as well as strumpet and harlot) seems to have designated a sexually free woman even more than a prostitute. Further, many women who participated in the public sphere were labeled whores: Aphra Behn provides another example of a financially successfully, sexually autonomous woman so labeled (Pearson *Prostituted Muse* 143). Transferring the language but not the meaning of seventeenth-century vernacular is one way historians elide the position of the Restoration actress.

Examining Restoration discourses of sexuality and theatricality demonstrates how historical narratives may limit the understanding of agency and power in the lives of historical subjects. Accepting the commonplace notion that all seventeenth-century actresses were whores extirpates the possibility that they exercised some measure of control over their lives and representations. In general, histories of Restoration theatre assume that actresses embarked on stage careers primarily to entice audience members into liaisons and even marriage, ignoring their theatrical skills and professional status as well as the economic conditions that might drive some women to seek paid labor of all kinds. J. H. Wilson's 1958 history *All the King's Ladies* is the first modern, comprehensive study of Restoration actresses and, as my epigraph demonstrates, proposes that the virginal actress was easily seduced by unscrupulous aristocrats. His account has been repeated and expanded in subsequent histories, and prevents historians from narrativizing the first generation as autonomous subjects. Even feminist scholars, such as Elizabeth Howe and Katharine Eisaman Maus, retain some of the biases that color Wilson's account.

A more complicated narrative proposes that "whore" mitigates the threat posed by the sexually and socially transgressive women of the Restoration stage. Though the whore stigma was deployed in order to limit the first generation, Boutell's narrative demonstrates how individual actresses may have claimed and exploited that position in order to wrest personal agency. Peter Stallybrass and Allon White suggest that "[p]oints of antagonism, overlap and intersection between the high and the low, the classical and its 'Other,' provide some of the richest and most powerful symbolic dissonances in the culture" (*Politics and Poetics* 25). The first generation troubled hierarchical categories of gender and class: as working women they seemingly rejected the domestic realm, and as mistresses of wealthy, aristocratic, and even royal men they rose above their prescribed station. Accusations of whorishness might better be regarded as discursive limits to female agency rather than empirical truth. Interrogating Betty Boutell's construction as exemplary actress/whore illuminates the class and gender tensions occluded by historiographic preoccupation with actresses' sexuality.

Historical focus on the actresses' bodies links to the conviction that during the Restoration the English rejected sexual restraint for sexual licentiousness.[1] According to traditional histories of English society, Charles II returned to England to free his society from the shackles of Puritanism. Charles' embrace of pleasure included regularly attending the theatre and engaging mistresses first noticed on the stage. The king "impressed the stamp of his personality upon his surroundings so deeply" that the rest of England was obliged to follow suit (Bloch *Sexual Life in England* 231). Accordingly, aristocratic influence seeped into the lives of even the lower classes and drinking, debauchery, gambling, and entertainments were presumably pastimes vigorously pursued by all. The Restoration playhouse has been made central to this construction of Restoration society; the entertainments provided on stage and the sexual licentiousness of the players offer concrete examples of sexual debauchery. Examining the discursive bond between playhouse and court suggests that the stage figured metonymically in notions of Charles II as dangerously debauched monarch and the Restoration as sexually obsessed. The first generation of English actresses is central to this metonymic reduction; as Stallybrass and White point out, "cultures 'think themselves' in the most immediate and affective ways through the combined symbolisms of psychic forms, the human body, geographical space, and the social order" (*Politics and Poetics* 3); thus, the playhouses, court, and actresses' bodies overlap existing tensions within the Restoration social order.

After Charles II decreed that all female parts were to be played by females in 1661, women populated the Restoration stage in numbers nearly equal to their male counterparts. The prominence of female actresses (who were often also mistresses of male audience members) signaled that London theatres, traditionally located near brothels and frequented by prostitutes, now seemed places where whores could be seen on the stage as well as in the audience and in the surrounding streets. In the public imagination at least, if a woman presented herself on stage, then she would present herself off stage, sexually, as well: lampoons, satires, and gossip perpetuated this assumption. Further, the narratives of the plays themselves suggested the sexual avail-ability of the actresses. Examining this discursive convergence suggests reasons for both contemporary and modern representations of the Restoration, as well as continued links between actresses and prostitutes.

Thus, the first generation of English actresses illuminates how the discursive formation of the actress/whore originated in the modern era. At the same time, the success of the actress/whore also suggests that "whorishness" was not always already negative during the Restoration. Boutell's designation as a whore implies that her audience might also have recognized her as a challenging and transgressive woman.

The slip between actress and whore is further complicated by the class position of many of the first English actresses. The Restoration court and the Restoration stage were intimately connected by the body of King Charles II; Charles' sexual relationships with actresses from working- and lower-middle-class backgrounds raised them from their base origins to a position of relative social esteem. Harold Weber suggests that Charles II's relationship with Nell Gwyn, which began "as an inequality of class, and an inversion of the proper relationship between the royal and the common, quickly becomes a matter of gender, and the subversion of the proper relationship between a man and a woman" (Weber "Charles II" 194). Charles II's obsession with his mistresses suggested an effeminate interest in romance, luxury, and pleasure, calling into question his ability to rule.[2] Further, his affair with Gwyn publicly unsettled class hierarchies: if the grandson of a brothel keeper and the son of an actress could be made a Duke, then the "natural" aristocracy was no longer safe. Traditionally, power and privilege were the rights of those who had earned them by birth, rather than labor, or especially sex. Labeling actresses as whores and publicizing their sexual peccadilloes was an attempt to limit the threat to class hierarchy their position as aristocratic mistresses indicated as well as downplay their entry into the public sphere. Designating actresses as whores insured that focus remained on their sexuality, not on their professional status or possible influence on statecraft.

More importantly, modern historians have maintained the actress/whore connection to limit the possible agency of Restoration actresses. Because very little is knowable about the players – few were literate enough to have kept diaries, sent letters, or written memoirs; the nascent print culture of the seventeenth century is scarcely preserved in archives and libraries; and playbills, advertisements, original play texts, and prompt books have mostly vanished – Restoration history is written primarily through the circulation of well-known anecdotes. This history is thus not a referential practice, but a performative one. That is, through the repetition and recitation of anecdotal evidence, the history of the Restoration theatre has been created. This historiography rarely includes representations of actresses as powerful or even autonomous, badly limiting present understandings of women's lives. Betty Boutell's status in Restoration theatre history reveals how women's biographies are ignored and their experiences subsumed into familiar narratives: accordingly, Boutell was promiscuous, instead of professionally successful.

The repetition of biographical anecdotes, focusing in the case of actresses on their sexual relationships, creates a discursive link between the first generation and prostitution. One account is written by one historian, and then (re)cited by another, and another. Stories, jokes, and memories which first only circulated orally were eventually included in Restoration diaries, memoirs, lampoons, and play texts; the shift from orality to print signals a shift in authenticity and validity. Following from Michel Foucault, these documents can be handled, examined, copied, and cited as evidence. The existence of documents seems to logically lead to the existence of the event. Because they were recorded, they are assumed to have happened. The discourse on the event is viewed as a tangible trace of that event, which can be made to speak, telling the story of the past. According to Foucault,

[e]very statement involves a field of antecedent elements in relation to which it is situated but which it is able to reorganize and redistribute according to new relations. It constitutes its own past, defines in what precedes it, its own filiation, redefines what makes it possible or necessary, excludes what cannot be compatible with it. And it poses this enunciative past as an acquired truth, as an event that has occurred, as a form that can be modified, as material to be transformed or as an object that can be spoken about. (*Archaeology* 124)

Historical narratives build on each other, and every time an event is recorded and redocumented, it appears more true than the time before. The link between the actress and the whore has been constructed historically through the repetition of anecdotal evidence. In his introduction to *The London Stage: Part One, 1660–1700* (a key source for Restoration scholars), William van Lennep states "[a]n actress was fair game . . . against her will, or often, willingly, for men of all classes including the monarch; for men of position, in Downes' inimitable phrase, 'erupted' the actresses from the stage" (xcvi–xcvii). Van Lennep's citation of Downes' inimitability clarifies the antecedence of anecdotal evidence and the sedimentary effects of historiography.

It is virtually impossible to pull apart the discursive construction – to imagine the actress as other than sexually suspect.[3] In fact, I am not trying to prove or disprove the extent of a particular actress' involvement in commercial sex. Whether Boutell took lovers for money or pleasure or at all is not the central question; rather, I focus on why this assumption has prevailed. Boutell's case history demonstrates that a crucial part of the production of history, distinct from the object revealed, are the very apparati of that revelation. While it is true that most primary source material comes from court records, Pepys' diary, John Downes' prompt book, and satires and lampoons and so tends towards the sensational, modern and contemporary accounts do not examine the limiting effect of focusing only on the actresses' sexuality.[4] Through the circulation of anecdotal evidence, an incomplete and often biased narrative of women's lives is reiterated and canonized.

The admittedly sketchy biographies of mid-range Restoration actresses demonstrate the citational effects of history. For example, the biography of Rebecca Marshall (a founding member of the King's Company and an actress of considerable talent and acclaim) included in the Highfill, Burnim, and Langhans *Biographical Dictionary of Actors, Actresses, Musicians, Dancers, etc. in London, 1660–1800* (*BDA*) focuses on her private life. Though Marshall is noted for her portrayal of vengeful, "evil" women and her acting partnership with Boutell, the *BDA* highlights her off-stage exploits. In this account, Marshall is primarily described as a promiscuous woman who complained about her treatment at the hands of actors and audience members. In 1665 she complained to the Lord Chamberlain that the actor Mark Trevor had sexually assaulted her both on and off the stage, and in February 1667 accused Sir Hugh Middleton of various offenses and assaults. Marshall was particularly upset that she had been followed by one of Middleton's men who threw feces in her face (107). The *BDA* and other histories that include this anecdote, such as Rosamund Gilder's *Enter the Actress* and J. H. Wilson's *All the King's Ladies*, use this event to prove that actresses were frequently assaulted, their bodies sexually used and grossly abused by audience members and actors who believed they were fair game for such treatment.

A counter-narrative for this anecdote is also available. Rather than viewing Marshall as the victim of male sexual predation, it is possible to interpret her actions as an attempt to stand against her antagonists. Marshall used her position as one of the King's servants – as an actress, she was entitled to his protection – to punish men who had made unwelcome sexual advances and metaphorically insulted her purity and morality by throwing excrement at her. This counter-narrative does not contradict that actresses were viewed as sexually available and low class, but rather suggests that there is more to their experiences than mere oppression. Traditional accounts tend to only consider the subjugation of actresses and not their potential for agency. In the case of Betty Boutell, historians have used the whore stigma to virtually erase considerations of her longevity, innovation, and popularity in accounts of her life.

I argue that Betty Boutell's case history offers an example of how the whore stigma might have been deployed and subverted in Caroline London. English actresses, often used to signal the shift from the golden age of Shakespearean drama to the highly sexualized Restoration theatre, registered a newly visible preoccupation with female sexual experience, parallel with the class and gender tensions of Caroline society. Placing histories of first generation English actresses in the context of histories of marriage, sex, and the family as well as histories of Restoration theatre demonstrates how potentially transgressive narratives have been limited by historical inquiry. At the same time, Boutell's case history illuminates how marginalized women may provide counter-narratives: Boutell used her epithet in order to draw attention to her own (and by implication, other women's) potential sexual agency.

PHILANDERS AND PRUDES: HISTORIES OF MARRIAGE, SEX, AND THE FAMILY IN RESTORATION ENGLAND

Many historians suggest that Restoration sexuality represents a break in attitudes toward sexual pleasure rather than a shift in actual behavior, and that anxiety over Restoration sexual license was rooted in a Puritan-influenced ideology of proper sexuality. Puritans certainly viewed sexual fulfillment as central to happiness, satisfaction, and even godliness. The Puritan household "consisted of a male and female who were structurally identical in that they were represented as active and passive versions of the same attributes" (Armstrong and Tennenhouse "Introduction" 9), and both parties were responsible for the maintenance of affection, production, and procreation. Within this framework, marriage was an ideal state providing support, comfort, and sexual satisfaction for both partners. The Puritan minister Henry Smith, for example, assured his flock that "marriage itself is not sin . . . the bed is honourable, . . . that is, even the action of marriage is as lawful as marriage" (in Keeble *Cultural Identity* 120). Thus, the Puritan ideology of sexuality testified to its importance for the well-being of godly men and women by stressing its centrality within marriage. This notion of proper sexuality remained current throughout the Restoration, as the debauchery of Charles II's court was contrasted with the more conservative, domestic sexuality of the middle class.

Rake sexuality may have been particularly offensive to more conservative commentators because of the waste implied by sexual relations outside of marriage. The primarily aristocratic Wits surrounding Charles II: John

Wilmot, Lord Rochester; Henry Jermyn; Charles, Lord Buckhurst; John Sheffield; Sir Charles Sedley; Harry Killigrew; and playwrights George Etherege and William Wycherley pursued pleasure, not marriage, privileging their own satisfaction rather than the mutual comfort espoused by Puritan rhetoric. Outside of Charles II himself, Rochester and Wycherley are perhaps most responsible for publicizing and popularizing "rake" masculine sexuality: Wycherley's Horner in *The Country Wife* is clearly the archetype for rake sexuality, and Rochester's widely circulated erotic poetry celebrates male desire and sexual prerogative. According to Harold Weber, this pursuit of pleasure suggested that the aristocracy was no longer fit to rule, and that Charles II needed to be reined in lest he abuse his royal authority. He was criticized specifically for failing to "subordinate royal pleasure to royal duty" (Weber "Charles II" 195). Further, Charles II's inability to produce a legitimate heir was tied to his indiscriminate "spending" of both royal semen and royal monies on his many mistresses. Several satires challenged Charles II's ability to rule; their popularity testifies to Restoration concerns over the shift of sexuality from prudent to indiscriminate use (even though actual sexual behaviors may not necessarily have changed). Obviously, some of this concern reflects growing antagonism between the aristocracy and the nascent middle class, who worked thriftily for their success.

Within the ideology of rake sexuality, women are aggressively constructed as objects available for pleasure. Unlike the ideal middle-class wife "whose value resides chiefly in . . . possessing psychological depth rather than a physically attractive surface," the aristocratic mistresses "represented surface instead of depth, embodied material rather than moral values, and displayed idle sensuality where there should be constant vigilance and tireless concern for the well-being of others" (Armstrong and Tennenhouse "Introduction" 10). The first generation of English actresses seemed to be particularly suited to the role of mistress. As actresses, they were trained to dissemble and hide behind a character mask, and their willingness to display their bodies on stage indicated their "idle sensuality" and lack of morality. The surface beauty of the actress, not her character or moral core, was her chief hallmark and constituted a further separation between the player and the ideal wife. By seeming to embody the attributes hailed by Rochester and other Wits and subject to the material conditions of the playhouse that encouraged audience/player interaction, the first generation was easily included in existing discourses of promiscuity.

Of course, as Weber points out, this discursive construction is informed by "male anxiety generated by the threat of female sexuality; and to establish

a male order that can marginalize or erase the specter of female power"
("Charles II" 197). Many of the Wits were brutally misogynistic and eager to
supplement their alliances with women through congenial and sexual relationships with other men. Rochester's poetic willingness to "bugger his
page" and his assertion that men who love women are "asses" who choose
"the silliest part of God's creation" over young servant boys who do "the
trick worth forty wenches" (37) does indicate an impulse to erase female
desire and pleasure from the template of masculine sexuality. In fact, the
Caroline focus on illicit sexuality tends to privilege the male perspective:
within rake sexuality women are objects to be used and within more
conservative, domestic models, women are objects to be protected. This
erasure of female power is preserved within modern histories of the family,
sex, and marriage in England. These histories demonstrate how contemporary
assumptions about historical subjects are preserved and reinflected by modern
historians. The conventional patriarchal thrust of late seventeenth-century
sexuality is largely unexamined or unchanged within late twentieth-century
historical narratives.

Within these histories, masculine experience serves as the norm for
understanding marriage, sex, and the family. Even when female experiences are represented, they most often confirm existing assumptions about
patriarchal sexuality. Because, as Michel de Certeau points out, history is
"made from ideological or imaginary structures" (*Writing* 8), it is important to consider the gender and class biases through which traditional
histories of marriage, sex, and the family are written. Representative
historians Lawrence Stone, Alan MacFarlane, and G. R. Quaife tend to
view female sexuality and desire as an aberrant emotion that must be
explained away. Interrogating their narratives illuminates how female
subjectivity is elided within traditional histories, an omission relevant to
understanding how Restoration theatre studies similarly elides narratives of
female agency.

Lawrence Stone's 1977 *The Family, Sex and Marriage in England,*
1500–1800 is the foundational text for most historians of the English
family. Though it is flawed, both factually and theoretically,[5] it is the
starting point for interrogating changing family patterns in early modern
England. Stone argues that during the three-hundred-year period under
consideration, massive shifts occurred in the make-up of the (primarily
aristocratic) English family, resulting in an increase of what he terms
"Affective Individualism," or private, separate subjects joined by emotion
and choice. Within Stone's history, the Restoration is a period of flux,
when the patriarchal authority of husband and father gave way to a more

egalitarian family structure. This family structure was characterized by strong affective ties between husband and wife, who married to affirm personal, emotional bonds rather than to cement financial or political alliances. Children were loved and respected and greater autonomy was granted to female and younger members of the household. Stone's history further suggests a progression from autocratic patriarchy to feminized domesticity, positing that by the end of the nineteenth century, the English family was a model of morality, equality, and virtue.

Though Stone argues that the male-dominated household formed through political and economic alliance slowly shifted to a loving partnership of separate equals, his interpretation of women's experience tells differently. Stone includes the marital history of Mary Granville (later Delany), culled from her autobiography. According to that memoir, in 1717 at the age of seventeen, Mary was married to Mr. Pendarves, "an excessively fat ... person rather disgusting than engaging" of sixty (Delany in Stone *Family, Sex and Marriage* 209). Pendarves became an alcoholic, a fact Stone blames on "his failure to win the affection of his wife" (210) and died in 1726. Three years later, the widowed Mary re-met Lord Baltimore, a former suitor. According to Mary's autobiography, Lord Baltimore asked her to marry him, but declared he was "determined never to marry unless he was well assured of the affection of the person he married" (Delany in Stone *Family, Sex and Marriage* 211). Mary refused; as a widow she chose to marry him and so declined to offer any further proof of her love. Lord Baltimore was unconvinced and he left Mary to marry another, wealthier heiress. Stone claims that after Baltimore's rejection, Mary "turned violently against the whole male sex" (211). Of course, Mary ultimately remarried and had a daughter, a difficult feat if she "violently" rejected all subsequent suitors.

Stone explains Mary's encounter with Baltimore two ways, both indicating "the see-saw battle between family wishes and personal choice, between interest, money and affection" (211). Either Mary refused to reciprocate Baltimore's depth of feeling through sexual intercourse "because she preferred flirtation to commitment, being basically frigid" or Baltimore wanted to marry a richer wife and "had used the demand for a declaration of love, and maybe a consent to fornication, as an excuse to get out of a difficult situation" (211). Throughout his reading of Mary's autobiography, Stone blames her for her own maltreatment. She married Pendarves against her will, but Stone blames her for his alcoholism and early death. Lord Baltimore intimated that Mary sleep with him to prove her love and when she refused – with good reason, as she was rightfully wary of premarital intercourse and its possible effect on her reputation and health – Stone determines she was frigid. Nowhere in his retelling of this anecdote does Stone suggest that Mary made the best of a series of bad situations or seem to understand that her choices were severely limited by her gender. Instead, ignoring the narrative presented in the autobiography, ignoring Mary's own voice, Stone characterizes her as a frigid, castrating bitch.

Other historians offer economic reasons for changing marriage patterns; despite this alternate emphasis, however, these historians tend to replicate Stone's inattention to female subjectivity. For example, Alan MacFarlane's 1986 *Marriage and Love in England: Modes of Reproduction 1300–1840* suggests that changing economic factors were responsible for the demographic shifts in marriage, birth, and mortality rates, rather than Stone's Affective Individualism. In short, by the late seventeenth/early eighteenth century, Englishmen and women were putting off marriage until it was economically feasible. The rise in industry and urbanization combined to make late marriage more commercially sensible, as men judiciously chose to wait until they were financially stable before committing to a bride.

According to MacFarlane, late marriages alarmed some commentators, as they suggested that men and women were rejecting the Puritan ideal of matrimonial chastity, a concern tied to tensions over shifting markers of class boundaries. Statistics demonstrate that men and women in late seventeenth-century English society married later (at approximately age twenty-five) than they had two hundred years earlier, and later than their Continental counterparts (MacFarlane *Marriage* 148–62). Later marriage implied a shift away from the partnership ideal of the Puritan marriage. As Michael McKeon argues, the domestic economy of husband and wife equally involved in the economic survival of the household gave way to a market economy with the familial income increasingly derived from labor (rather than goods) produced by the male members of the household ("Historicizing Patriarchy" 299). Strict differences between men's (public, paid) employment and women's (private, unpaid) labor developed and the roots of nineteenth-century domestic ideology are evident in the shifting economics of the late seventeenth and early eighteenth centuries. Further, the preoccupation with class difference is coextensive with sexual and gender difference. Delaying marriage until the man was financially secure suggested that women's role in marriage was for pleasure rather than mutual aid and comfort: women were the reward for hard-working men.

MacFarlane's research suggests that in the seventeenth century husbands in particular were in short supply, a problem that was both lampooned and legislated against. A late seventeenth-century ballad opined that

> A young man need never take thought how to wive
> For widows and maidens for husbands do strive
> Here's scant men enough for them all left alive
> They flock to the Church, like Bees to the hive.
>
> (in MacFarlane *Marriage* 150)

This quatrain, and others like it, suggest that women were desperate to marry, although male and female populations remained relatively equal throughout the period. MacFarlane's anecdotal evidence stressing feminine desire to marry is supported in part by legal strictures targeting single men. A 1695 Act taxed men over twenty-five who remained bachelors and widowers who did not remarry were taxed at an even higher rate (MacFarlane *Marriage* 150). MacFarlane reads this legislation as an example of attempting to control and regulate male sexuality; it seems equally likely that unmarried women posed a similar concern. Women, who rarely controlled their own property, could not be taxed for remaining single; thus, the legislation addressed female reluctance to marry by default.

Non-traditional histories do offer a fuller account of female sexuality. G. R. Quaife's 1979 *Wanton Wenches and Wayward Wives* offers a prurient view of specifically rural Puritan and Restoration sexuality. As the title suggests, Quaife focuses on female sexuality and the problem of transgressive women. Tracing sexual behavior in Somerset, England, 1601–60, Quaife argues that Restoration "bawdiness" is contiguous with rather than opposed to the sexual behavior of the Puritans and other early Englishmen and women. Quaife's narrative covers a shorter historical period and features titillating accounts of peasant sexuality to closely describe a social and geographic group left out of more traditional histories. Using depositions to the Quarter Sessions of the County of Somerset and the Consistory Court of the Diocese of Bath and Wells, Quaife persuasively argues that (rural) Puritans were as bawdy as their (primarily aristocratic and urban) descendants. Studying rural, primarily peasant-class men and women,[6] Quaife offers an important counter-history of English sexuality, suggesting that sexual practices were in fact fairly constant between the Puritan and Caroline eras and between urban and rural groups. However, his focus on "wanton" women demonstrates that he too posits female sexuality as a threat to normative patriarchal family structures.

Quaife's study demonstrates that the peasants of Somerset took advantage of every opportunity to engage in sexual relations. Most advanced sexual activity consisted of the manual stimulation of the penis, clitoris, and vagina (Quaife *Wanton Wenches* 165), an activity that was possible to perform even on horse back: "he carried her beside him upon his horse or mare from Wells . . . and did feel her by the privy member twenty times by the way" (Weare Parish Records, Vol. 300; in Quaife *ibid.* 49). While these activities were sometimes punished by fines, public floggings, and even imprisonment, Quaife argues that penalties exacted for illicit sexual behavior seem based on maintaining order within the community rather than breaking a Church- or State-prescribed code of morality. Fornication or other sexual activity became a problem only when it threatened the financial and social harmony of the peasant community. Quaife demonstrates that "[s]exual behavior often invoked comment and action not because it breached secular or ecclesiastical law but because it flew in the face of custom" (43). Frequently, unmarried men and women who were caught engaging in illicit sex were hastily sent to church, married without the customary reading of the banns or even family and friends present (59–88). Further, the declaration of intent to marry was as binding as formal marriage vows within most rural communities; sexual intercourse without the blessing of the church but with the promise of an eventual formal ceremony was not illicit sexual activity, as (at least in the eyes of the community) it occurred within marriage (61).

Wanton Wenches is colored by conflicting assumptions about women and their sexual agency. Quaife tends to view illicit sexual activity as actions perpetrated on and against the female, who is seduced by sweet words and promises of everlasting devotion into surrendering her honor. In his history, men seduced and "innocent spinsters . . . lost their virginity" (58). On the other hand, Quaife characterizes widows and some unmarried women as prostitutes and promiscuous women who actively solicited sex. Quaife divides rural prostitutes into four categories: the poor, wandering vagrant whore; the public whore working out of an inn or tavern; the private whore, or kept mistress; and the village whore "who ranged from the slut to the almost respectable protector of the chastity and fidelity of other village women" (146). One notable village whore, Mary Combe, offers an opportunity to further interrogate feminine sexual agency and peasant attitudes about female sexuality. Combe publicly solicited sex "in the highway between Axbridge and Crosse, and called to all persons passing, by spreading her legs abroad, saying: 'Come play with my cunt and make my husband a cuckold'" (in *Wanton Wenches* 157) but was never penalized for her behavior. Though Quaife denigrates Combe and ranks her with the lowest village whores, her behavior suggests another possible interpretation. Perhaps her blandishments to cuckold her husband are an attempt to wrest sexual prerogative from an errant spouse. Though Combe's story is sketchy, Quaife (like Stone and McFarlane) foreclose possibilities for female sexual agency.

Lois G. Schwoerer's 1984 feminist critique "Seventeenth-Century English Women Engraved in Stone?" calls for a broader understanding of female sexuality across the classes during this period. She faults Stone primarily for his masculinist assumptions: "[women] are not to be studied as individuals, but only in their relationship to others, men and children; or in other words, that their lives can be understood only in the private sphere of the family" (390), a critique many echo. Schwoerer questions Stone's fundamental assumptions, arguing that his family models are doubtful because of the dearth of data reflecting a female experience. Schwoerer's critique illuminates how female sexual agency is elided within traditional histories of marriage, sex, and the family.

In particular, Schwoerer refutes Stone's assumptions about romantic love. Noting that Stone suggests romantic love in marriage existed only after 1780, only among the upper classes, and only after the spread of novel reading, Schwoerer asserts that romantic love "struck all persons in all classes throughout the seventeenth century, and earlier" (398).[7] Indeed, female love and even sexual desire are recorded and thus available for analysis. Schwoerer's research demonstrates that some (aristocratic) women were clearly able to assert their sexual and romantic desires, although notably within the trope of courtly love (401).

Reading these representative histories of marriage, sex, and the family in early modern England makes obvious the difficulty in accounting for female sexual agency.[8] In the absence of much significant primary source material, most historians subsume female sexuality either within the discourse of rake sexuality, which posits women as objects, or within nascent domestic ideology, which insists on separation of feminine and masculine sexuality. The absence of sustained inquiry into feminine subjectivity within these histories might be understood through de Certeau's theories on the writing of history. "Modern Western history," he writes, "essentially begins with differentiation between the *present* and the *past*" (*Writing* 2). These representative histories, with their emphasis on masculine sexuality, attempt to mark a difference between the late twentieth century and the Restoration. The brutal misogyny of rake sexuality and the hierarchical separation of female and male spheres of Puritan domesticity are implicitly contrasted with the presumed equality of the post-sexual revolution era. Leaving these absences unexamined, however, modern historians reinscribe notions of female passivity.

Though most Restoration historians agree that "[t]he chief advantage of the Restoration actress over the boy player of the Elizabethan stage lay in her looks" (Styan *Restoration Comedy* 93), this understanding suggests that the ideal male spectator was the one looking. Within the plays themselves, the passive heroines seem to mask tensions about sex and gender by presenting women as objects and victims. More importantly, the recirculation and repetition of anecdotal evidence about actresses' sexuality constructed actresses as being as passive as the characters they portrayed. Here, I examine material shifts in Restoration theatrical production to illuminate its ideological meanings. As Stuart Hall insists, "no social practice or set of relations floats free of the determinate effects of the concrete relations in which they are located" ("Problem" 45). The new theatre instituted major changes: revisions of standard texts; advances in theatre technology; and the inclusion of women guaranteed that the theatre enjoyed by Restoration audiences was radically different from the theatre enjoyed by their grandparents. These literary, technical, and physical differences suggest that the uses, pleasures, and meanings of theatre for Caroline society were different as well. Not surprisingly, there has been a great deal of critical inquiry[9] into Restoration theatre; however, positing the actress as the focus for inquiry and assuming a monolithic (male) audience response colors theatre histories in much the same way as traditional histories of marriage, sex, and the family are influenced by male narratives; the assumptions of both kinds of history obviously mirror each other. In short, Restoration theatre studies has participated in the reinscription of the discourse of the actress/whore to the exclusion of alternative interpretations. Here, I offer both that traditional history and a discussion of its limits.

For nearly twenty years, from 1642–60, the theatre was outlawed in England; until Charles II's restoration to the throne, theatrical production and performance were underground at best and non-existent at worst. In 1660 Charles II awarded patents to Thomas Killigrew, who had written plays prior to Puritan rule and had accompanied the court to France, and William Davenant, who had remained in England producing "musical entertainments" during the Interregnum. These patents guaranteed the two managers a virtual monopoly over all theatrical production in London. Killigrew headed the King's Company and hired many professional, experienced actors[10] and Davenant headed the Duke's Company, principled with younger, new actors.[11] The patent system led to fierce competition between the companies, each adding technical, literary, and histrionic improvements to their companies. Of course, the inclusion of women was an important facet of the competition. Killigrew staged *The Moor of Venice* with his female Desdemona, probably Ann Marshall or Katherine Corey, in January 1661. Davenant too began to capitalize on the presence of actresses, and both companies commissioned new plays and revised the canon in order to include more female roles (Milhous and Hume *Producible*, 36–37). For example, John Dryden's 1667 adaptation of *The Tempest*, renamed *The Enchanted Island*, added sisters for both Miranda and Caliban, gave Ariel a fiancée, and introduced Hippolito, a man who had never before seen a woman (Howe *First English Actresses* 63). These additions tripled the number of female characters, and Hippolito's naïveté provided opportunities for commenting on female characteristics and physical attributes. This refashioning of canonical texts suggests that theatre companies took every opportunity to exploit the novelty of the female body.

For the most part, the body of the actress is assumed to have precipitated shifts in theatre design as well as revisions to play texts. Jill Dolan argues that "[t]he lighting, setting, costumes, blocking, text – all the material aspects of theatre – are manipulated so that the performance's meanings are intelligible to a particular spectator, constructed in a particular way by the terms of its address" (*Feminist Spectator* 1). Though Dolan is writing about twentieth-century realist theatre, her criticism is relevant here. Traditional Restoration theatre histories demonstrate how production changes in three key areas – playing space, lighting, and scene changes – are assumed to have privileged an ideal male spectator who was particularly interested in the actresses' bodies and sexual availability. Though more recent histories have begun to complicate these assumptions, they bear rehearsing here, as they demonstrate how the link between acting and prostitution has influenced interpretations of Restoration stagecraft. Killigrew, Davenant, and their successors improved their theatres regularly, in part to highlight the bodies and personalities of the actresses.

In general, Restoration theatres were based on the same design. The stage was truncated by a proscenium arch with acting areas and scenic devices behind the arch; the primary acting area extended in front of the arch into the seating area, or pit, where most audience members sat on benches (Howe *First English Actresses* 3). In addition, tiers of boxes extended away from the stage: side boxes along the walls of the theatre and front boxes along the back. There was a gallery above the front boxes and pit (Styan *Restoration Comedy* 25). The use of playing space is hotly debated by scholars, but most agree that the majority of the action took place before the proscenium arch. Significantly, actors and actresses played in front of the scenery, close to the audience. This division of playing space suggests that actors and actresses played to and with the audience, physically close to the benches and gallery boxes. Further, the backstage area was probably connected to the auditorium by passages through the wings, and the dressing rooms were probably accessible to the actors by a set of stairs on either side of the stage (Jordan "Restoration Playgoers" 67–68). Audience members were free to go backstage to the tiring, or dressing, rooms and visit with or watch the actors and actresses as they prepared for performance or rested afterward. The physical intimacy of the actors and audiences arguably decreased the social barriers between them and, within the theatre at least, is presumed by most historians to have broken down the hierarchical divisions between aristocrat and artist.

As the above examples demonstrate, Restoration theatre studies assume that stagecraft held specific meanings for the audience (and that the audience's response can be adequately gauged despite few primary sources). According to Judith Milhous and Robert D. Hume, the audience for Restoration theatre was primarily made up of a core group of only a few hundred people (*Producible* 38). Further, this core is assumed to be primarily male, and theatre-going is viewed as a male activity.[12] Most historians agree with J. L. Styan "that for a particular social group the playhouses were on a pleasure circuit that included the parks and the brothels, the gaming-houses and the bagnios" (*Restoration Comedy* 7). In addition, the theatre was intimately connected with the court of Charles II and part of his and his courtiers' daily routine. The audience therefore was relatively small and relatively insular. If Pepys is taken as an authority – and he usually is – most audience members were recognizable to each other and used the playhouse to further their business and congenial relationships. The fraternal character of the playhouse seems to support assumptions that actresses appeared for the pleasure and titillation of the primarily male audience. In addition, the ideal spectator is constructed as male; not only because men seemed to make up the majority of the audience but also because, as Dolan points out, the "ideal spectator [is] carved in the likeness of the dominant culture whose ideology he represents" (1). Thus, understandings of the first generation of English actresses are drawn from the position of this ideal, male spectator.

Of course, information on the Restoration audience is severely limited, and the experiences and attitudes of regulars like Pepys are extrapolated onto all audience members. The discussion of female audience members is even less adequate. David Roberts, who bases *The Ladies: Female Patronage of Restoration Drama 1660–1700* on the experience of Elizabeth Pepys as reported by her husband, argues that women, though present, were largely ignored. Some support for this position comes from Restoration prologues and epilogues, which were opportunities for players to directly address the audience, bringing them into the action. Women were mentioned in only forty percent of prologues and epilogues, compared to men who were mentioned more than twice as often (28). Prologues and epilogues that did mention women often suggested that the theatre was not intended for ladies, as Boutell insinuated in her prologue to an all female production of Dryden's *Secret Love*: "The ladies we shall not so easily please. / They'l (sic) say what impudent bold things are these / That dare provoke yet cannot do us right." Women may well have been actively excluded from the community of the playhouse audience.

Further, many critics argue that the spectatrix was narratively excluded as well. Plots that constructed women as "objects of rude fancy, mere referents of sexual experience, in the banter of playwright and male audience" (Roberts *The Ladies* 28) seem to offer little to female audience members. Pat Gill argues that the spectatrix was entertained by representations of women as sexual objects, but not allowed or able to recognize that representation as referring to herself (*Interpreting Ladies* 11); following from Gill, women found pleasure in watching the female on stage not as an extension of themselves but as an Other, constructed for their viewing pleasure, with little to ground her as referent to their own lives. The differences between the whorish actress, the vulnerable character, and the morally and socially secure spectatrix determined that for women, Restoration theatre was only entertainment.

These explanations, however, seem inadequate to fully describe interpretative practices. Almost certainly the "ideal" audience member was joined by women (and men) reading differently. For example, Restoration heroines, though often sexually assaulted and used, did

commonly insist on making their own affective, erotic, and marital choices, offering identifactory opportunities for female audience members that suggest the ambivalence of both representations of female sexuality and the material conditions of (at least) the elite female audience members. (Rosenthal "Reading Masks" 203)

Behn's heroines are often as sexually aggressive as their male counterparts, and characters like Wycherly's Margery Pinchwife develop throughout the plays, moving from the position of innocent bystander to worldly player in the games of sexual intrigue marking Restoration comedy. Further, the presumed sexual transgressions of the actresses may have fascinated and even inspired female audience members. If Rebecca Marshall could face her accusers in court, demanding apology and reparation, what might more socially powerful audience members be able to ask from their husbands and from society? Perhaps most importantly, the sexual appeal of Restoration actresses, especially those who appeared in breeches, may not have been limited to male audience members. Queer historian Kendall suggests that, especially during the reign of Queen Anne, some spectators would have read plays such as Catherine Trotter's *Agnes de Castro* as "the lesbian love story it is" ("Ways of Looking" 109); her work on this and other Restoration texts is an important corrective to traditional theatre studies that suppose the male audience member as the only interpretative position.

Notwithstanding that audiences held different interpretations of and interests in the actresses' bodies, their familiarity with conventions of Restoration performance suggests complicity with a system of representation that favored certain meanings. In particular, audiences were encouraged to correlate between actor and role. According to Katharine Eisaman Maus, "[a]ctresses as well as actors were praised not for their ability to depict any character with equal skill, but for their ability to inform their dramatic portrayals with the force of their personal talent and idiosyncratic vision" ("Playhouse" 598). Stage roles were presumed to be an extension of the actors' and actresses' personalities. Anne Bracegirdle, for example, was noteworthy for her refusal to take a lover; her off-stage reputation lent credence to her portrayals of innocent virgins. On the other hand, Elizabeth Barry, mistress to the notorious Lord Rochester (among others), was laughed off the stage for playing Cordelia "arm'd in . . . virgin innocence" (Chetwood *History of the Stage* 28). According to Milhous and Hume, playwrights often wrote with specific actors in mind, as the "mad couple" comedies of the late 1660s were written for off-stage lovers Nell Gwyn and Charles Hart (*Producible* 51). In addition, actors and actresses probably used typecasting to create and bolster their reputations, especially in the early days of their career. For example, Boutell played more breeches roles than any other actress of her generation, which enhanced her popularity and was an important component in her construction as a whore, as I demonstrate below. Further, actors and actresses usually kept their roles until they retired from the stage (Milhous and Hume *Producible* 48). Therefore, Boutell probably played the breeches-clad ingenue Fidelia in William Wycherly's *The Plain Dealer* for twenty-five years, though she had switched companies twice, retired once, and aged considerably during this time period (Downes *Roscius* 117). Spanning several decades, her association with ingenue and breeches roles was particularly strong and cemented her reputation as beautiful and desirable.

Though actors and actresses played similar roles over again, concretizing a specific persona, many historians, such as Thomas A. King, argue that audiences remained aware of sharp distinctions between player and role, especially regarding class. The appetite for comedies based on the foibles of the aristocracy demanded that actors and actresses play above their station regularly: a simple, untutored girl or ill-bred, vulgar young man might impersonate the queens and kings of legend as well as society wives and rake-heroes. In addition, theatrical wardrobes for both men and women were frequently supplemented by the castoffs of wealthy patrons (King "Reconstructing" 79). The stage provided both actors and actresses with entrée to a wealthier and more elite circle than they would have enjoyed had they stayed with their families, presumably remaining in their fathers' profession or marrying men of their class. Downes' chestnut about Moll Davis singing so "Charmingly, that not long after, it Rais'd her from her bed on the Cold Ground, to a Bed Royal" (Downes *Roscius* 55) bears repeating here; by convincingly and charmingly impersonating an innocent virgin dressed in the clothes of a Restoration lady, Davis became mistress to a king. The actors' and actresses' dissimulations, then, fueled fears of increasingly permeable boundaries between Caroline classes.

Actors and actresses enjoyed other class privileges. They were granted the right to liveries, "elaborate scarlet cloaks with crimson capes to be worn on state occasions" (Howe *First English Actresses* 27). In addition to being a mark of status, the right to wear liveries identified actresses as servants of the king, signifying that creditors could not arrest and sue them for debt without the permission of the Lord Chamberlain of the Household, raising them above most lower- and middle-class audience members.

The tension surrounding actresses' class position was exacerbated by the first generation of English actresses' bids for professionalization. At a historical moment when the female labor market was narrowing, women working in the theatres enjoyed more financial autonomy than most other working women, who were almost exclusively domestic servants or prostitutes. Although actresses were never so well paid as their male counterparts, they did have some input into their careers (and notably, acting is a career where whoring and servitude are not); Mary Saunderson Betterton and Anne Bracegirdle's co-management of Lincoln's Inn Fields exemplifies the pinnacle of career control any actor could hope to attain. Many feminist histories highlight the actresses' professional status, suggesting they were set apart from other early modern women workers, enjoying the respect and admiration of their society because they were skilled workers in a field traditionally dominated by men.[13] While this interpretation is certainly refreshing, it elides the merciless attention given to actresses' bodies and personal lives, suggesting that professionalization and sexuality are incommensurable. Betty Boutell's case history, however, suggests that the first generation may have used the intense interest in their sexuality as a career strategy. While the whore stigma was deployed to limit actresses' autonomy and mitigate their inroads into Restoration class hierarchy, Boutell's narrative suggests that some actresses may have used their own spectacular sexuality to carve out a performance niche and guarantee theatrical success.

FUCKING BETTY BOUTELL: CONTEMPORARY AND HISTORICAL CONSTRUCTIONS OF THE ACTRESS/WHORE

The discursive convergence of the actress and the whore permeated the lives of all Restoration players. Thomas Betterton's wife Mary played den mother to many of the actresses in her husband's company, attempting to maintain their innocence and moral purity. According to her husband's biography,[14] she found it a "[t]ask more laborious and difficult than any Hercules had" (Betterton *History* 23) since audience members frequently took advantage of their access to the tiring rooms – and then took advantage of the actresses changing or resting there. Regardless of whether or not actresses welcomed these advances, they were represented as sexually available, and this representation dominated the popular imagination. Betty Boutell's construction as a whore establishes how the discursive, narrative, and visual images of the first English actresses worked to limit their agency by relegating them to an object position, a nomination modern historians have generally upheld. The circulation of anecdotes about Boutell's sexual availability, both during her life and in the historical record of that life, testifies to the way the whore stigma is deployed in order to limit female sexual agency and the way history, especially the history of women, is written.

Though Boutell was not as famous as Barry, Bracegirdle, or Gwyn, she had a particularly long career (ca. 1662–97) and was an important player. She was particularly successful in her acting partnership with Rebecca Marshall. During the 1670s, the two were frequently paired as rivals for the hero's affection, with Boutell playing the innocent virgin willing to sacrifice for love and Marshall the evil, lustful villainess. Their pairing, like

Nell Gwyn and Charles Hart's influential "mad couple," started the vogue for rival tragic heroines. Their rivalry was imitated by Mary Betterton and Mary Lee of the Duke's Company, and revived by Elizabeth Barry and Anne Bracegirdle's "she-tragedies" of the 1680s and 1690s. Boutell and Marshall's first successful pairing featured Marshall playing Fulvia opposite Boutell's Aurelia in William Joyner's 1670 *The Roman Empress*. After the first performance, Joyner commented that "Fulvia . . . has been ever much extoll'd: if my art had fail'd in the writing of it, it was highly recompenc'd in the scenical presentation; for it was incomparably acted. . . . Aurelia, which though a great, various and difficult part, was excellently performed" (xii). The two were paired again in Wycherley's 1676 *Plain Dealer* and Nathaniel Lee's 1677 *Tragedy of Nero* and *Alexander the Great*. Significantly, Boutell played most of these roles in breeches, and her duplicitous assumption of masculine dress was always discovered and understood as an expression of her sacrificial love. Marshall, who did not cross-dress, was motivated by lust and jealousy. Her disguise was emotional rather than physical. Where Boutell's heroines resorted to trickery only when forced by circumstance, Marshall's villainesses were duplicitous by nature. At the end of the drama, both were emotionally and/or physically exposed, and Boutell got her man.

Despite Boutell's theatrical success, she is best remembered as a whore. Again, "whore" seems to mean differently in the Restoration; rather than suggesting commercial sexuality, especially as reclaimed by the prostitutes' rights movement, whore is better understood as sexually visible. Thus, though Boutell was never named the mistress of an aristocratic man, nor are any specifics about her illicit sexual activities available to modern historians, she was included as a Restoration actress/prostitute by her contemporaries. This designation is not particularly remarkable: with few exceptions the first generation was subject to this accusation. However, " . . . chestnut-maned Boutell, whom all the Towne fucks" (quoted in Howe *First English Actresses* 35), seems to have engendered especially close sexual scrutiny. A Restoration lampoon promises

> Betty Bowtall[15] is true to whom she pretends
> Then happy is hee whom she Chuses for friend
> Shee faine would hang out Widdows peak for a signe
> But ther's noe need of Bush where there is so good wine.
>
> (in Wilson *All the Kings' Ladies* 97)

This quatrain asserts that Boutell was so well known as sexually promiscuous that she did not need to advertise; further, it implies that she was a particularly practiced and skilled whore. A 1688 satire calls Boutell "that whore . . . poor Armstrong's life betrayed / And passed upon Maccarty for a Maid" (in Milhous "Elizabeth" 127). Thomas Betterton's memoirs also suggest that Boutell was popular both on-stage and off.

> Mrs. Boutel [sic] was likewise a very considerable Actress: she was low Stature, had very agreeable features, a good Complexion but a Childish Look. Her Voice was weak, tho' very mellow. She generally acted the young Innocent Lady whom all the Heroes are mad in Love with; she was a Favourite of the Town; and besides what she saved by Playing, the Generosity of some happy Lovers enabled her to quit the Stage before she grew old. (21)

Here, Boutell is described as a good actress, but Betterton primarily focuses on her physical attributes. Of course, as a theatre manager, Betterton was likely to comment on any actor's or actress's appearance. Unfortunately, he does not give the same attention to the "happy Lovers" who supported Boutell. Perhaps, as the above lampoon suggests, Boutell's offstage exploits were so well known he did not need to name names; perhaps he was displaying a gentlemanly discretion, perhaps he was repeating unfounded gossip. His comments seems facile and dismissive for an actress of Boutell's importance, especially in what is ostensibly a collection of actors' biographies and critical comment on their performances.

Betterton's other anecdote about Boutell also focuses on her personal life. He remembers an incident between Boutell and Elizabeth Barry. Barry and Boutell quarreled over a scarf before a performance and Barry stuck a dagger about one-quarter inch into Boutell's side as the two actresses played a scene together. The audience, according to Betterton, believed "Mrs. Barry was jealous of Mrs. Boutel and Lord Rochester, which made them suppose she did it with Design to destroy her" (22). The audience's assumption that Boutell was involved in a love triangle, with Lord Rochester no less, points to their belief that she was sexually promiscuous. This story is probably apocryphal: it is unlikely that Boutell was ever the mistress of Lord Rochester as he never mentions her in any of his poems or writings, and because Barry and Boutell are only recorded as having played together three times, in 1695 and 1696, when Boutell was playing supporting roles to Barry's star turns with Anne Bracegirdle. However, this incident is recounted in several biographies of the first generation, further indicating how anecdotes and oral culture pass into texts and are so accorded the status of documentary evidence. Based on her roles, her status within several lampoons and satires, her contemporaries' accounts, and the assumption of Restoration audiences, Boutell by the late twentieth century is constructed as the exemplary actress/whore.

The actual extent of Betty Boutell's illicit sexual activity is unclear. The complete "truth" of her life is unknowable given the absence of much documentary evidence; rather, examining how anecdotes have positioned Boutell within theatrical history is more fruitful. Facts about the historical Elizabeth Boutell do little to refute or support her construction as a whore. Judith Milhous has conducted the only sustained inquiry into Boutell's life, and even her copious research provides little more than a sketchy biography. According to Milhous, Elizabeth Boutell is the daughter of Christopher Davenport and Frances, née Ridley. With her sister Frances, Boutell joined Killigrew's King's Company in the early 1660s as a teenager under her maiden name ("Elizabeth" 124–25).[16] Sometime after 1669, Elizabeth Davenport married Barnaby Boutell, the son of Barnaby Boutell of Parham Hall, Suffolk. The Boutells were a fairly well-to-do and well-respected family ("Elizabeth" 124–25). Boutell's first part under her married name was Aurelia, a breeches role, in William Joyner's *The Roman Empress* in 1670 (van Lennep *History* 46). Boutell's success as Aurelia may have typed her as an actress willing to expose herself on stage. She played many roles from 1670 to 1677; ten of them were breeches parts. No record of Boutell acting exists from 1678 to 1688. She may have been living in a convent in France (Milhous "Elizabeth" 126) or accompanying Barnaby, who was commissioned by William III in Holland (Highfill, Burnim, and Langhans *BDA* 260).

Though Boutell seems to have led a relatively prosperous and respectable married life in the 1670s and 1680s, she sporadically continued her theatrical career. Boutell returned to the stage in 1688 and stayed until 1690, although few roles, and none of them breeches parts, are recorded for her during this period. However, she may have been allowed to reclaim some of her old parts (Milhous "Elizabeth" 126). She traveled back and forth from England to Holland several times in the early 1690s, often with her friend, the actress Elizabeth Price. In 1695 Boutell returned to London to help Price in her unsuccessful lawsuit against the Earl of Banbury (Milhous "Elizabeth" 127–28). After the lawsuit, Boutell stayed in London, probably to care for her sister Frances, who was seriously ill. She joined Thomas Betterton's rebel company at Lincoln's Inn Fields and was often cast as Anne Bracegirdle's sister or friend (Milhous "Elizabeth" 128). Nearing fifty, she was cast in a breeches role, Constantia in George Granville's *The She-Gallants*, and her final role was the ingenue Francillia in *Love's a Jest* (Howe *First English Actresses* 182). She probably permanently retired from the stage in 1697.

Betty Boutell lived a relatively cosmopolitan life, traveling throughout Europe, consorting with minor members of the peerage, and playing on the stage for over twenty-five years. Because she had an active career and married a prosperous man, Boutell was probably relatively wealthy. When Boutell testified for Elizabeth Price in 1695, she told the court she had "Lately bought an Annuity for life of £25 per Annum and that she was heiresse to an Estate of £200 of her Sisters and an interest in her Uncle Ridleyes Estate as Coheire with her Sister when her Uncle dyes" (quoted in Milhous "Elizabeth" 126). She received money from the estate of John Chamberlain, her sister Frances's first husband, and collected a debt of £300 from Justin Maccarty, the third son of the Earl of Clancarty, in 1692; according to one lampoon, he was her lover. When she died in 1715, she left bequests worth about £800, a solid but far from extravagant sum. Her husband Barnaby, to whom she was married for over thirty years, had died sometime before 1711 and she left her money to friends and relatives. There were no bequests to theatre people, people who were likely former lovers, or children (Milhous "Elizabeth" 130–31). Her biography suggests Boutell was a particularly successful and independent woman who managed her own considerable finances and was controlled by neither her husband nor lovers.

Because the historical record on Boutell is incomplete, it is impossible to determine with any certainty her actual sexual life. Instead, it seems more salient to focus on how and why her whore status was constructed within her own time and maintained through the historical record than to attempt to prove or disprove the extent of her sexual affairs. One explanation for her status may lie in the perceived correlation between Boutell's stage roles and her off-stage personality. Though Boutell generally played "the young Innocent Lady whom all the Heroes were mad in Love with" (Betterton *History* 21), she played that role in figure-revealing breeches more than any other actress of her day. I argue that this exposure, more than her promiscuity, marked Boutell as a whore.

Three of Boutell's characters exemplify how the conventions of the breeches role facilitated display of the female body. In William Wycherly's *The Country Wife* (1675), Boutell played the innocent and beautiful Margery Pinchwife, a role she originated. Her husband brings her to London, but is afraid both that she will be spoiled by the luxuries and freedoms she sees there and that other men will fall in love with her. He finally agrees to take her around town, but insists she disguise herself as a man. Unfortunately for him (and following the generic conventions of the play), the scheme backfires. Horner, the very man Mr. Pinchwife hoped to avoid, easily sees through Margery's disguise. In front of her husband, who is unable to protest without giving away his wife's identity, Horner kisses Margery three times, then invites his friends Harcourt and Dorilant to kiss her as well before taking the "boy" back to his chambers (Wycherly *Country Wife*

III.ii.483–99). Ultimately, as in many plays, the breeches character is sensationally unmasked: Margery is exposed both as a woman and as a willing player in Horner's games of sexual intrigue. In this play, the breeches role exists solely for the enjoyment of Pinchwife, Horner, and the audience. In order to satisfy her husband, Margery agrees to dress in boy's clothes. Then, at the mercy of Horner's advances because she is in disguise, Margery suffers his attentions. The audience enjoys the spectacle of the beautiful actress displaying her body and being manhandled by the actors in the play.

One of Boutell's earliest breeches roles is equally gratuitous. Boutell created Benzayda in John Dryden's *Conquest of Granada* in 1670. Benzayda is a Moorish noblewoman, who loves Ozmyn, a member of another tribe. When he is taken prisoner, she dresses as a man both to follow him and prove her worthiness. When she meets him in prison, she proclaims:

> Ozmyn, no.
> I did not take on me this bold disguise,
> For ends so low to cheat your watchmens eies.
> When I attempted this; it was to doe
> An Action, to be envy'd ev'n by you.   (130)

Her courage and faithfulness demonstrate her love and the two eventually marry. Interestingly, Dryden does not show Benzayda acting bravely or tricking the guards in her costume. She appears to Ozmyn "dressed in the habit of a man" (129) and remains so for the rest of the play, although she is not mistaken for a man by any of the characters Dryden shows interacting with her. She appears in breeches only after the need for them is over. The breeches costume is completely gratuitous, showing the lengths Restoration heroines had to go in order to prove their love as well as the lengths Restoration actresses might go in order to insure their inclusion on the stage.

As Fidelia in William Wycherly's *The Plain Dealer*, a part written for her, Boutell spends the entire play in breeches. Fidelia disguises herself as a young boy so she can follow her beloved Manly to sea. Manly, unfortunately, is in love with Olivia, and sends Fidelia to woo Olivia for him. Olivia falls in love with Fidelia. When Olivia's husband Vernish finds out, Fidelia is nearly raped and Boutell is fondled on stage in order to prove she is a woman and therefore incapable of making love to Olivia.

FIDELIA: I am a woman, sir, a very unfortunate woman.
VERNISH: How! A very handsome woman, I'm sure then. Here are witnesses of it too, I confess – (Pulls off her peruke and feels her breasts).
     (Wycherly, *Plain Dealer* IV.ii 377–80)

Eventually Manly discovers Olivia's falseness and marries Fidelia. The unmasking scene in *The Plain Dealer* typifies such scenes in Restoration comedy. Several Restoration plays, such as *The Rival Ladies* by Dryden and Aphra Behn's *The Younger Brother*, call for actresses to open their bodices and actually expose their breasts to the audience. Thus, the breeches role is traditionally assumed to be symptomatic of male sexual domination.

Though the breeches role and its necessary display seem to underscore the sexual exploitation of the actress, here again the ideal male spectator sets the terms of debate. Though contemporary theories of cross-dressing and transvestitism both on and off the stage suggest that the cross-dressed female assumes masculine privilege,[17] Restoration breeches roles are generally understood as reinforcing sexual stereotypes: "It was attractive actresses who were given the chance to play breeches parts" (Rogers "Breeches Roles" 248). Cross-dressing provocatively highlights the hips, buttocks, and legs, as

[t]he breeches part of the Restoration was introduced first for the youthful actress to display as much of the female anatomy below the waist as a man's dress would allow; in an age when women wore their skirts to the ground, a shapely ankle or calf was provocative and a pair of Holland thighs would be sensational. (Styan *Restoration Comedy* 134)

Most agree that women in men's clothes were read as sexually alluring during the Restoration. Thus, contemporary theories of cross-dressing are presumed to be inadequate to explain Restoration convention; if the ideal (male) spectator sees sexual titillation, then other explanations for cross-dressing are unimportant. In addition, scholars assert that the importance of breeches roles and the accusations of promiscuity that followed Restoration actresses made them as exposed and passive as the heroines they portrayed. According to feminist critic Jean Marsden, women in Restoration plays, like the actresses who play them, are generally governed by love ("Rewritten Women" 47). Further, a female character donned breeches in order to pursue her beloved. Once she found him and/or won his love, she usually returned to her feminine clothes and a conventional female role (Howe *First English Actresses* 59). In a parallel construction, female actresses in breeches wore those figure-revealing clothes with the full knowledge they attracted male attention. When they received that attention, they accepted a role as mistress. Accordingly, Betty Boutell, playing at least ten different breeches roles several times over the course of her career, must certainly have been particularly sexualized.

The breeches role frequently entailed an unmasking scene, which may have further underscored Boutell's construction as a whore. Unmaskings are common in the exposure narratives of many Restoration plays, where heroes are revealed as duplicitous villains and secret ambitions motivate the action. In the case of female roles, such exposure typically marks a previously chaste character as sexually available: the breeches role raises the stakes of convention. Accordingly, within many narratives, the breeches actress, already sexually provocative because she exposes her legs, eventually displays her hair and breasts as well; in every way, the actress' body is on display. Further, Boutell's signature heroines, such as Fidelia, Christina, and Constantia, were written as passive, virtuous, and governed by love. Marsden suggests that "[t]he scenes of near-rape . . . problematise the helplessness characteristic of the idealised Restoration woman. Perversely, it is a woman's purity that attracts her ravisher" (Marsden "Rewritten Women" 53). Thus, the actress who portrayed the "nearly raped" woman was physically exposed and her chastity was revealed as a character mask.

According to Michael Ketchum, the Caroline self "is characterized through the multifarious encounters and social performances of the city where the private self is depicted as an interior 'core' of selfhood lying somehow behind a public surface" ("Setting" 401). In the case of actresses, this understanding may have augmented audience assumptions that actors' "true selves" were lurking behind the character. Following from Ketchum, some audience members were particularly interested in seeing virginal characters unmasked: chastity was a pretense, and the partially nude body was the "truth," especially as bodies are generally understood to mean more than words. Thus, working both narratively, as secrets were revealed by the plot, and materially, as hair and breasts were exposed, audiences were encouraged to believe they saw the "true" Boutell: a sexually promiscuous whore who exposed her body and emotions to anyone willing to pay the admission price.

Despite critical insistence on sexual exploitation, the Restoration breeches role, however, might also be read as a (limited) subject position. Reading from the position of a particular actress rather than an ideal audience member suggests alternative interpretations. First, breeches roles were very popular and several plays were written or revised to include cross-dressed women. In June 1672, Thomas Killigrew's *Parson's Wedding*, Dryden's *Secret Love* and John Fletcher's *Philaster* were produced by the King's Company with all-female casts. Boutell delivered the revised prologue to *Secret Love*, implying that financial difficulties necessitated the gender switch.

> Accept us these bad times in any dress
> You'l find the sweet on't, now old Pantaloons,

> Will go as far, as formerly new gowns,
> And from your own cast Wig, expect no frowns.

Boutell, who had one of the longest careers of any of the first generation, certainly must have known how to market herself and remain popular. Taking her cue from the King's Company management, she may have specialized in breeches in order to enhance her commercial viability. Second, because breeches roles offered actresses the chance to openly display their physical beauty, Boutell and other first generation actresses might have used them to attract wealthy lovers, assuming that was their objective. The primacy of breeches characters guaranteed stage time to actresses who specialized in them and masculine clothing showed off a neat figure. Though breeches roles are traditionally read as exploitative, it is possible to view them as self-conscious bids for commercial viability and aristocratic liaisons.

Though the breeches role is generally assumed to have been directed toward a male audience, it doesn't necessarily foreclose the possibility of female pleasure and identification. Restoration heroines (especially those characters played by Boutell) did make bold choices and enjoyed some masculine privilege. For example, Fidelia took care of all of her master's financial and personal business, traveling to court, club, and shops traditionally closed to women. Certainly some audience members might have enjoyed the spectacle of female liberty as much as female sexual display. Further, Boutell's heroines risk all for love and are rewarded by a conventional happy ending. Audience members may have identified with her characters' motivation if not behavior. Finally, some audience members might have experienced the queer pleasures of seeing women making love together, even if the plot insisted their romance would be revealed as a sham and the characters embarrassed into making more conventional, heterosexual choices. By shifting the interpretative lens away from conventional explanations and from an ideal male spectator, the breeches role is more open than previously assumed.

Restoration prologues and epilogues also produce ambivalent and contradictory interpretations, as these curtain speeches seemed to give the audience a certain knowledge of the actresses. According to Elizabeth Howe, "[t]hey constituted spicy and intimate pieces of theatrical gossip, freely discussing personalities, politics, the rival company, current scandal and the latest improvements in scenery" (Howe *First English Actresses* 91–92). The curtain speeches invited audience speculation as well. Many of Boutell's plays included prologues that assured the audience that she was not the virgin she appeared. For example, Charles Hart gave the prologue to the premiere of *The Country Wife*, reminding the audience that

> We set no guards upon our tiring-room,
> But when with flying colours there you come,
> We patiently, you see, give up to you,
> Our poets, virgins, nay, our matrons too.
>
> (Wycherley *Country Wife* 25–28)

Likewise, the prologue to *The Conquest of Jerusalem*, which featured Boutell and her partner Marshall, promised that the actresses "shall be Saints no where but on the Stage."

In the previous examples, the prologues were delivered by men; however, women delivered the majority of prologues and epilogues. According to Howe, over 180 epilogues and prologues written between 1660 and 1710 were delivered by women, and "of the eighty or so women who became actresses before 1689, at least twenty-six were entrusted with one or more prologues and epilogues; this was far in excess of the number of named male players so entrusted" (*First English Actresses* 94). While it is true that playwrights wrote these lines, and so the actresses cannot be considered the authors of their curtain speeches, it seems possible that actresses knowingly used prologues and epilogues to advance their popularity and advertise their sexual availability, especially since they were usually assigned to specific performers. Thomas A. King asserts that "[t]here was an obvious correlation between the alleged sexual availability of the actresses, their popularity, and the assignment of prologs and epilogs" ("As if" 87). Boutell gave at least two curtain speeches, fewer than some of her contemporaries, but a number that bespeaks her status in the playhouse. She gave the epilogue to John Corye's *The Generous Enemies* (1671) in breeches implying her own sexual availability:

> 'Tis worth your Money that such Legs appear
> These are not to be seen so cheap elsewhere
> In short, commend this play, or by this light
> We will not sup with one of you tonight.

This epilogue suggests that Boutell was aware of actresses' – and her own – reputation and so teased the audience with the suggestion that applause might win companionship for the evening. Thus, Boutell might be viewed as participating in her own construction as an actress/whore. She performed feminine sexuality, playing to an audience which enjoyed seeing a woman in sexually enticing clothing.

Finally, Boutell's pictorial representations may have contributed to her construction as a whore. The frontispiece to volume VI of Nicholas Rowe's

Works of Shakespeare depicts the dying Cleopatra from Dryden's *All for Love* (Howe *First English Actresses* 113). Boutell originated the role, and whether or not the illustration is a literal rendering (no definitive portrait of Boutell is extant), readers would have recognized the engraving as a representation of her as the dying queen. In this illustration, Cleopatra reclines on a luxurious bed, a man (Antony?) dead at her feet and her maid to her right. Cleopatra presses the asp to her naked and well-defined breasts, her dress pulled down to her torso and pushed up above her thighs. In the illustration, her stomach and pelvis are swathed in a filmy fabric that highlights the contours of her body. By modern standards, the image is nearly obscene, and even within the context of other Caroline illustrations of raped and dying theatrical characters, it is intensely sexual. In the image, Cleopatra is utterly passive and vulnerable to the gaze of the audience. She is depicted at the moment of death, after her act of suicide. The circulation of this image may well have fueled Boutell's reputation for sexual vulnerability and availability.

The evidence from plays, satires, and visual images certainly suggests that Boutell was a whore. Focusing on this facet of her biography, however, elides her other professional and personal accomplishments. Boutell is largely forgotten in theatre studies, despite her remarkably long career, origination of major roles, and trend-setting partnership with Rebecca Marshall. Thus, linking Restoration actresses to prostitutes restricts current understanding of these women as historical subjects. When contemporary historians speak of Boutell at all, they tend to dismiss her as little more than the average Restoration actress/whore. Elizabeth Howe calls Boutell a whore (*First English Actresses* 57) without noting the role discursive convention plays in that designation. Katherine Maus states "Elizabeth Boutell played the field" ("Playhouse" 603) despite her insistence that Restoration actresses should be reconsidered in light of their professional achievements. Judith Milhous states that "[h]ow profitable Bowtell found her extramarital love life we cannot tell" ("Elizabeth" 131) but fails to acknowledge that, as her own research indicates, Boutell may not have had an extramarital love life. Designating Boutell a whore, contemporary scholars perpetuate the notion that Restoration actresses were little more than pretty faces and warm bodies.

Nominating Betty Boutell and other first generation actresses as whores places them in a passive role. Conventional wisdom implies that only weak, "bad" women are whores, and so the first generation is subject to assumptions about their limited agency. The traditional biography of Elizabeth Boutell thus focuses on sexual exploitation, rather than the potential her

Figure 2.1 A Possible representation of Elizabeth Boutell as Cleopatra in Dryden's *All For Love* (Courtesy of AMS Publishing)

breeches roles may have offered or the relative independence of her life. Clearly, Boutell received a negative and sexualized reputation in her own time and modern historians have upheld it; each narrative of her life builds on the preceding narratives, until it is nearly impossible to distinguish between successive layers of representation. By the late twentieth century, Betty Boutell is constructed as the perfect actress/whore.

Reading against the grain of Restoration studies, however, it seems possible that the first generation of English actresses exercised considerable agency over their lives and careers. Counter-narratives and alternate inter-pretations are available even within traditional accounts of Restoration sexuality and theatre. Other anxieties, especially regarding class, gender, and the decadent Charles II and his court, contributed to the discourses of prostitution implicating the first generation. Thus, accusations of whorish-ness might better be viewed as an attempt to contain the threats embodied in the consanguinity between the first generation of English actresses and the aristocracy, rather than an indication of actresses' sexual passivity and victimization. Betty Boutell, whose reputation is based on anecdotal evi-dence, demonstrates how assumptions about the first generation of English actresses have reduced their measure to their sexual behavior. Further, alternate readings suggest that Boutell may have used her whore designa-tion in order to attract an audience and hold their interest for over twenty-five years. Instead of assuming that lampoons, gossip, and the breeches role pushed Boutell to the sidelines of the Restoration stage, it is at least possible to imagine that she transformed the whore stigma into a place from which to speak women's sexuality. In the eighteenth century, this position was emphatically taken up by female memoirists. Margaret Leeson and Charlotte Charke use their writing to construct a version of female sexuality that stands as marked alternative to contemporary ideologies of female experience and sexuality.

CHAPTER 3

Memoir and masquerade: Charlotte Charke, Margaret Leeson, and eighteenth-century performances of self

This [the success of female playwrights, novelists, poets, and translators] convinces me that not only that barbarous custom of denying Women to have Souls, begins to be rejected as foolish and absurd, but also that bold Assertion, that Female Minds are not capable of producing literary Works, equal even to those of Pope, now loses Ground, and probably the next Age may be taught by our Pens that our Geniuses have been hitherto cramped and smothered, but not extinguished . . . our natural Abilities entitle us to a larger Share, not only in Literary Decisions, but that, with the present Directors, we are equally intitled to Power both in Church and State.

(Centlivre in Jones *Women* 169)

Susanna Centlivre, in the preface to her *Works*, argues that women are entitled to a more prominent role in politics, society, and culture, because of the merits of their writing. Centlivre supported herself as an essayist, poet, and playwright; her commentary on Whig politics was widely circulated during her life and her plays *The Busy Body* (1709) and *The Wonder: a Woman Keeps a Secret* (1714) were performed well into the nineteenth century (Pearson *Prostituted Muse* 202). Centlivre's literary career drew on her earlier struggles for education, financial security, and respect. After her parents' deaths, Centlivre cross-dressed to follow a lover to Cambridge University, then worked as a strolling actress, and finally wrote plays. Married in 1707 in her mid-thirties, she continued as a playwright, using her plays to champion "the Whig values of liberty, property, and constitutional monarchy" (206). Like many eighteenth-century women, Centlivre wrote her way into the public sphere. And like many eighteenth-century women writers, it was her notoriety as much as her ideas that first allowed her access to that sphere. Actress Charlotte Charke and prostitute Margaret Leeson (also called Peg Plunkett) were other public women who wrote to the mainstream from a marginal position, capitalizing on their sexual notoriety in order to find an audience. From their marginal position they

55

offered alternative understandings of female experience and sexuality; thus, they stand as paradigms of how women's narratives can reflect and transform dominant social constructions of gender.

Like Elizabeth Boutell, Leeson and Charke occupied the whore position. As the previous chapter makes clear, Boutell was labeled a whore in order to limit her agency. Charke was also an actress, and like Boutell her sexuality was her most notable feature. Her sexual notoriety, however, was based on her cross-dressing rather than her promiscuity: tales of her "Adventures in men's Cloaths" fascinated her contemporaries as well as current historians. Charke thus wrote as a "whore," narrating a life that suggested even sexually transgressive women could function within a community. Her print and everyday performance of femininity stood in sharp contrast to traditional representations, providing an alternative to other eighteenth-century women struggling to define their lives. Leeson also wrote from the whore position, suggesting that mainstream depictions of prostitution were inadequate to explain the nuances of her experience. Leeson refused to play the victim, instead insisting on autonomy, power, and pleasure. Like Charke, Leeson suggested an alternative model of female behavior that was widely read and circulated.

Leeson and Charke used specific strategies in order to construct a new subjectivity for themselves, and, by extension, for other eighteenth-century women. Much critical writing on the eighteenth century focuses on the formation of the modern subject; a paradigm of the age was the "autonomous individual, testing rules imposed from without against a sensibility nourished from within, demanding as a matter of right to flourish in his or her own way" (Coleman "Introduction" 3). Memoir and masquerade are two strategies through which Georgian men and women tested themselves against society. On one hand, masquerade suggests the self is performed; the interior, private subject is masked by outwardly visible signs. When those signs are decoded as the inverse of the true character (as when Leeson dressed at balls as the virgin goddess Diana), the inner core is revealed. On the other, autobiographical memoir offers individuals a means to construct subjectivity; by narrating a life, its meaning is made clear. But that memoir, as Charke's autobiography demonstrates, is always only partial, revealing no more and no less of the subject than the domino worn by the masquer. In the eighteenth century, these two practices condition how and why the self is performed; examining Leeson's and Charke's biographies suggests both the range and the limits of memoir and masquerade.

For many historians, the eighteenth century is characterized by the rise of print culture; that is, the increased availability of newspapers, pamphlets, poems, broadsides, cartoons, and, of course, books. The spread of ideas engendered by the spread of reading material is usually understood to have given rise to a "public sphere" of men (and some women) debating and challenging the legitimacy of traditional authority. Old structures gave way to new concepts of society and self; the circulation of conduct literature, political treatises, travel narratives, poetry, and fiction offered models of behavior and surrogate experiences that ambitious readers could exploit for social and cultural gain. Literary historian Patrick Coleman asks, "what was the 'public' itself, if not the domain constituted by the self-representation of private individuals in print and other media?" ("Introduction" 5). As he suggests, writing constructs a public self. By writing the life story, individuals perform and enact themselves. Leeson and Charke share strategies of performative writing[1] to put forth a specific image of eighteenth-century female experience. Both seek to persuade their reading audience that they are not transgressive women. Leeson and Charke write to convince that they have a developed moral code. At the same time, their protestations of innocence offer alternatives for thinking through female experience, especially sex and gender roles: they use their autobiographies to rework female subjectivity. In their memoirs, Leeson and Charke offer descriptions of an "other-world" (Pollock "Performing Writing" 83), where women are autonomous, proud, and in community with each other, facilitated by reading and writing the memoir.

Charlotte Charke, daughter of playwright, memoirist and poet laureate Colley Cibber, is well known to feminist, theatre, and queer scholars. Her *Narrative of the Life of Mrs. Charlotte Charke (Youngest Daughter of Colley Cibber, Esq.) Written by Herself* was published in serial form in the *Bristol Weekly Intelligencer* in 1755; the full-text edition was published later that year. Charke was born in 1713, the youngest of eleven children. In 1729, she married musician Richard Charke against her father's wishes. The Charkes had a daughter, Catherine (called Kitty), but in 1737 Richard Charke abandoned his family to immigrate to Jamaica. Both before and during her marriage, Charke pursued a theatrical career. For a time, she was a moderate success in comic plays, playing ingenues as well as breeches parts and male roles, but by 1739 "had so antagonized the managers of the London theatre district and alienated her father" (Barros and Smith *Life-writing* 128) that she was forced to quit the London stage. Since the Licensing Act of 1737 had reduced the number of legal theatres to the two Charke had been thrown out of, she became a strolling player, practicing on the legal margins of her profession. She also worked as a pastry cook, sausage-seller, waiter, puppeteer, and valet before turning to writing to support herself. The *Narrative* was written at least in part to persuade her father to forgive his prodigal daughter and welcome her back into the family fold; when he refused, Charke continued to write for a living until her death in 1760. Though her financial and familial motivations for writing are clear, the *Narrative* also presents Charke as a performer, both on- and off-stage, who takes up the pen as one in a series of costumes.[2]

Charke's *Narrative* is an important and well-studied document: as Cibber's daughter, she is a notable figure by association; with the success of her memoirs, plays, and novels she takes her place in the canon of female eighteenth-century writers; histories of cross-dressing dwell on her remembrance of dressing in her father's wig and coat as a very young girl; and theatre scholars turn to the *Narrative* for one of few first-person accounts of life as an eighteenth-century actor outside the Licensing Act. Though Charke's narrative deserves study from all these perspectives, in this chapter I consider her as a woman writing from the whore position. Though Charke is careful to distance herself from the prostitutes with whom she often lived and worked, and is not generally believed to have traded sex for money, her contemporaries understood her as a whore: a public women defined primarily by her sexuality. I tease out the implications of labeling Charke a whore below; for now, it is important to note that her perceived sexual transgressions were a large part of what interested her audience. She capitalized on her sexual notoriety, especially after her father's rejection, in order to sell her *Narrative*.

Margaret Leeson was a whore in letter as well as spirit. Born in Killough, Ireland in 1727 to a successful land-owner, Matthew Pilkington, she was raised in a solidly middle-class family and educated well. After her mother's death, when Leeson was about twelve, her father turned all family decisions over to his eldest son, Christopher. Leeson was seduced by a family friend, Mr. Dardis, and turned from her home; accordingly, she blamed her family both for her initial seduction and for the economic privation which drove her into formal prostitution. Leeson moved from admirer to admirer, ultimately opening a succession of "flash houses" (brothels) in Dublin. Her houses were well known and well respected, catering to the large, urban, male market who could not afford the expense of keeping a courtesan but wanted more than a streetwalker. Leeson continued as a successful brothel-keeper and prostitute until 1792, when she underwent a religious conversion. Though she assumed that her old friends and clients would continue to support her, and, more importantly, to pay the debts they had incurred, she was mistaken. By 1794 she was running out of money, and wrote *The Memoirs of Mrs. Leeson, Madam* in order to make a living. She spent her initial payments, and subsequently spent time in a debtor's prison. Several old friends and charitable acquaintances helped her through this difficult period, urging her to complete her memoirs. Living in extreme poverty but writing regularly, Leeson was gang-raped and contracted venereal disease: she died soon after, in 1797. The third volume of *Memoirs* was published posthumously.

Though Leeson's autobiography has not received as much attention as Charke's, it is equally significant. *Memoirs* is one of the earliest first-person accounts of a prostitute's life written in English; only Ann Sheldon's memoirs predate Leeson's, and those by less than a decade. Further, Leeson tells stories of her life as a streetwalker, a kept woman, and a brothel keeper, illuminating all types of Georgian prostitution. Though Leeson was not a professional actress, metaphors of performance structure her autobiography as much as Charke's. Specifically, Leeson performs penitence, contrasting anecdotes which celebrate her life as a courtesan with confessions of piety and devotion to a Christian god. In her writing, she is both chaste and debauched, penitent and unrepentant. In both detail and tone, *Memoirs* offers a striking alternative to typical narratives of fallen women, whether written by themselves, their critics, or contemporary novelists.

Charke and Leeson wrote *mémoires scandaleuses*, a popular sub-genre flourishing around mid-century, that offered first-person narratives of sexual transgression. Scandal memoirs were usually written by women who had lapsed from a chaste and socially respectable position. Writers like Ann Sheldon, Teresa Constancia Phillips, Laetitia Pilkington, and Elizabeth Gooch used their memoirs to beg forgiveness from both the reading public and the fathers, husbands, and brothers they had wronged through their sexual transgressions. Further, scandal memoirs excuse the writers from blame in an attempt to restore them to their original class and gender position. Though the *Narrative* and *Memoirs* offer apologies, they are equally marked by joyful accounts of the transgressions that earned their writers a dishonorable status. For example, Charke regrets that her intransigence toward the patriarchal code estranged her from her father, but nonetheless recounts particularly damning episodes, such as parading through their neighborhood on a donkey and working cross-dressed as a sausage higgler. In this way, Charke and Leeson offer scandal narratives that both depend on and subvert generic expectations.

For contemporaries, these scandalous women could not be trusted (Barros and Smith *Life-Writings* 11). Further, the autobiographical form itself has been called into question by post-structural theorizing on subjectivity. Sidonie Smith suggests that autobiography depends on the fiction of the unified "I" doing the telling. The fragmented, storytelling I is only one possible I, constructed in part through the telling itself, not existing apart from the tale. Beyond the poststructuralist critique of the subject, there are more concrete challenges to autobiography as truth. Charke's record is necessarily partial: if autobiography is some *one* telling what happened, she can only tell her part of the story. The adventures in men's clothes include the marriage proposals she received from wealthy women but do not directly identify her traveling companion, Mrs. Brown, nor characterize their relationship. Even if a "lost chapter" settled once and for all questions of Charke's sexual orientation, her explanation and understanding of that relationship would be necessarily partial, eliding Mrs. Brown's story of the events.

Like memoir, masquerade offered a space for the negotiation of female agency. Terry Castle has done the most sustained work on the trope of masquerade; her 1986 *Masquerade and Civilization* details the origins of masquerade, its eighteenth-century English manifestations, and its impact on eighteenth-century cultural life.[3] Throughout most of the eighteenth century, members of all social classes regularly attended masquerade balls. Dressed as historical and mythological figures; representatives of "exotic" countries; in the fancy dress that included popular ecclesiastical, milkmaid, and cross-dressed costumes; or in the anonymous black domino cloak, masquers ate, drank, danced, and gossiped at public and private balls. Importantly, the balls were popularly understood as spaces where women could exercise a certain degree of sexual agency and enjoy sexual freedoms. Harriette Wilson remarked that she "love[d] a masquerade because a female can never enjoy the same liberty anywhere else" (in Castle *Masquerade* 44). While masked, married women could presumably have intercourse with men other than their husbands and unmarried girls could make assignations with young men; the *Weekly Journal* went so far as to opine that "Fishes are caught with Hooks, Birds are ensnar'd with Nets, but Virgins with Masquerades" (in Castle *Masquerade* 43). Though this witticism likely overstates the erotic possibilities of masquerade balls, it seems clear that masquerades did provide some women with more physical and intellectual freedom than other, more traditional social activities. Importantly, the relaxation of gender roles and behaviors associated with masquerades evidences a climate favorable to the literary advances of a prostitute and a cross-dresser.

I suggest here that masquerade offered an interpretative strategy for understanding the negotiation between public and private selves. The ubiquity of masquerade as a social activity as well as a literary trope offered some a way to exercise narrative and material agency. Both Leeson and Charke participated in masquerade, performing a variety of selves in everyday life as well as print. Leeson's *Memoirs* include detailed references to her attendance at and sponsorship of masked balls, and she often cast her interactions with admirers as a kind of masquerade. Charke's crossdressing can be understood as a long-term, successful masquerade. Most strangers and even some long-time friends reportedly took her for a man when she was in masculine attire.

Leeson and Charke traded on their perceived sexual deviance, using the whore position to offer alternative narratives of female experience. In this chapter, I place Leeson and Charke into the context of eighteenth-century women's engagement with the public sphere. With this background in mind, I consider Margaret Leeson's *Memoirs* as anti-conduct manual, tracing her use of tropes of the fallen woman, her everyday and print performances of femininity, and her celebration of female sexuality. Leeson provides an early, first-hand account of the agency offered women who willingly occupy the whore position. Acknowledging Charlotte Charke's centrality to theatre historians and queer theorists, I place the actress within the tradition of performing women who used their sexuality to gain an audience. On the page and in her daily life, Charke performed for an audience delighted with her "transgressive" adventures. As whores, both Charke and Leeson offer examples of performative writing meant to make a difference, suggesting new ways to think through female experiences, both for historians of the eighteenth century, and for other eighteenth-century women themselves.

ENGAGING THE PUBLIC SPHERE: WOMEN WRITING AND PERFORMING

The shift to new modes of production engendered by the eighteenth-century industrial revolution suggests commerce is the defining characteristic of eighteenth-century Britain: "When we think of Augustan England we immediately think of the Bank, the Stock Exchange, the Insurance Company" (Sharpe and Zwicker "Refiguring Revolutions" 6). Commerce was an insistently masculine endeavor; it was men who visited the bank, traded on the exchange, and purchased insurance against disaster. Most historians agree that as capitalism developed, "women were increasingly marginalized, confined, and made subject to men" (Barker and Chalus "Introduction" 10). Despite a continued insistence on masculine privilege, women were more visible in the eighteenth century than in previous decades; they took their place on stage, in print, at the theatre and coffee houses, and within public debates on the nature of the self. Feminism began in the eighteenth century: Mary Wollstonecraft's 1792 *A Vindication of the Rights of Woman* provides the capstone to the century's increased recognition of female accomplishments and claims.

Many Georgian commentators believed that men and women were "naturally" different, their gender suiting each for specific roles. Conduct literature[4] attempted to reconcile women to their natural role as wife and mother. At the beginning of the century, George Savile, Marquis of Halifax, reminded women to be diligent in "Government of your *House, Family,* and *Children*" since this realm was the "Province allotted to your Sex" (in Jones *Women* 21). Women were "designed by the great Author of Nature for the Vehicle thro' which the human Species should be propagated" (*Ladies Dispensory* in Jones *Women* 83) and, after giving birth, women were expected to nourish their children, both physically by breast-feeding, and emotionally by tender moral instruction. Though nineteenth-century commentators were even more preoccupied with relegating women to the domestic realm, during this period, "the English nation came to represent its eighteenth-century woman as . . . happiest as mother" (Nussbaum *Torrid* 1). In fiction as well as conduct manuals, maternity was the condition to which all eighteenth-century women were assumed to aspire.

Convention dictated that a woman had to marry to become a mother. Stone's theory of the rise of Affective Individualism suggests that eighteenth-century women married for love. Love was dangerous, however, because women were "much more amorous than Men" and "too susceptible of Love" ("A Physician" in Jones *Women* 82). It is not coincidental that the novels exemplifying the eighteenth century (*Pamela, Clarissa, Fanny Hill, Tom Jones, Tristam Shandy*) often focused on the seduction of middle-class women. Female chastity before marriage and moderation after was a pressing concern for moralists who feared that women's "natural" propensity to romance left them open to immorality. The most marriageable women (and thus the most fit for motherhood) were chaste. Wetenhall Wilkes' *A Letter of Genteel and Moral Advice to a Young Lady,* first published in 1740 and then republished in at least eight subsequent editions, is one conduct manual among many that defined femininity by chastity. The ideal young woman was chaste because of her "delicate soul" and rejection of "wantonness." In fact, according to Wilkes, "[c]hastity is so essential and natural to your sex, that every declination from it is a proportionable receding from womanhood" (in Jones *Women* 30). Sexually active women were unfeminine and unnatural.

Chastity corresponds with modesty. Eighteenth-century women were expected to be seen and not heard. John Gregory reminded his daughters in 1774: "One of the chief beauties in a female character is that modest reserve, that retiring delicacy, which avoids the public eye, and . . . will naturally dispose you to be rather silent in company, especially in a large one" (in Hill *Eighteenth-Century Women* 18). Further, this "natural" modesty indicated that women would readily submit to any constraints placed on their behavior and thought. Married women were advised to submit to their husband's will, even if it was wrong (Jones *Women* 46), and daughters were governed by their fathers. Because of their "retiring delicacy," they were grateful for the guidance of men. Ultimately, the "natural" eighteenth-century woman was constructed as maternal, chaste, and submissive.

Feminists[5] argued that there was nothing "natural" about these characteristics. Though early feminists often disagreed about what women should and could do best, they all rejected the silent and obedient position. Vivien Jones reads Wollstonecraft's *Vindication* as insisting that "the characteristics ascribed to women are not natural but constructed, the result of limited education and experience" (Jones *Women* 5). In general, most eighteenth-century feminists argued that inadequate education kept women from developing their intellectual and emotional potential, insisting along with Mary Robinson that, "in activity of mind" women were equal to men (in Jones *Women* 239). It was the lack of education, not rational minds, that barred women from full participation in the public sphere: "Why is learning useless to us? Because we have no share in public offices. And why have we no share in public offices? Because we have no learning" ("Sophia" in Pearson *Prostituted Muse* 19).

Eighteenth-century women's writing is feminist writing, as female novelists, essayists, and playwrights "had to rebel against a pervasive sense that language and literature were in the keeping of men" (Pearson *Prostituted Muse* 3). Publishing was a transgressive act that threatened the social order: as writers, women took on the "masculine" characteristics of creativity, imagination, and logic (Jones *Women* 140). By taking up the pen, women crossed gender boundaries and reversed the natural order. The published memoir[6] offered women special opportunities to negotiate identity in a mass medium. Autobiography is generally understood as an attempt to inscribe a self, to write a specific "I" into existence (Nussbaum *Autobiographical* xiv). For women in particular, memoir crosses the boundary between private and public speech, demonstrating a desire to influence and affect both representations of their selves and all women.

Women were seen as the primary market for novels and conduct literature. Further, as feminist literary critic Vivien Jones reminds, "women's supposed capacity for sympathy and feeling is assumed to make them peculiarly fitted for literary pursuits" (*Women* 11). Eighteenth-century women wrote poetry, plays, travel narratives, and memoirs from a variety of ideological positions. In 1773, an editorial in the *Monthly Review* complained that "[t]his branch of the literary *trade* appears, now, to be almost entirely engrossed by the Ladies" (in Turner *Living by the Pen* 31). Hyperbole aside, women did publish novels throughout the period. Many, like Delarivière Manley and Eliza Haywood, wrote scandal narratives that exploited the potentials of predatory male lust coupled with female innocence. In Haywood's novels like *Love in Excess; or The Fatal Enquiry* (1719) and *The Fatal Secret; or Constancy in Distress* (1724), female characters partake in love and romance wholeheartedly. Other women wrote more moral narratives. According to Cheryl Turner, novelists like Penelope Aubin strove to distance themselves from writing women whose lives and works were too passionate, instead crafting narratives with a "purity of style and manners," that instructed on moral behavior through the punishment of vice (*Living by the Pen* 48–49). These sentimental novels offered heroines who upheld the virtues of community, family, and femininity. Finally, some novelists bridged between scandal and sentimental fiction in order to reflect feminist concerns. Wollstonecraft wrote novels as well as essays; her *Mary: A Fiction* was understood as autobiographical, feminist, and fictive. Other eighteenth-century feminist reformers, such as Priscilla Wakefield, Elizabeth Inchbald, Mary Ann Radcliffe, and Hannah More, also used fiction to present feminism to their readers.[7] These are the literary traditions on which Leeson and Charke profitably drew.

The world of letters also included the theatre, and plays about the middle class (rather than historical and contemporary noble characters) were increasingly popular, in part precipitated by the success of George Lillo's *The London Merchant*. In an age defined by commerce, theatre was a business, and, as George Winchester Stone, Jr. suggests in "The Making of Repertory," audience tastes for both particular genres and actors dictated the repertoire. Sentimental comedies, most associated with playwright Colley Cibber, were usually applauded. His plays, widely imitated, tended to feature libertine characters who pursued pleasure until they underwent a fifth-act conversion and resolved to mend their ways, often with the loving support of virtuous if dull sweethearts.

Female playwrights were willing to follow Cibber's lead, though often with some differences. Sophia Lee's *The Chapter of Accidents* kept the libertine into penitent formula, but depicted a female heroine whose "remarkable sensibility redeems the social crime she has committed in yielding her virginity to her lover" (Smallwood "Women and the Theatre" 240). Though eighteenth-century sentimental comedy was much less sexually explicit than Restoration productions, it was still attacked for immorality; some managers probably included plays by women in order to increase the seeming morality of their playhouses. In fact, some women chafed against this presumption: Hannah Cowley complained that she was "encompassed in chains when I write" (in *ibid.* 241) because critics assumed that she was unwilling and unable to freely and accurately depict human emotions such as lust, greed, and envy.

Despite constraints placed upon them, female playwrights flourished in the eighteenth century, devising "strategies, open or covert, for expressing a vision which was inevitably different from that of their male colleagues" (Pearson *Prostituted Muse* xi). Women wrote about 20 percent of the new plays staged in London theatres, a particularly remarkable statistic since women comprised only about 5 percent of all working playwrights (Smallwood "Women and the Theatre" 239). Not surprisingly, given the centrality of theatre to cultural debate, many of these plays directly engaged mainstream representations of women. Women frequently wrote afterpieces and epilogues which mocked and undercut the themes of the main play, as when Frances Sheridan's epilogue to *The Discovery* (1763) concluded with the actress playing Lady Medway noting that her character was "out of nature – never drawn from life, / Who ever heard of such a passive wife" (in Smallwood *ibid.* 255). Obviously, such afterpieces contradicted not only the previous play but also dominant constructions of marriage and modesty.

Women also engaged gender in full-scale productions. Centlivre's *The Beau's Duel* included Mrs. Plotwell, a powerful woman with a sexually dubious past who is sympathetically treated by the other characters. According to Jacqueline Pearson, Plotwell "ends the play triumphantly and happily unmarried" (*Prostituted Muse* 215), offering a depiction of women which directly contradicts normative ideology. Women also adapted older plays, rewriting narratives to highlight female experience. In 1779, Hannah Cowley adapted Centlivre's *Stolen Heiress* to feature young women in central, active roles. Working within a system that privileged adaptation, women inscribed old narratives with more feminist characters and ideology.

Of course, women were most visible and influential as actresses. On the Georgian as on the Restoration stage, the actress "figures discursively as the site of an excessive sexuality" (Straub *Sexual Suspects* 89), and the conflation of the actress/whore described in the previous chapter remained current throughout the century. Popular actresses such as Lavinia Fenton, Hestor Santlow, and George Anne Bellamy "had reputations for exchanging their sexual favors for a price" (Crouch "Public Life" 61), and Susannah Cibber was at least as well known for her adulterous affair with William Sloper (instigated by her husband) as for her acting. The same assumptions about promiscuity that dogged Elizabeth Boutell and other members of the first generation also attached to Georgian actresses.

Even so, as both Kimberly Crouch and Angela Smallwood point out, actresses' status was on the rise, and links to "ladies of quality" as well as ladies of the night characterized their social position. Some women, especially the imminently respectable Sarah Siddons and Katherine Clive, "were able to establish personal friendships with members of the aristocracy who had initially served as their patrons" (Crouch *ibid.* 71). Further, star actresses like Frances Abdington were noted as particularly fashionable. Of course, fashion was a preoccupation of aristocratic women; Abdington's evident superiority of dress made her the "delight of the fashionable world" (Smallwood "Women and the Theatre" 248). Playing aristocratic women on stage, actresses like Abdington and Siddons crossed class boundaries. Off-stage, these relatively wealthy and educated women participated in the Georgian "expansion of leisure and consumerism" whereby the emergent middle class "consciously cultivated social activities associated with their betters, and emulated many aspects of upper-class lifestyles" (249). Thus, eighteenth-century actresses straddled several class positions, ones that encompassed larger concerns about fashion, class, and morality.

The career of Margaret (Peg) Woffington consolidates many of the tensions about gender and class exemplified by Georgian actresses. Woffington achieved fame and fortune through her portrayal of Sir Harry Wildair in George Farquhar's *The Constant Couple*, a role which both increased her reputation as an actress and, at least anecdotally, increased box office whenever she played it (Straub *Sexual Suspects* 132). Pat Rogers uses Woffington's Wildair as the paradigmatic eighteenth-century breeches role, one which "serves to confirm rather than discredit [gender] conventions" ("Breeches Roles" 257). She characterizes Woffington as "[t]he smooth-thighed Mercury, 'fiery' in charms but poised ready to soften and quiver" (257), a description that places emphasis firmly on Woffington's femininity while in masculine dress. As actor James Quin remembered in his memoirs, "it was a most nice point to decide . . . whether she was the finest woman or the prettiest fellow" (*Life* 67). On stage, Woffington was not only an actress, but an object of sexual appeal.

Representations of Woffington's sexuality extended off-stage as well. Her *Memoirs*, almost certainly not written by herself, were published at roughly the same time as Charke's.[8] Rather than Charke's performance of female autonomy, Woffington's *Memoirs* instead read much like *Fanny Hill*, as in the following passage:

[Woffington], unable to resist so mighty a Champion, sank in his Arms, and gave him Kiss for Kiss, and sigh for sigh. Her breast now beat with tumultuous Throbbings. Her Eyes flashed Fire; her Knees knocked together; and her whole Frame was so agitated, she could not speak, nor had the strength to resist. In that critical, that soft moment, the vigorous BOB taking her in his Arms, threw her on the*** ** Oh happy Bob!**** (in Straub *Sexual Suspects* 91).

The excessive sexuality of a popular breeches actress like Woffington was underscored in her *Memoirs*, but her success enabled her to purchase Teddington Place Hall, originally built for Sir Charles Duncombe, Lord Mayor of London, as a retreat and a sign of her position. She installed her sister Polly at the house, sparing "no expense to fit [her] sister for an elevated position in society"(Dunbar *Peg Woffington* 135). Woffington's purchase paid off, and her sister eventually married the Honourable Robert Cholmondeley, a minor member of the peerage. By conforming to conventional expectations of actresses, Woffington secured a place for her family (if not herself) in more socially secure circles. On the contrary, Leeson and Charke offered new ways to narrate and describe how femininity is lived. As their autobiographies demonstrate, normative constructions of women as chaste, maternal, and submissive, or actresses as sexually suspect, fail to adequately describe female experience. Of course, neither Leeson nor Charke was as socially respectable as Woffington, but their influence potentially reached further.

PUBLIC PROSTITUTE: THE LIFE OF MARGARET LEESON

The Memoirs of Mrs. Leeson, Madam tell an already familiar story, of virtue once abandoned but ultimately redeemed, and they tell it in a conventional manner. First-person prostitution narratives were a "popular sentimental topos" (Jones "Placing" 204), and ranged from fictions such as *Fanny Hill* and *Pamela* to widely circulated "letters" from penitent prostitutes, such as those published by the Magdelan Hospital, a charitable organization for reformed prostitutes. Leeson relied on these narratives, using familiar tropes from sentimental fiction in order to shape her autobiography. At the same time, she troped discourse, describing prostitution as perform-ance, asserting her pride in her accomplishments, and offering an account of female sexual pleasure not available in other texts written by and for women. In all, *Memoirs* describes a world of female experience existing alongside dominant notions of female subjectivity, both capitalizing on and subverting those norms.

That *Memoirs* follows convention demonstrates the power of autobio-graphical discourse to shape the life it narrates. Prostitute narratives were an important genre in eighteenth-century fiction and non-fiction; that Leeson's story conforms so closely to generic expectations suggests that she understood her life in the tropes made available by dominant discourse. Jürgen Habermas' explanation of the relationship between reading and eighteenth-century bourgeois selfhood explains the process Leeson as reader and writer went through:

The psychological novel fashioned for the first time the kind of realism that allowed anyone to enter into the literary action as a substitute for his own, to use the relationships between the figures, between the author, the characters, and the reader as substitute relationships for reality. (*Structural Transformation* 50)

Thus, Leeson understood her life as conforming to a set of generic expect-ations about prostitution: the young girl seduced and abandoned, the woman at first delighting in sensual pleasure but ultimately recognizing her sin; the final repentance and concomitant plea for forgiveness. For Smith, this reliance is unsurprising, as the scandal memoirist

brings to the recollection of her past and to the reflection on her identity inter-pretive figures (tropes, myths, metaphors) ... always cast in language and ... always motivated by cultural expectations, habits, and systems of interpretation pressing on her at the scene of writing. (*Poetics* 47)

Clearly, Leeson cast her story in a way that was familiar and accessible to her readers and herself.

This conventionality is troubling for some modern critics, however, as autobiography makes obvious truth claims: after all, the events happened to the one doing the telling. Truth in memoir presses especially for women, who are spoken for more often than speak themselves. As Betty Boutell's case history so aptly demonstrates, once an event (or behavior) is docu-mented, it is taken for truth regardless of whether or not it took place. In many cases, scandal memoirists are writing against a particular truth, explaining their sexual sin as an act perpetrated against them rather than rising from their own deviant natures. Rather than suggesting a weakness in her writing, however, this reliance on convention suggests instead that Leeson shaped her life story according to her audience's (and, following Habermas, her own) expectations.

Further, despite the familiarity of her subject matter and her attitude toward it, Leeson's voice is distinct. Within the conventional eighteenth-century prostitution narrative, Leeson presents herself as a woman who enjoyed a great deal of independence and autonomy. What is most striking about *Memoirs* is Leeson's pride in her wit, her position as well-respected whore, her own sense of justice and morality, and her power to influence others. Several times she remarks that she "ever found it hard to overlook insults that touched [her] pride" (72), and in fact offers several extended anecdotes of "punishing" those she felt insulted her. In a catalog of sins, Leeson's pride is at least as great as her profligacy; unlike the latter sin, however, she feels no guilt for defending and celebrating her accomplishments. Clearly, Leeson offers further ways of thinking not only female sexuality but also female subjectivity; she is far from the ideal chaste, modest, submissive woman. Further, Leeson presented those possibilities to other eighteenth-century women. Her *Memoirs* were sold by subscription and then later published; after her death, the third volume was sold to a public eager for more revelations of this penitent but proud prostitute. Writing from the margins, her life story might well have influenced how mainstream British women conceived of their subjectivity and sexuality.

As a prostitute, Leeson was barred from full participation in bourgeois society that nonetheless "tolerated and accepted" prostitution as part of urban life,[9] (Bullough "Prostitution and Reform" 61). As a brothel keeper and kept woman, Leeson was on the highest economic rungs of the profession; most prostitutes lived in poverty. Out-of-work servants, underemployed women working in the clothing trades, and wives and daughters of struggling tradesmen made up the majority of eighteenth-century prostitutes (Hill *Eighteenth-Century Women* 110–11). Further, most of these women worked as streetwalkers rather than in brothels, often soliciting in pairs for their own safety and comfort (Henderson *Disorderly Women* 36). And, as was true in the nineteenth century, many prostitutes were occasional workers, supplementing low wages from legitimate jobs with streetwalking (16); in fact, Tony Henderson's research demonstrates that the majority of prostitutes had given up the trade by their mid- to late twenties, presumably marrying and/or finding more stable employment (48).

The regulation and reform of street prostitutes was a pressing issue for many Georgian commentators (an issue that became even more troubling over the next hundred years); tolerance only attended to some, and then only so far. In eighteenth-century London, private "suppression societies" were formed in order to remove streetwalkers from residential areas and shut down bawdy houses (Henderson *ibid.* 86–87). For the most part, prostitutes and madams were arrested and charged with vagrancy, being loose and disorderly, or keeping a disorderly house (see 76–103). Other reformers, like Bernard Mandeville, whose 1724 *A Modest Defence of Public Stews: or, an Essay upon Whoring,* remained influential throughout the century, suggested regulating prostitutes, controlling their effect on bourgeois neighborhoods and society through segregation, regular medical treatment, and specialized recruitment. Finally, many reformers simply suggested that women be taught greater virtue and chastity. Daniel Defoe, in *Some Considerations upon Street-Walkers with A Proposal for lessening the present Number of Them* called on his fellows to "let us by gentler Allurements to Virtue, destroy the Hopes of any Succession of such miserable Sinners" (in Jones *Women* 70). Ultimately, it was reformers like Defoe who had the most impact on understandings of the prostitute, casting her as a victim of both her own easy virtue and the seduction of unscrupulous men.

As the innocent victim of seduction, prostitutes were capable of redemption; in the literature of the period, "the figure of the innocent, penitent, and redeemable prostitute emerges . . . as an increasingly powerful cultural myth" (Jones "Eighteenth-Century" 127). This understanding of the prostitute is significant to understanding the success of Leeson's *Memoirs.* Though by the early nineteenth century the prostitute was a "repulsive figure who threaten[ed] to corrupt the very core of bourgeois society" (Norberg "From Courtesan to Prostitute" 46), during Leeson's career, reformers "regarded [the prostitute] more as a victim" than as the carrier of disease and disorder (Bullough "Prostitution and Reform" 61). Leeson was self-consciously careful to conform to this understanding of prostitution and to cast herself as victim.[10] Specifically, she blames the abuse she suffered from her oldest brother, Christopher, for her profligate life:

It must be obvious to every one that my wanderings, and every occurrence that may appear blamable in me, were originally owing to his behavior. Had I been treated with the same humanity and tenderness that other girls of like condition experience, my youth had glided pleasantly along. I might have been honourably married, and settled in life; might have made some deserving man happy, and received from him mutual content. (*Memoirs* 14–15)

When she became pregnant as a result of her initial seduction by Mr. Dardis, a family friend who she believed would marry her, Leeson explained that her innocence and naïveté led her to make further bad choices. As represented in prints such as the first plate of Hogarth's *A Harlot's Progress* and in novels like *Clarissa*, naïve girls could be easily tricked into further error: the pregnant Leeson compounded her difficulties by unknowingly lodging with "one of the impure ones, and therefore, not a fit habitation for the recovery of character" (Leeson *Memoirs* 21). Because she innocently lived with other prostitutes, Leeson excused herself for her subsequent "easing into" prostitution; again, this pattern follows representational convention.

After her baby was born and she was abandoned by Mr. Dardis, the desperate and repentant young woman appealed to her brother and sisters for help; they all refused even to see her (see *Memoirs* 26–29). Of course, this final rejection virtually guaranteed Leeson would have to make her own way in life.[11] Women alone in eighteenth-century Great Britain had few choices, and most contemporary commentators understood that women entered prostitution through severe economic need. In fact, some observers, such as James Boswell, who seemingly visited every kind and class of London prostitute, and Richard Steele, who used *The Spectator* to comment on urban life, insisted that prostitution was only a last resort; most women longed to be rescued and redeemed (Radner "Youthful Harlot's Curse" 59–60). Accordingly, more liberal eighteenth-century prostitution reform focused on offering repentant prostitutes alternative occupations. John Fielding proposed a public laundry that would "reform those Prostitutes whom Necessity has drove into the Streets, and who are willing to return to virtue and obtain an honest livelihood by severe industry" (in Bullough "Prostitution" 69). Female reformers also focused on providing prostitutes with economic alternatives. Mary Ann Radcliffe suggested that women were subjected to "great evil" when deprived of the human right to make an honest living; others, such as Priscilla Wakefield, demanded that repentant prostitutes be offered a variety of occupations which would suit their upbringing, talents, and needs (Jones "Placing" 208).

Of course, such occupations were virtually non-existent in the real eighteenth-century world, and for a middle-class woman like Margaret Leeson, employment was even harder to come by than for a poor woman. Mary Wollstonecraft, who perhaps saw most clearly the pressures facing impoverished bourgeois women, detailed the supposed plight of the seduced middle-class girl:

A woman who has lost her honour, imagines that she cannot fall lower, and as for recovering her former station, it is impossible; no exertion can wash this stain away. Losing thus every spur, and having no other means of support, prostitution becomes her only refuge, and the character is quickly depraved by circumstances over which the poor wretch has little power, unless she possesses an uncommon portion of sense and loftiness of spirit. (in Jones "Placing" 202–203)

According to conventional depictions, middle-class woman had little hope of gaining any kind of legitimate employment; and as Leeson asks her readers "How could I have gone into service? Bred up as I had been, for what service was I fit? Who would have taken a servant without a character? and who had I to give me one?" (*Memoirs* 32). Further, the stigma of premarital sex was greater for middle-class women, who usually believed (as Leeson's experience bears out) that their family and friends would never accept them after their indiscretion.

Wollstonecraft does suggest that some lofty and sensible women may be able to find a way back to virtue and community. Leeson recovered as well, albeit in atypical ways. From her initial naïveté, she transformed herself into a clever businesswoman who rose to the top of her profession and became a figure of some respect in Dublin. And, as her *Memoirs* bear out, she certainly had "an uncommon portion of sense" if not a "lofty" spirit. As Bullough suggests, "[p]rostitution was one of the few ways a woman could make it on her own, and if she had intelligence, sophistication, talent, and the right contacts, she could go far" ("Prostitution" 72). Leeson's middle-class upbringing, which virtually ensured she turn to prostitution, also enabled her success. With her middle-class manners, education, and tastes, she was well positioned to become a high-class, expensively kept courtesan. Thus, although economic conditions and gender bias suggested that Leeson, like nearly all seduced girls, was forced to continue as a prostitute, she seems to have made the best of a difficult and limiting situation.

By the end of her life, however, Leeson apparently regretted her success. Sometime around 1792, when Leeson was about sixty-five years old, she was apparently overcome by guilt for "shar[ing] her charms indiscriminately with every ruffian who could afford a price" (Leeson *Memoirs* 222). Broken-hearted to find herself alone, without children, friends, or husband to comfort her in her old age (*ibid.*), she drank opium in a suicide attempt. When she didn't die, she decided to reform. Though her penitence seems sincere, and Leeson included the fourteen-stanza poem she wrote expressing her new devotion to Christ in her *Memoirs*, it is significant that this conversion also followed narrative convention: "[t]he deft backflip by which the whore-text reverses itself and becomes a religious penitential text is one at which eighteenth-century English writers became particularly adept" (Nelson "Women of Pleasure" 184). Again, if literature suggests scripts for readers to follow, it is ultimately unsurprising that Leeson underwent an eleventh-hour conversion, especially one so filled with melodrama. The "whore-texts" with which it is fair to assume Leeson was familiar structure her life-writing as well as her life. In its treatment of sin and redemption, then, Leeson's *Memoirs* followed a familiar and comfortable pattern, one that undoubtedly played a part in its commercial success. A penitent whore makes more appropriate bourgeois reading material than a still promiscuous one, and Leeson is better able to inspire identification as well as titillation by casting herself as one made wiser by her youthful indiscretions.

That Leeson casts herself initially as victim and then as penitent should not suggest that her *Memoirs* were either overly self-pitying or moralizing. In fact, it also conforms to another conventional representation of Georgian prostitution: the cheerful, friendly, and merry whore. The appellation "woman of pleasure," made popular by John Cleland and others, suggests that eighteenth-century whores were known for their fun. Though representations of prostitution are clearly ambivalent,[12] literary historian T. G. A. Nelson points out that expectations of "a woman both giving and receiving pleasure" increased in the latter half of the eighteenth century ("Women of Pleasure" 192). Further, Elizabeth C. Denlinger's study of late eighteenth-century prints of prostitutes suggests that even though novels, essays, and polemical tracts often forecast a desperate end for sexually active women, visual representations of prostitutes show them as "jolly and inviting" and as "game companions" ("Wink" 71). Leeson's *Memoirs* certainly offers a similar portrait. For example, she describes a trip she made to Killarney with a fellow prostitute, Mrs. M'Clean, and their "keepers." She describes the area as the perfect place for love, swears that the food and drink are the most delicious she has ever tasted, and fondly remembers an afternoon spent on a secluded island with Purcell where "just when the sun was in its highest meridian, did we refine upon extatic (sic) luxuries, like our first parents in the Garden of Eden; we sauntered through this beautiful paradise . . . and with great regret, after spending upwards of three hours in this divine place, we left . . . " (188–89). The reader believes she enjoyed her life as companion and madam, and took genuine pleasure in being with her clients, traveling, going to the theatre, and hosting masquerade balls.

Though the jolly prostitute was an important figure in eighteenth-century print culture, this representation was undercut not only by counter-representations of poverty-stricken, pathetic prostitutes but also by questions about the authenticity of the whore's emotion. As Denlinger points out, the conventions used in eighteenth-century prints underscore "one of the oldest complaints about prostitutes: that they are faking it, that the good humor shown in these prints is just show" (79). Further, discourse about prostitution continually referred to the performance of pleasure enacted by the whore. As early as 1683, *The Whore's Rhetorick* claimed that a prostitute "may give [her] Mate to believe, that [she is] melted, dissolved, and wholly consumed in pleasure, though Ladies of large business are generally no more moved by an imbrace (sic) than if they were made of Wood or Stone" (in Nelson "Women of Pleasure" 182). In the eighteenth century, then, most understood that the prostitute was likely to feign emotion in order to please her clients. Leeson's obvious delight in her excursion to Killarney notwithstanding, other parts of her *Memoirs* suggest she self-consciously performed for her clients. She describes her relationship with Mr. Leeson, one of her first "keepers" (whose name she took, though the two were never legally married), as being based on the appearance of affection rather than genuine emotion. She recalls that when they lived in the country she seemed happy with their bucolic lifestyle, but "however I might have carried myself outwardly, a recluse and retired way of life was not agreeable to me" (Leeson *Memoirs* 36–37). Further, she suggests that as a prostitute it was her nature to mislead him: a man "can have no confidence in an affection, *however strong it may appear*, that is not founded on Delicacy and Virtue" (41, emphasis added). Leeson here admits that she was capable and willing to act a particular part for an admirer. Throughout *Memoirs*, she is careful to distinguish between the "real" affection she feels for her lovers such as Mr. Lawless and Bob and less favored clients, feigning for the latter what she reported feeling for the former.

Though it is unsurprising that Leeson did not fall madly in love with all of her keepers or with her flash-house clients, her understanding of herself as playing a part was undoubtedly fueled by an understanding of a performing self engendered by the ubiquity of masquerade. According to Castle, masquerade structured eighteenth-century life and thought, its influence spreading beyond the balls to both literature and society at large. For those, like Leeson, who attended masquerades, even in everyday life "theatrical selves displaced supposedly essential ones; masks, or personae, obscured persons . . . . The true self remained elusive and inaccessible – illegible – within its fantastical encasements" (Castle *Masquerade* 4). Thus, the performances Leeson (and other whores) enacted with her clients may have been expected within this entertainment-focused stratum of society.

In Dublin as in London, prostitution was closely linked to masquerade balls. Not only middle-class and aristocratic women attended masquerades, but also prostitutes and the demi-monde. Castle suggests that both common sense and evidence from both fictional and non-fictional writing affirm that "thieves, sharpers, and prostitutes" frequented masquerades in order to ply their criminal trades in relative anonymity (31). Though she is careful to cite many reports of prostitutes frequenting masquerade balls – the *Weekly Journal* complained that "all about the Hundreds of *Drury*, there was not a single *Fille de Joie* to be had that Night, for Love nor Money, being all engaged at the Masquerade" (34) – Castle's argument seems overstated. If, as she claims, masquerade ticket prices ranged from five shillings to four guineas (29), most prostitutes walking London streets, and even those working in brothels, would have been hard-pressed to afford masquerade tickets on a regular basis. As social historian Tony Henderson points out, prostitutes made around two shillings for each sexual transaction (*Disorderly Women* 36). Regardless of how many prostitutes actually attended the balls, their perceived link with commercial, non-reproductive sexuality is clear.

As a Dublin whore, Leeson attended many masquerades, including a grand 1785 ball held for the benefit of one of her friends and colleagues, the gambling impresario Hughes. She "employed all [her] industry, to engage four of the prettiest *impures* [she] could select in all Dublin, whom [she] introduced as VENUS and the GRACES" (Leeson *Memoirs* 147). Leeson herself

thought the character of the Goddess of Chastity, Diana huntress of the woods, would best suit me, as we were all in *masquerade*, for had I appeared in the character of *Cleopatra, Messalina*, the Ephesian matron or any such, it surely could not be deemed *masquerade*; as to be in masquerade is undoubtedly to be in an *assumed character*; thus I sported that of the goddess of *Chastity*. (147)

Clearly, Leeson understood the conventions of masquerade, and portrayed a "world upside down" where the most notorious brothel-keeper was best represented as the chastest goddess. When Dublin city officials prohibited public balls a year later, Leeson held her own at her Wood Street brothel, in order to "shew how much [she] disregarded all law or order" (92–93). She sold and gave away two hundred tickets, and she reports that her ball was the talk of town. Though some friends tried to "dissuade or frighten" her from throwing the ball in defiance of official policy, she "had gone to considerable expence [and] resolved to go on" (93). On May 1, in front of a large crowd of envious onlookers, she and her guests enjoyed supper and dancing until six the next morning, "of which government took not the least notice" (94).

The myriad conduct manuals of the period taught Georgian women that to be feminine meant to be silent, submissive, and chaste; Leeson's *Memoirs* might be seen to function as a different sort of conduct manual. Clearly, Leeson was submissive neither to Dublin laws nor to an ideology that suggested women should meekly accept restraints on their freedom of thought or movement. Instead, she took great pride in her reputation as a wit, including several *bon mots* in her *Memoirs*. She also literally left her mark in many of the places she visited (see 200–03), using her diamonds to inscribe witty epigrams on windows, mirrors, and other glass surfaces. In Wexford she wrote on a window in order to protest her mistreatment

> 'Tis surely a bore,
> That a favourite wh—e,
> Praised by wits for her humour and fun,
> Should with *cash* in her purse,
> As if God sent a curse
> Want lodgings in hungry Taghmon. (202)

In general, Leeson suggested that it was her spirit, her wit, and her independence that attracted her myriad keepers, undercutting claims that a modest reserve was the hallmark of the ideal woman. Her performance of unredeemed feminine conduct was certainly at odds with conventional representations, and cannot simply be recuperated as counter-example.

Of course, modest women were also assumed to be chaste women. As a whore, Leeson was paradigmatically unchaste. Instead of chastity, *Memoirs* express a particular enjoyment of sex that suggests women's right to their own sexual pleasure. For example, Leeson recalled her first encounter with Purcell, the young man with whom she later traveled to Killarney, in terms that make clear she expected her sexual needs to be met by her customers. She initially charged Purcell ten guineas to spend the evening with her, but promised to give back one guinea for each orgasm she enjoyed. Purcell agreed to the bargain, though he was very drunk. In the morning, Leeson returned one guinea, commenting ruefully "that, I must confess, was owing to my own wonderful exertions, as I wished to lose *a guinea or two* if possible" (186). By openly discussing her sexual response, and suggesting that women had some control over their sexual pleasure, Leeson again provided an important alternative to the conduct manuals, one that undoubtedly titillated and inspired some of her readers.

Though Leeson was clearly unchaste, she was not necessarily immoral. In fact, she strongly condemned her society's hypocrisy:

Can the presence of [chastity], render all the others of no avail? Or can the absence of it, make a woman totally incapable of possessing one single good quality? . . . One woman may indulge in frequent inebriation, she may ruin her husband, neglect, beggar, and set an evil example to all her children – but she arrogates to herself the character of a *virtuous woman*—truly, because she is chaste . . . and the wife of the parson of the parish will take her by the arm and appear with her in public (4–5).

Leeson insisted on her own moral code. Perhaps in reaction to her own family's rejection, she held generosity and charity to be the hallmarks of true character. *Memoirs* includes many stories of her giving money, food, and lodging to others less fortunate than her. When Moll Hall, another brothel-keeper, died, her creditors "came down upon the house, and seized even upon the very bed she lay waking on" (172). Leeson paid some of her debts and "had her decently interred in St Anne's Church-yard," hiring six coaches, paying for a funeral supper, and bringing several friends and acquaintances to the funeral. Leeson concludes this anecdote: "if charity covers a multitude of sins – honest Peg, thy only failing, of making use of what God gave, must be forgiven" (173). Others are also judged by their generosity, such as Captain Matthews. Matthews, one of her former lovers, operated the sponging house where she lived at the end of her life. Matthews fed Leeson and her companion, Mrs. Edwards, whenever they were short of funds. Perhaps in deference to his wife and in gratitude for their mutual generosity, Leeson refrains from discussing Matthews as a lover. As his charity marked his moral superiority, she avoided any counter-representations. Thus, in her discussion of charity vs. chastity, Leeson reworks official codes of conduct, performing morality despite her supposed immoral core.

Further, though Leeson was uninterested in her own chastity, she was careful to protect other young women. When a beautiful and well-bred girl applied to Leeson for a position in her Wood Street house, Leeson refused: "I never in my life was accessary (sic) or instrumental to the corruption of any girl; nor ever received in my house any one who had not already been deluded" (103). Importantly, this directly contradicts the construction of the eighteenth-century brothel keeper familiar to readers. As Tony Henderson points out, the "brothel keeper or bawd occupied the lowest place in the reformers' moral universe" (*Disorderly Women* 27), blamed for bringing innocent young women into prostitution. On the other hand, though Leeson would not "corrupt any girl," she wrote that she helped those who were turned out of their homes for sexual indiscretions. Some she put to work in her flash houses, others she introduced to potential patrons, and those she believed not suited for professional prostitution but were guilty only of a single transgression she either hired as companions or placed in legitimate occupations. Throughout, Leeson performs a version of Lady Bountiful, taking care of the young women who applied to her for work, money, or emotional support (see especially 103–05, 227–29, 246–47). In extending charity to seduced young women cast out by family and friends, Leeson rejected the example of the parson's wife who will excuse any sin as long as the woman is chaste.

Leeson's interest in helping other women, and the strong community of women to which she belonged, is evident throughout the *Memoirs*. Of course, she detailed several love affairs, and wrote about strong emotional connections to several men, including Purcell, Bob, and Mr. Lawless, but it is striking that her life story so emphasized her friendships with women. In this way, Leeson also provides an alternate narrative through which to understand eighteenth-century female experience. Unlike the conduct manuals, popular fiction, and plays which stress that a woman can only find happiness as a wife and mother, Leeson suggested that her female friends sustained her. She was particularly close to Sally Hayes, and grieved at her death even more than at the end of her romantic affairs: "Sally Hayes was my constant companion whilst she lived, and the woman I loved best, as she had a spirit congenial with my own" (113). She also mourned her "amiable friend, the good, the kind, the humane Betsy Edmonds," who was her companion in Matthews' sponging house, and who "breathed her last in [Leeson's] arms" (239). Leeson also acknowledged the business acumen of several rivals, including Moll Hall and Katherine Netterville. Leeson had a contentious relationship with Netterville, who was one of her chief rivals not only in trade but also personally; the two competed for the attention of several of the same men. Though Leeson seems to have disliked Netterville, she expressed regret that as she aged "Kitty-Cut-a-Dash" was unable to retain her position as one of the most popular and celebrated courtesans (152). Even when discussing her rivals, Leeson stresses the important connections women make among themselves.

Ultimately, though *The Memoirs of Mrs. Leeson, Madam* tells a fairly conventional story of the prostitute redeemed, Leeson also suggests a counter-narrative. As she performs her self in her autobiography, she constructs a female figure of tremendous pride, wit, and generosity. If *Memoirs* is in many ways conventional, Leeson's emphasis on female experience places it outside mainstream depictions of feminine subjectivity.

Further, she expresses an understanding of the self as performed, suggesting that she, and by extension other women, may play the roles demanded by society while constructing an interior self that undercuts those roles. Writing emphatically from the whore position, Margaret Leeson resists normative constraints on her life and narrative to offer a powerful counterpoint to eighteenth-century fictions about women.

PUBLIC WOMAN: THE LIVES OF CHARLOTTE CHARKE

Charlotte Charke has been variously identified as a "prodigal daughter" (Spacks *Imagining* 74), a "sentimental heroine" (Smith *Poetics* 104), a "passing woman" (Friedli " 'Passing Women ' " 241), a "cross-dressing failure" (Mackie "Desperate Measures" 846), a consummate performer (Strange "Charlotte Charke" 55, Wanko "Eighteenth-Century Actressess" 81), a "disorganised, impetuous Moll Flanders" (Charke *Narrative* ix), a much maligned author (Churchill " 'I was' " 74), a "freak" (Moore " 'She was Too Fond' " 94, Folkenflik "Gender, Genre and Theatricality" 101), a "chimera" (Peavy "Chimerical Career" 1), a potential lesbian (Moore " 'She was Too Fond' " 97), and a proto-feminist (Fields "Charlotte Charke" 225, Nussbaum *Autobiographical* 197). The label I have given her, "whore," encompasses all these understandings. Charke was a public woman who exposed her triumphs and mistakes to a paying audience. As Jean Marsden points out, Charke "[constructed] public identities through the semblance of private revelation" ("Charlotte" 65). This disclosure of private, even intimate, moments parallels the intimate disclosures a whore makes to her paying audience. Charke, who proudly detailed her refusal to sell her body (Charke *Narrative* 73), proudly sold her life. Further, as the biographer of actress Anne Catley suggests, "[t]he word *Prostitute* does not always Mean a W – ; but is used also, to signify any Person that does any Thing for *Hire*. In this Sense Miss C – Y may be said to be a *Prostitute Player*" (quoted in Straub *Sexual Suspects* 102). Like Catley, Charke did "any Thing for Hire," and was open to the charge that a woman prepared to make her writing public would be prepared to expose herself in other ways: the sale of her life story might well have been understood as the sale of her self.

As suggested by the multiple and overlapping positions Charke occupied, the *Narrative* encourages contradictory interpretations. In her description of her youth and first marriage, these contradictions are especially apparent. Charke fashions a narrative of parental love and lenience, making her adult separation from her father all the more cruel and unfair. Of course, as Sidonie Smith points out "autobiography is understood to be a process through which the autobiographer struggles to shape an 'identity'" (*Poetics* 5). Thus, her recollections frame her education, activities, and marriage as the gifts of doting parents, and Charke writes herself a recipient of unconditional love, even when other narratives seem more plausible. In this way, her writing is a performative act, meant to call into being a happier childhood than the "facts" suggest she actually experienced. Not only does her text perform a self and subject, but also a history.

Biographer Fidelis Morgan, among others, suggests difficulties in the Cibber household. Despite Charke's very real desire to "move his Heart to Pity and Forgiveness" and finally receive his "BLESSING, and his PARDON" (Charke *Narrative* 8), Colley Cibber was an indifferent parent at best. He grabbed his wife Katherine's inheritance in order to pay his gambling debts, sold his shares in the Drury Lane Theatre outside the family, and left Charlotte and another of her sisters only £5 in his will. Cibber was also a notorious womanizer, arrested for profligacy and impregnating spinsters on several occasions (Morgan *Well-Known Troublemaker* 23–24). Further, though Charke insists she was her mother's favorite, her late birth may have dismayed her forty-five-year-old mother. In fact, Katherine was frequently ill, and Cibber occupied with his writing and business; Charke often stayed with friends and relatives when her parents were unwilling or unable to care for her (27). Despite her performative insistence on a happy home, Charke's childhood may have been difficult.

Even so, the *Narrative* constructs a blissful childhood. Charke's position as daughter of the poet laureate ensured that her early life was one of relative comfort and privilege. In the *Narrative*, she notes that she was given an excellent education "sufficient for a Son instead of a Daughter" (Charke *Narrative* 10). As a teenager, Charke took on roles such as doctor, groom, gardener, and man-at-arms. Though most critics have rightly interpreted these activities as evidence of Charke's identification with masculinity, they also suggest a young woman restless for activity, company, and stimulation. Charke seems to have performed these occupations in order to earn parental approval. Living alone with her mother, she worked as gardener and groom, spending "the most Part of [her] Time every Day" (22) planting, digging, and weeding. When her mother saw Charke at her gardening, Charke "ask'd, Whether she imagined any of the rest of her Children would have done as much at my Age?" (23–24). It seems clear that Charke wanted her parents' approval badly, and her stories of her "indulged" childhood suggest neglect rather than benevolence.

Charke's account of her marriage suggests a performance of "belovedness" undercut by visible alternate interpretations. When Charke was seventeen, she married Richard Charke, a violinist much like her father: spendthrift, philandering, indifferent. Charke suggests that her father allowed the two to marry because he loved her too much to deny her anything, but her description of the courtship suggests another interpretation. Charke recalled that in another attempt to prove her value to her parents' household (she tried to purchase a horse for her father, but could not control the animal) she nearly killed a child. After this incident, Charke sank "into a Kind of Melancholly (sic) . . . Miss *Charlotte* became for a little while, I believe, rather stupidly dull, than justly reflecting" (27). In this state, she was courted by Richard Charke and believed his protestations of love. Though Charke characterizes her father's consent as springing from his "tender" concern, it seems as likely that Cibber was happy to marry off his increasingly intractable daughter to the first man who asked for her. In her performance of beloved daughter, Charke proves to be an unreliable narrator; her unreliability is especially troubling when the *Narrative* engages questions of gender, legitimacy, and sexuality.

Though details about Charke's romantic life are somewhat murky,[13] the *Narrative*, as well as other sources, is clear about her career as an actress. For much of her life Charke worked in the theatre, on and off the legal, London stage. According to biographer Fidelis Morgan, she began with her father's company in Drury Lane in 1730, playing several small roles and serving as general understudy. In 1733, after her father sold his share of the Drury Lane patent to John Highmore, Charke joined her brother Theophilus in his rebel company at the Haymarket. She worked as an actress in the Haymarket theatre, Drury Lane, and Bartholomew Fair, and managed several booths, small companies, and individual productions in London for the next several years. She also alienated her father by working with his rival, Henry Fielding. According to traditional accounts, her early theatrical career established her reputation as a rebellious if talented actress who seemed to have an over-investment in male roles, especially her father's; unfortunately, by the time of the Licensing Act of 1737, she had destroyed her connections with the licensed theatres. She managed a puppet theatre, worked in unlicensed London theatres and in fair booths (Morgan *Well-Known Troublemaker* 50–65), and generally tried to avoid debtor's prison until 1746, when she went on the road as a strolling player. She returned to London in 1753, tired of fighting for a career as an actress, and turned her attention to writing (Charke *Narrative* 96). She published the *Narrative*, as well as the short novels *The History of Henry Dumont Esq., and Miss Charlotte Evelyn; The Mercer, or the Fatal Extravagance;* and *The Lover's Treat.* She died in 1760, still estranged from most of her family, and still probably living with Mrs. Brown, the woman she began traveling with as a strolling player.

After the Licensing Act of 1737[14] effectively ended her career, Charke struggled to perform. She worked in illegal companies and in a booth at Bartholomew Fair, as well as evaded the act by staging "rehearsals" and presenting "free" performances with the purchase of a pint of wine, a ruse she originated (Morgan *Well-Known Troublemaker* 130). In a more legitimate vein, in 1738 Charke also set herself up as the manager of a puppet theatre company. Her licensed puppet-show "was allowed to the be the most elegant that was ever exhibited" (Charke *Narrative* 43).[15] Charke dramatized the effects of the Licensing Act by styling her puppets as actors and producing Fielding's satires, which had contributed to its passage in the first place (Baruth "Who is Charlotte Charke?" 33). Charke appropriated the conventions of the legitimate stage – her puppets were elaborately costumed and styled as actors – in order to highlight the effects of the Licensing Act. Puppet shows are another strategy through which Charke negotiated dominant codes, reworking and resignifying them for her own benefit.

Charke also resisted the Licensing Act by becoming a strolling player. Theatres outside the City of Westminster were unlicensed, but several companies circumvented the law or simply ignored it. Provincial theatres in Cambridge, Bath, and Liverpool, continued to produce plays even after the Act, and Charke details stories of playing in smaller towns and even villages as well. As a strolling player, Charke played several roles from the contemporary stage; one of her most revealing stories concerns the "Wild-goose Chace (sic) through all the dramatic Authors" she took with a fellow actress, Mrs. Elrington (Charke *Narrative* 106–107). Far from upsetting the audience, their decision to combine *Cato* with *Jane Shore* with *The Beaux Strategem* was unnoticed: their performance gained "the Universal Satisfaction of that Part of the Audience who were awake, and were the reeling Conductors of those, who only *dreamt* of what they should have *seen*" (107). In many ways, the Licensing Act of 1737 occasioned counter-performance. In the above example, Charke created a new script, offering a performance that responded to her audience's needs, making do with the materials and audience she was given. Away from the constraints of the legal stage, Charke was able to pursue characters, interpretations, and activities that would have been denied her at Covent Garden or Drury Lane.

Though breeches roles, which were designed to draw attention "to [the actress'] charms" (Rogers "Breeches Roles" 255) or to offer a "playfully

Mrs Chark daughter of Co: Cibber

Figure 3.1 A feminine, hopeful Charlotte Charke, around the time of her marriage
(Courtesy of David Garrick Club ET Archive)

ambiguous sexual appeal" (Straub *Sexual Suspects* 129), were a convention
of the Georgian stage, Charke used her marginal theatrical status to subvert
expectations. Though Charke appears to have been an attractive woman,[16]
she did not trade on that attractiveness as did first-generation actresses such

as Betty Boutell nor her contemporaries Susanna Cibber, Hester Santlow, or Peg Woffington. As the previous chapter makes clear, breeches actresses were usually physically appealing and assumed to be physically available. Charke was a very different kind of breeches actress, one who, according to feminist critic Polly S. Fields, directly "negated the Barbie-in-high-boots image or that of the kitten with a whip," ("Charlotte Charke" 234). Instead, Charke played male characters rather than breeches roles. Biographer Fidelis Morgan explains that by 1734, when she joined her brother's rebel company at the Haymarket Theatre, she played exclusively male roles, including Macheath in *The Beggar's Opera*, Lothario in *The Fair Penitent*, and George Barnwell in *The London Merchant*. A year later, in what was perhaps her most notorious performance, she appeared in Lincoln's Inn Fields as Lord Foppington, the role most closely associated with her father (Morgan *Well-Known Troublemaker* 52–55). Joining Henry Fielding's company in 1737, her first role was Lord Place in Fielding's satire *Pasquin*; Place was modeled on Cibber (60).[17]

Though Charke's performances are obviously open to the kinds of pleasures associated with traditional breeches performance, it appears that her contemporaries viewed them differently. First, she played *male* roles, rather than *breeches* roles such as those made popular by Boutell and subsequent eighteenth-century actresses. The unmasking scenes so central to the appeal of most breeches performance are missing in Charke's portrayal of characters such as Macheath and Falstaff. Second, Charke's male repertoire was extensive; unlike Woffington, who made her career playing a particular male role and reportedly shading it with feminine overtones, Charke played a variety of roles, as did the male actors in her companies. Though of course the unauthorized companies with which she worked may well have cast Charke out of necessity (Strange "Charlotte Charke" 55), it is nonetheless striking that she worked so extensively in men's parts. Further, as a strolling player, Charke apparently lived cross-dressed, and her parts were probably all male at this point. Finally, Charke was most notorious for roles modeled on or taken from her father.[18] The titillation, then, was more in watching the rebellious daughter mock her disapproving father rather than in "playfully ambiguous sexual appeal."[19]

Because Charke was so closely associated with cross-dressing on- and off-stage, and because her *Narrative* was advertised as containing anecdotes about "her Adventures in Mens Cloaths," her masculine performances also point toward her possible appeal to a lesbian audience. As with Betty Boutell, it is difficult to determine how many female audience members might have watched Charke with desire, and even more difficult to determine how many of them might have identified in some way as lesbians. But, as with Boutell, it is dangerous to assume that female audiences didn't take pleasure in Charke's representation of a feminine masculinity and her ability to play with gender. Further, her commitment to transvestite roles suggests that watching Charke's take on Lothario was very different from, say, Woffington's. Straub suggests that Charke's performances undercut the basic assumptions of the breeches role: "(1) the subjugation of a feminine spectacle to the dominance of the male gaze and (2) the exclusive definition of feminine sexual desire in terms of its relation to masculine heterosexual desire" (*Sexual Suspects* 128).[20] As such, Charke's performances provide an opening for homoerotic desire. Charke's roles "in small clothes" were likely intended and read differently than those of her cross-dressed contemporaries.

Further conjecture about Charke's appeal to women is supported by an increased awareness of what is now recognized as lesbian behavior and desire, as well as an increased link between the cross-dressed actress and "deviant" female sexual desire (131). Lillian Faderman demonstrates that passionate, romantic friendship characterized female relationships during the eighteenth century; these relationships comprised erotic elements if not sexual elements as traditionally conceived (*Surpassing the Love of Men* 78). John Cleland's *Fanny Hill* contains perhaps the most famous literary example of eighteenth-century lesbianism. Other pornographic and scandalous texts included similar scenes. These literary representations had real-world counterparts. As queer historian Randolph Trumbach demonstrates, the eighteenth century opened new categories of gender and sexuality, adding the male sodomite or molly and female sapphist or tommy ("London's Sapphists" 112–13). Though "sapphists" were most frequently understood as hermaphrodites (117) and so their desires came from a physical rather than emotional source, Trumbach suggests that by the end of the eighteenth century there was "no need of a separate biological category in which to place such women" (121). In many ways, then, Georgian audiences were more aware of a range of female sexual desires than Restoration audiences. Ultimately, "Charke could have been a living fantasy of lesbian possibilities for women readers" (Donoghue *Passions between Women* 100) and audience members. Different from other cross-dressed actresses on the eighteenth-century stage, she was almost certainly a powerful figure for women looking for representations of alternate sexuality.

A further crucial distinction between Charke and other cross-dressed actresses, obviously, is that she cross-dressed off-stage as well.[21] As with Leeson, masquerade may have supported her understanding of the self as performed. *Travesti* is an important characteristic of the balls, and the transvestite Charke traversed gender boundaries and class boundaries as did *travesti* masquers. As Marjorie Garber suggests, the transvestite occasions "category crisis," that is, the "border crossing from one . . . category to another: black/white, Jew/Christian, noble/bourgeois, master/servant, master/slave" (*Vested Interests* 16). Cross-dressed, Charke worked as a waiter for Mrs. Dorr, a successful tavern- and inn-keeper, and neither her employer nor customers were aware of her "true" position. At the tavern, she performed "cosmopolitan gentleman," crossing gender boundaries to obtain the job in the first place, and then class boundaries. Though a waiter, she conversed with foreign guests in their native tongue; they took her for a well-bred and well-traveled young man who had fallen on hard times. Her cross-dressing, supported by masquerade's insistence that the self is performed, allowed her to further cross class and national boundaries.

Of course, Charke did not cross-dress in order to disturb class and gender boundaries but for a variety of personal reasons. Most contemporary critics and biographers focus on Charke's cross-dressing as central to understanding her conflicted identities, and they offer a variety of explanations: Charke cross-dressed to avoid debt, to usurp (her father's) masculine power, or to facilitate lesbian relationships. Whatever the reason, her cross-dressing marked her as a particularly sexualized and notorious public woman; in effect, it marked her as a whore. Garber argues that the transvestite "marks the trouble spot" (17), explaining how a focus on cross-dressing indicates cultural crisis somewhere else. That Charke's contemporaries read her transvestism as whorishness suggests that her life as well as the *Narrative* highlighted a rising crisis in appropriate femininity. Like Leeson, Charke's representation of alternate female sexuality and experience questioned normative gender constructions, and like cross-dressed Betty Boutell before her, Charke was labeled a whore.

Again, the suggestion that Charke is a whore refers to her discursive construction rather than her actual experience. Though Charke certainly knew prostitutes, she insists that she was never one. Thus, labeling Charke a whore acknowledges both the conflation of the actress and prostitute still prevalent in the mid-eighteenth century, as well as the collapse of the two senses of "public woman." Charke figures discursively as a whore because she is outside of mainstream understandings of femininity. Though her narrative makes passing reference to her role as wife, and though she exhibits maternal affection and concern for her daughter, Charke is otherwise unidentified with traditional female roles. Rather than viewing this as evidence of her desire to be a man, as many readings of the *Narrative* imply, I would suggest that Charke remains closely aligned with that other eighteenth-century female figure, the prostitute. Roy Porter explains how the eighteenth-century emphasis on "woman's special role as mother" (*Rewriting the Self* 16) was a strategy used to decrease her sexual independence. Charke, identified most consistently as an actress and a cross-dresser, seems to have given up her "special role," leaving her open to accusations of excessive sexuality. Further, "her avid exploration of every role save that of wife" (Friedli " 'Passing Women' " 240) suggests that she constructed herself as an independent woman, one who rejected the domestic sphere in favor of a more public role. Emphatically a "public woman," Charke is also a whore.

Charke's cross-dressing also aligns her with prostitution. Not only does it suggest an unnatural and even whorish sexuality, as we shall see in the nineteenth century, cross-dressing sartorially links to prostitution. Some prostitutes cross-dressed in order to attract and interest clients; Margaret Leeson details her own "adventures in men's clothes" (see Leeson *Memoirs* 113 and 192). Ironically, the very clothes which suggest masculine privilege and autonomy also suggest excess female sexuality. Her *travesti* costume and masculine performance might also have been read as indicative of feminine hypersexuality, as it did for both prostitutes and those women who cross-dressed at masquerade balls. This is not to say that Charke wore pants because she was a prostitute or to mark her solidarity with what she terms "the sisterhood," rather that her cross-dressing may have had many meanings.

Charke's cross-dressing was probably motivated at least in part by economic necessity. She was constantly on the brink of financial ruin; nearly all of her businesses failed, and she wrote that when she was able to raise some cash, "as long as the Money lasted, [she] was the worthiest Gentleman in the County" (Charke *Narrative* 122). The *Narrative* details many of her attempts to avoid creditors by leaving London or keeping a low profile; this suggests she took pains to avoid being recognized. And, as she asserts over and over, strangers took her for a man when she was dressed in men's clothes (see 52, 56, 82, 121). If she wanted to avoid creditors looking for Charlotte Charke, her alter ego Mr. Brown provided an easy disguise. Further, it was easier to find work as a man. Cross-dressed, she worked as a waiter, strolling player, and valet. In fact, she lost her position as Lord Anglesea's gentleman when some rivals told Anglesea that he was immoral for "entertaining one of an improper Sex in a Post of that Sort" (71). Clearly, her employment opportunities increased when she was taken for a man. Charke's interest in making her own money, though fueled by necessity, was unusual for eighteenth-century women. This interest suggests another link with prostitution, as it recalls other middle-class women forced into sexual "deviance" by financial crisis.

Making her own way in the world also suggests that Charke wanted the power and privilege of being a man. As Joseph Chaney suggests, "[t]he pleasure of the costume, the immediate relation to the material signifiers of the masculine body, supersedes the necessity of disguise in her motivation for cross-dressing" ("Turning to Men" 220). Charke did seem to enjoy both masculine privilege and its signifiers. As a man, she was able to walk the streets after dark, and could better protect her daughter and her companion, Mrs. Brown (DeRitter " 'Not the Person she Conceived Me' " 15). She enjoyed the company and financial support of Elizabeth Careless, a prostitute, as well as several other "Ladies who kept Coffee-Houses in and about [Covent Garden]" who helped bail her out of debtor's prison (*Narrative* 48). Her pleasure that these women knew her as "Sir Charles" is evident in the text, and she is especially proud that her jailers see her surrounded by so many female admirers. Finally, Charke assumed masculine prerogative in her relationship with Mrs. Brown. When the latter received an inheritance, the two set out cross country to retrieve it. Charke made the plans, and, after the inheritance was claimed, took charge of the money (119–22).[22] In many ways, then, Charke's masculine clothes allowed her new pleasures and new powers.

Finally, Charke cross-dressed in order to facilitate her relationship with Mrs. Brown. The question of Charke's sexual identity is a contentious one. Pat Rogers states that "[s]he was in all probability homosexual" ("Breeches Roles" 252). Fidelis Morgan is equally certain that Charke is not lesbian. The epilogue to Morgan's *Well-Known Troublemaker* is little more than her explanation of how and why those who suggest anything "improper" in Charke's cross-dressing and relationships have grossly misread the text.[23] Robert Rehder, among others, suggests Charke was bisexual, as she was married twice and bore a child, and because "[t]here is no evidence that she disliked men" (Charke *Narrative* xxviii). Most historians and critics are more tentative in their approach to Charke's sexuality, however: Lisa Moore suggests that her text "provide[s] evidence about the *possibility* of a female homoerotic sexual identity formed through the unsystematic adoption of various class and gender practices and identities" (" 'She was Too Fond' " emphasis added 93). The general consensus is that it is as foolish to rule out behaviors, emotions, and attitudes now associated with lesbianism as it is to insist on Charke's heterosexual identity.[24] At the very least, Charke's friendship with Mrs. Brown is analogous to the "romantic friendships" detailed by Lillian Faderman, and this friendship, along with her relationship with her daughter, was clearly the most important and enduring emotional attachment of Charke's life. Like her cross-dressing and her financial independence, Charke's relationship with Mrs. Brown points toward sexual "deviance" and links her discursively with prostitution.

Labeling Charke a whore is especially important when considering the impact of her *Narrative* and its salient potential to offer an alternative model of female sexuality and agency. Like all scandal memoirists, Charke is writing from a marginal position, and, like many, her work was widely read. The *Narrative* was first released in installments in April 1755; because of their success the *Narrative* was collected and sold as a book, which went through two printings (Morgan *Well-Known Troublemaker* 182). The *Narrative* was also summarized in three issues of the 1755 *Gentleman's Magazine*, a kind of Georgian *Reader's Digest* that included excerpts and transcriptions of popular novels, essays, and scientific treatises (Turley "Masculine Turn of Mind" 180). Both eighteenth-century men and women had access to Charke's *Narrative*.

Importantly, the *Narrative* constructs an "other-world" almost entirely populated by professional women. Charke constructs this world through the parodic resignification of familiar theatrical scenes. Della Pollock suggests that performative writing in general depends upon citational practice ("Performing Writing" 92). Though "[i]dentity cannot escape its discursive construction in/as iteration...through performance it may exert a counter pressure. It may repeat with a vengeance" (92), recasting the normative in order to undercut its force. In particular, Charke uses theatrical convention in order to contrast her life with representations of the female, describing her experience as a wife in terms of the character, Mrs. Sullen, she played in *The Beaux Strategem* (Charke *Narrative* 29). As Marsden points out, her story's "most emotional moments are couched in theatrical scenes with which her audience would have been familiar" ("Charlotte Charke" 77). When her father rejects her latest overture, Charke responds by quoting his own play: "I'M SORRY THAT I'VE LOST A FATHER" (Charke *Narrative* 62). The reference to her father's work and the hyperbole of the all-capitalized lament suggest an ironic undertone to this no doubt distressing event. It takes nothing away from Charke's desire for familial comfort to note the playfulness with which she invests the scene. In its reliance on theatrical quotations, the *Narrative* challenges the trope of the sentimental heroine,[25] subverting normative constructions of female subjectivity. Instead, Charke performs comic hero.

Though Charke very rarely follows convention, she certainly knew that the ideal eighteenth-century woman was submissive, pliant, and patient but rejected those behaviors for herself. Despite her poverty, illness, and frequent despair, Charke remained in control of her fate, and narrated herself triumphing over career and family setbacks. Though Charke was sometimes bitter about her experiences, she consistently contrasted an example of her trials with a humorous story. She also refused to give up and wait for others to help. For example, when she returned to London after nine years of "the general Plagues of Disappointment and ill Usage, that are the certain Consequentials of a strolling Life," she was eager to open an "oratorical Academy" (Charke *Narrative* 138–39). Though she was frustrated by her own experiences on stage, she believed that theatrical careers offered significant opportunities to those who were willing to work hard. Throughout the *Narrative*, when one venture fails (which it almost inevitably does), she tries another. Charke emphatically denies ideas about the natural characteristics of women, offering an alternative model remarkably similar to Leeson's presentation of mastery.

Where Leeson's *Memoirs* makes clear that women have a right to sexual pleasure, *Narrative* suggests that female desire does not merit mention. Charke's first love is presented very dryly: "Mr. *Charke*, who was pleased to say soft Things" (27). This relatively subdued episode comes closest to romantic sentiment in Charke's autobiography. By erasing any discussion of romantic love and sexuality, Charke again offers a generic alternative. Though the *Narrative* is usually grouped with other eighteenth-century scandal memoirs, "a unique canon in which issues of aberrant sexuality are directly addressed by the eighteenth-century women" (Moore " 'She was Too Fond' " 93), Charke focuses on female friendship, instead writing an autonomous female community. Sue Churchill notes Charke's "considerable interest in female roles and the powerful female presence in the text" ("I was" 81), something ignored by most other critics. Her focus on her sisters, mother, and female friends represents feminine power and agency. First, Charke's mother remained a stable and loving presence "to the latest Moment of her Life" (Charke *Narrative* 42). Charke characterized her mother as "possessed of every personal Charm" (42) and insists that despite her age and illnesses, Katherine Cibber steadfastly supported her daughter, Charke suggests that if her mother were still alive, she might have remained part of a loving family. Her sisters Anne and Elizabeth, as well as her sisters-in-law Jane and Susanna Cibber, are also regarded fondly (see 37, 54, 89).

She also had close female friends, including the whores of Covent Garden who visited her in prison and women she met while strolling, including her frequent scene partner, Mrs. Elrington, and the "Lady, who lived within a Quarter of a Mile of *Chepstow*, and often favoured me with friendly Letters" (115). She spoke fondly and respectfully of the "heiress," who fell in love with her (56–59), and Mrs. Dorr, who ran the tavern where Charke worked as a waiter (82–86). For the most part, Charke described her community as peopled with friendly and supportive women, many on the outskirts of conventional society. Of course, her relationship with Mrs. Brown is another example of Charke's supportive female friendships; whether or not the two were romantically and sexually involved, it is clear from the *Narrative* that both she and Mrs. Brown preferred their makeshift family (which included Charke's daughter, Kitty) to a more conventional household. On the whole, the *Narrative* introduces its readers to a world where women work and live together. This especially suggests its potential for offering alternative narratives of female experience.

Importantly, though Charke constructs a supportive world of women, she also recognizes that not all women accept her lifestyle. Most notably, Charke battles with her "cruel" (64) sister, Catherine, whom she blames for her break with her father. Catherine also chastises her for wearing breeches and disgracing the family (73) and for contaminating their niece, Jenny (89). Throughout the *Narrative*, Catherine is the only person, male or female, who disapproves of Charke's life and choices. Importantly, Catherine seems to enjoy the happy marriage and parental affection that Charke lacked; she is a much more traditional model of eighteenth-century femininity. In her disapproval as well as her steadfast domesticity, Catherine seems to stand in for all those conventional women who might disavow Charke and her relatively autonomous lifestyle. Ultimately, Catherine's negative portrayal balances out the sympathetic portraits of virtually all other female characters, providing a richer and more realistic representation of women's relationships with one another.

The Narrative of Mrs. Charlotte Charke stands as an example of a public woman – in every sense – constructing her own narrative. It resists convention as it tells the story of an unconventional life. The text breaks from existing models of female autobiography: for a scandal memoir, it is remarkably free of any real scandal. Instead, as Fields asserts, "Charke is quite possibly not interested in our knowing why she was marginalized" ("Charlotte Charke" 233), but rather offers a narrative of the effects rather than the cause of her marginalization. As such, Charke offers a model of alternative femininity to her readers and her audience, whether we fix that alternative as lesbian, or feminist, or whore.

If, as Susanna Centlivre promises, women will prove by their writing that they are more than soulless fools, both Margaret Leeson and Charlotte

Charke exemplify how alternate narratives of female experience and sexuality might circulate within the public sphere. Like Elizabeth Boutell, though with an even greater reach and impact, Charke and Leeson demonstrate how the whore position offers women a space from which to speak. Further, their writing functions as a performance of character, constructing themselves as proud, autonomous, and powerful women. Their struggle to offer an alternative to conventions of sex and gender is taken up by another performing, public woman: Lydia Thompson.

CHAPTER 4

Burlesque, breeches, and Blondes: illegitimate nineteenth-century cultural and theatrical performance

[Lydia Thompson and the British Blondes] have made an unnecessary and lewd exhibition of their persons, such as would not probably be tolerated by the police in any bawdy-house; that they have made use of broad, low, and degrading language, such as men of any self-respect would repudiate even in the absence of ladies; that their entertainments have been mere vehicles for the exhibition of coarse women and the use of disreputable language, unrelieved by any wit or humor; these things and much more can be proved by anyone of respectability who has attended any of their performances.

(Storey "Blondes in a Nutshell" 4)

Like the first generation of English actresses, the first generation of female burlesque performers instigated public debate on the proper display of female sexuality and forever changed the face of (US-American) theatre. Female burlesque performers re-interpreted what had previously been an all-male variety entertainment (Dressler "Burlesque" 17) and the inclusion of women into an all-male form illuminated tensions about the kinds of theatrical entertainments in which women could participate. Like Boutell, Charke, and Leeson, Lydia Thompson and the Blondes struggled to influence and control their own discursive representation. At the same time, Thompson labored within constraint; her case history parallels the struggle of other nineteenth-century women, like prostitutes and feminists, who were limited by dominant discourses of female sexual agency. Lydia Thompson and the British Blondes[1] were reviled in the press and from the pulpit as real threats to both US-American womanhood and theatrical tradition. The Blondes, inadequately described by labels of actress, whore, or feminist, offered new ways to think female sexuality, ones that exceeded familiar narratives.

Lydia Thompson and the British Blondes embodied mid-Victorian American tensions, especially those surrounding the construction of the feminine ideal embedded within the ideology of the Cult of True Womanhood.

The True Woman was pious, sensitive, emotional, and dependent. Her "natural" role was as wife and mother, and her natural sphere was the family and home (Smith-Rosenberg *Disorderly Conduct* 110–12). Of course, the Cult of True Womanhood was challenged from a variety of other locations and marked by a central ambivalence, as the work of feminist historians such as Carroll Smith-Rosenberg makes clear. In part, Thompson and the Blondes were successful because they exploited existing ambivalences within the ideology of the Cult of True Womanhood. Alan Sinfield argues that "dissidence operates, necessarily, with reference to dominant structures" and that dominant discourse allows its own subversions (*Faultlines* 47–48). Lydia Thompson was not only a symbolic signifier of challenges to domestic ideology, but also directly threatened that ideology.

Following from Peter Stallybrass and Allon White's oft-cited assertion that "what is *socially* peripheral is so frequently *symbolically* central" (*Politics and Poetics* 5), the burlesquer is pressed into the service of other discourses. Stallybrass and White, though primarily concerned with class rather than gender, argue that those socially designated as "low" occupy a "powerful *symbolic* domain *despite* and *because of* their actual social marginalization" (24). Thus, although the Blondes' entertainment and Thompson herself were relegated to the periphery of US-American theatre as well as society, the hysteria greeting their performances suggests they constituted a significant cultural challenge. That hysteria demonstrates how Thompson and the Blondes participated in what Michel Foucault terms "the incitement to discourse" (*History I* 18). That is, although social critics attempted to contain the Blondes' sexual threat, the proliferation of discourses around them in fact generated the Blondes' transgressive potential. Thus, "Lydia Thompson"[2] existed within discourse, and was in fact, in Foucauldian terms, a "specific type of discourse on sex" (97), multiply disseminated and circulated through various sites of power. Though she pressed against the boundaries of domestic ideology, she was embedded within that ideology. Further, Lydia Thompson is an example of Foucault's "speaking sex," that which seems to reveal the truth of the body and self. Costumed to highlight her legs, hips, and bosom, Thompson revealed far more of her body than fashionable dress allowed and put her secondary sex characteristics on stunning display. In her performances as well as in her interactions with her critics, Thompson spoke sex with a frankness that disturbed her audiences. Labeled and speaking as a "whore," Thompson offered alternative female sexuality to mainstream audiences.

Early in their US-American tour, the Blondes were an enormous popular and critical success. On September 28, 1868 they first appeared at George Wood's Museum and Metropolitan Theatre[3] in New York City.

The theatre was sold out on opening night, and the Blondes were an overnight sensation. Thompson arrived from London already a celebrity. Thompson, her publicist Archie Gordon, and her husband/manager Alexander Henderson had mounted a massive publicity campaign based on Thompson's physical beauty and personal charm, engineered to guarantee sold-out houses and constant press attention. Initially, critics approved of Thompson and her troupe, audiences of respectable men and women regularly attended the theatre, and several imitation troupes sprang up, mimicking the Blondes' physical appearance and theatrical style. But the tide quickly began to turn as the characteristics the publicity machine had stressed were turned against them. Less than six months after their initial success, the Blondes were targets of vitriolic public criticism. Scantily clad and sexually candid, the British Blondes seemed to denounce established gender norms by displaying an excessive and even masculine sexuality.

Nineteenth-century anti-burlesque hysteria is generally explained as a reaction to the hypersexual female image presented by Thompson and her troupe. Understanding Thompson as a cross-dressed performer in the tradition of Boutell, Charke, and others, however, complicates this understanding. Cross-dressed – albeit in tights, short pants, and tight corsets – Thompson talked like a man but walked like a woman. She was neither fully male nor female, but, in the words of critic William Dean Howells, "an alien sex, parodying both" ("New Taste" 642). Thompson transformed burlesque from an all-male theatrical form and used male clothing and attitudes not to impersonate men but to underscore her femininity.

The female burlesque performer was also particularly threatening because she overturned conventions of theatrical female sexual display. The nineteenth-century theatre included many dancing women; the long-running *Black Crook* had a chorus of dozens of dancing girls and ballerinas had previously appeared on US-American stages in tights and diaphanous skirts. Critics assumed important differences between the burlesquer and the ballet girl, however, and strove to articulate the Blondes' threat vis-à-vis the ballerina. Feminist actress Olive Logan, one of the most outspoken critics of burlesque, argued that the ballerina

is a dancer, and loves dancing as an art. That pose into which she now throws herself with such abandon is not a vile pandering to the taste of those giggling men in the orchestra stalls, but is an effort which, to her idea, is as loving a tribute to a beloved art as a painter's dearest pencil touch is to him. (*Apropos*, 112–13)

Burlesquers, on the other hand, were outspoken exhibitionists rather than artists. Unlike the ballet dancer and living tableau model who exhibited their bodies mutely, or the conventional actress whose words and actions were restricted by narrative, the burlesque performer looked at and talked back to the audience. As burlesque historian Robert C. Allen[4] points out, the female burlesque performer, "out of control and unable to control [herself]," insisted on calling attention to her body, actions, and words (*Horrible Prettiness* 128), presenting a more threatening, direct sexuality, one that reflected tensions over the nineteenth-century prostitute and feminist.

On stage and in her well-publicized daily activities, Lydia Thompson "performed" both female and male characteristics. As Judith Butler points out, the female performance of feminine behavior can illuminate the constructed nature of gender (*Bodies* 124), while the female performance of masculine behaviors signals "a monstrous ascent into phallicism" (103). On stage, Thompson frequently appeared cross-dressed as an amorous and aggressive suitor for the other Blondes' affections. Thompson's publicity transgressed expected feminine behavior even further. She not only "spoke" onstage, she spoke in public as well, writing letters to the editor, planting stories, and holding press conferences. In Butler's framework, this discursive production threatens the "normative dimension of the constitution of the sexed subject" (106–07). Most nineteenth-century women eschewed this kind of public intervention; further, many of those who did, like Olive Logan above, were careful to frame their exchanges within the ideological bounds of the Cult of True Womanhood. Though Thompson worked closely with Henderson and publicist Gordon, her words and actions were publicized as being in "her own voice," and the public generally understood her to be the author of her written communications with the press. However, at other times the press denied Thompson discursive participation, demonstrating the difficult battle she waged to be viewed as the author of her life's narrative.

Efforts to contain Lydia Thompson underscore the parallels between the burlesque performer and the prostitute. The Blondes, who "made an unnecessary and lewd exhibition of their persons," were easily slotted into existing discourses of promiscuity and prostitution. The standard nineteenth-century narrative of prostitution suggested that the prostitute had "fallen" into a moral and physical abyss that led swiftly and inevitably to disease and death. Dr. William Sanger, whose 1859 *History of Prostitution* traces the career paths of New York City prostitutes, stated unequivocally that *"The average duration of life among these women does not exceed four years from the beginning of their career!"* (455).[5] Critics of burlesque used the metaphor of contamination to explain the effect burlesque performances exerted on audiences. Symptoms of "burlesque mania," according to the *New York Times* anonymous theatre critic on February 5, 1869, included performers "dispossess[ing] themselves of their clothing," uttering "piercing screams called comic singing, distorted and incoherent ravings called puns, and finally, strong convulsions and denominated break-downs and walk arounds" ("Burlesque Mania" 5). Female burlesquers were like prostitutes because their words and actions belonged in "a bawdy-house," and because, like prostitutes, they could contaminate the social body. By framing burlesque performance within existing discourses of prostitution and venereal disease, commentators attempted to mitigate its threat.

Nineteenth-century feminist movements also problematized conventionally and normatively secured systems of gender relations. Feminists aimed to place women within other discourses than the family, domesticity, and property and to end the sexual subjection of women. Thus, although feminists addressed the problem of sexuality from another angle, like burlesquers and prostitutes, they challenged the sexual status quo and domestic ideology. One of the most contentious issues for the nineteenth-century feminist was the sexual double standard: middle-class women wanted to end the sexual promiscuity men took for granted, and enforce celibacy before and monogamy during marriage for both men and women (Hill *Their Sisters' Keepers* 66). Therefore, the feminist unsettled sexual standards as much as prostitutes and burlesquers, though she approached sexual inequality from the opposite angle. The public sexuality of the prostitute and burlesquer suggested that both men and women were equally interested in sex, and equally able to participate in even promiscuous sexual activity. The moral reform campaigns of the new bourgeois feminist, on the other hand, suggested that both men and women should practice restraint and moderation. Both groups of women were thus promoting sexual equality: equal license or equal chastity. Despite the difference in their representations and agendas, both feminists and prostitutes threatened the sexual standards of Victorian America and questioned the assumption that sexual desire and promiscuity were the natural right of men. Burlesquers put this struggle on the stage; cross-dressed and otherwise masculinized, Lydia Thompson and the British Blondes entered the discursive sexual arena.

The Blondes' cross-dressing further linked them to feminists and prostitutes, as well as to the breeches tradition explored in previous chapters. What women chose to wear, and what those choices signaled to Victorian society, suggests that the link between fashion and femininity was particularly strong during the Victorian age. According to media critic Jennifer

Craik, "[b]ecause western culture has been so preoccupied with the 'problem' of femininity, women's fashions have responded frequently to discourses about sex" (*Face of Fashion* 56). As the discussion on masquerade makes especially clear, women are presumed to signal hidden sexual identities through costume. In the eyes of conservative critics, feminists, prostitutes, and burlesquers all wore pants, and thus all were unnatural, masculine monsters. Feminists frequently stressed dress reform, and some adopted Amelia Bloomer's creation, wearing pants or a split skirt in protest of the "disabling" fashions middle-class women wore. Prostitutes cross-dressed in order to attract clients, and female burlesque performers appeared on stage either cross-dressed as male characters or in short pants and tights. The controversy over burlesque was directly linked to their assumption of male attire: in 1869 William Dean Howells, writing about Ada Harland's Boston off-shoot of the British Blondes, described burlesquers as "not like men" but equally "unlike women" ("New Taste" 642–43). The British Blondes, like other gender-bending nineteenth-century women, seemed to cite both (hyper)feminine and masculine norms.

Howells' "alien sex" can also be understood as a woman who does not fit into dominant discourses of feminine sexuality and identity. Rather, burlesquers, feminists, and prostitutes strove for self-definition outside dominant discourse. Although feminists and female moral reformers wanted burlesque performers off the stage and prostitutes off the streets, at least some burlesquers and prostitutes enjoyed the economic independence and personal freedom that feminists wished to secure for all women. Putting on pants, burlesquers, prostitutes, and feminists also put on some of the freedoms associated with masculinity at mid-century. Female burlesque performers co-opted a theatrical form that had previously been associated with male entertainers[6] and were financially and sometimes critically rewarded for their efforts. Prostitutes took over the public space of city streets and sidewalks and participated in the financial infrastructure of urban life. Feminists worked to secure equality between the sexes in financial, familial, and political transactions. That all three groups of women adopted male clothing while taking on male roles – both literally and figuratively – suggests that sartorial similarities are not in fact coincidental, but part and parcel of these women's attempts to claim male privilege. These three groups of women all struggled to attain what had previously been only masculine privilege through their clothing, their economic independence, and their discursive agency.

In this chapter, I examine several of the discourses deployed to contain Lydia Thompson and her struggles to assert her own voice, gauging the extent to which her attempted interventions paralleled similar movements among "legitimate" actresses, feminists, and prostitutes. To that end, I first provide a narrative of Thompson's first season in New York and the discourses proliferating around her. Then, I place the Blondes in the context of other mid-nineteenth-century theatrical entertainments, paying particular attention to the use of breeches roles and their meaning in the new hierarchy of US-American theatre. Extending the discussion of the breeches role into everyday life, fashion and the female dress reform movement demonstrates that both practice and discourse determined the True Woman: this ideal was challenged both by the interventions of feminists and prostitutes as well as by internal contradictions. Finally, I return to Thompson's narrative, discussing how both her contemporaries and historians shaped her notorious battle with *Chicago Times* editor Wilbur Storey to tell a particular story about burlesque, nineteenth-century femininity, and transgressive female sexuality. Lydia Thompson exploited existing ambivalences in Victorian American notions of femininity. Both on stage and in public, Thompson flaunted her unconventional behavior and critics – both historically and in the contemporary period – have seized on her as a signifier of both low theatre and transgressive sexuality in Victorian US-America. At the same time, she reacted against the whore stigma to focus a particular, personal narrative of female sexual agency.

CONSTRUCTING LYDIA THOMPSON

In New York in 1868–1869 Lydia Thompson labored to control and influence her own discursive representation. She was generally understood to have creative control over her troupe's performances, spoke to members of the press about her biography and theatrical style, and defended herself when attacked.[7] In addition, it seems that Thompson, Henderson, and publicist Gordon courted controversy; in both New York and Chicago they attacked the newspaper editors who maligned them, capitalizing on the attendant publicity in order to fill theatre seats.

Lydia Thompson's biography is an example of her attempts to control public perception: the narrative of her early life stresses her middle-class background, filial responsibility, youthful beauty, talent, patriotism, and success. The details of Thompson's life before her US-American tour are sparsely documented: dates, productions, and liaisons are variously attributed or omitted, especially regarding her age and her marriage. The composite biography,[8] which relies heavily on Thompson's statements to the press, suggests that Thompson was a genteel young woman who turned to the stage in order to support her mother and eventually attained both financial success and the adoration of her extensive audience. Most accounts agree that Thompson was born in 1836 in London. Her father died when she was very young; her mother's remarriage to a prosperous Quaker businessman enabled Thompson to receive dancing and singing lessons. When her stepfather died, Thompson put her skills to work: at the age of ten she supported her mother by playing ingenue and breeches roles in a variety of London and provincial venues. In 1854 Thompson challenged a Spanish dancer, Perea Nina, to a competition, matching her step for step and endearing herself to patriotic British audiences. According to Bernard Sobel, she married "a well-fed young man by the name of Tilbury" (*Burleycue* 25) in 1853 or 1854; biographer Kurt Gänzl corrects Sobel by dating her marriage to John Christian Tilbury to 1863. She had a daughter, Zeffie, who herself became a moderately successful actress. In 1864, Tilbury was killed in a riding accident, and after a brief mourning period Thompson returned to the stage to great public sympathy and acclaim (Gänzl *Lydia Thompson* 59–61). Alexander Henderson managed Thompson's return to the stage, and steered her into burlesque; she apparently married Henderson in 1868. Thompson developed her burlesque, premiering *Ixion* and *The Field of the Cloth of Gold* for approving London audiences. Thompson and her blonde co-stars Pauline Markham, Alice Logan, Ada Harland, Lisa Weber, and lone male troupe member Harry Beckett capitalized on their London success, bringing their version of burlesque to US audiences. In September 1868 Thompson opened in New York at George Wood's theatre before moving to the more prestigious Niblo's in December. In July, the British Blondes took their version of burlesque on the road, visiting St. Louis, New Orleans, and Chicago.

Recognizing that the Blondes' appeal rested on their physical appearance as well as their theatrical skills, Thompson and Henderson hired publicist Archie Gordon to promote the Blondes' US-American debut; his advance work focused on Thompson's reputation as a heart-breaking beauty. The New York press received an eight-page biography of Thompson , detailing the passion she inspired in audiences; in addition to strewing her path with roses and carrying her through the streets, at least one audience member committed suicide in despair of her love (Allen *Horrible Prettiness* 7). Thompson's self-promotion continued beyond this initial press release. When the *Spirit of the Times'* anonymous drama critic mocked Thompson's hyperbolic life story, she answered the attack, attempting to control the discourse around her. In a letter to the *Spirit*, Thompson defended her biography – "it was compiled *entirely* from newspaper extracts upon my return to London from the Continent, which had to be translated from French, German, and Russian" and was "perfectly true" – but she was embarrassed and annoyed by the "insane instances of suicide and dueling" her performances had caused. Thompson further character-ized herself as a "very humble little individual" who worked "to *try* and merit all the flattering things [other newspapers] have said of me." She hoped American audiences would find her entertaining, but if they did not, it would be "the first time such a calamity every befel [sic]" her (96). Thompson used the drama critic's attack in order to repeat the sensational portions of her biography, portray herself as a hard-working and talented actress, and make a personal appeal to her potential audience. Like Charke and Leeson, Thompson performed humility, intelligence, and honesty while titillating her reading public.

With such a contentious and exciting introduction, it is not surprising that the Blondes were given regular coverage by the *Spirit* as well as other New York papers. The *Times* noted Thompson's arrival in New York, gave advance notices of the Blondes' debut at both Wood's and Niblo's, and printed editorials and reports of the Blondes' activities, as well as several letters from Henderson and Thompson regarding burlesque in general and the Blondes in particular. The *Spirit* mentioned the Blondes repeatedly; 65 percent of the *Spirit*'s weekly editions from September 1868 to February 1869 mentioned the Blondes, more coverage by far than any other theatrical troupe. In addition to reviews of the Blondes' openings at Wood's and Niblo's, these notices ranged from box office reports heralding the Blondes as New York's biggest money-maker for the fall season ("Theatres" 14 Nov. 1868, 208) to the gently satiric "at Wood's Museum, Management still takes the customary precautions that no-one is allowed to speak to the 'Man at the Wheel,' although the man at the wheel has spoken by this time to nearly everybody in town" ("Theatres" 17 Oct. 1868, 144). This frequent coverage by both the regular and entertainment press suggests that the British Blondes courted publicity; the receipts for Wood's suggest that the publicity paid off.

Press coverage tended to focus on the Blondes' personal lives and the performers' physical features, especially in the case of Thompson and her seeming rival, Ada Harland. On October 24, 1868 the *Spirit* reported that "Miss Harland has yielded to the vulgar clamor and sunk her individuality in a yellow wig – unwisely, we think, as it distracts from her beauty. No amount of false hair, however, can destroy the effect of her peculiar and attractive dancing" (160). Two separate June 1869 columns detailed Harland's split with the Blondes, informing its readers that she had formed her own troupe in Boston, much to the chagrin of Henderson, who, the critic intimated, had been romantically involved with Harland (272, 288). Like most of the notices in "Theatres and Things Theatrical," the Blondes' publicity was primarily gossip. As media scholar John Fiske points out, gossip connotes "triviality and femininity" (*Television Culture* 77), a distinction that was as valid in the nineteenth century as it is today. Thus, Lydia Thompson used traditionally female avenues of discourse in order to spread news about herself and her troupe. Further, using gossip as publicity, Lydia Thompson fed the public's appetite.

These media manipulations influenced both her troupe's success and the way their performances were read. Reviews usually noted the physical beauty of troupe members before critiquing their performance. Reviewing the premiere of *Ixion,* in the October 1, 1868 edition, the *Times* cautioned that "the whole success of the piece depends on dressing up the . . . good looking young ladies as immortals, lavish in display of person and setting them to dance and sing in the most reckless burlesque fashion." Sartorial display, not theatrical talent, was the focus of the review. The *Times* described Thompson's performance as "lively, vivacious, and spirited," but noted her masculine behavior and costume with some alarm: "although some exceptions may be taken to her costume, and that of her companions, no one can do so from artistic reasons; . . . nature has her own" (6).

Like the *Times,* the *Spirit*'s review noted that the show was a "great popular hit" and then detailed the physical charms of the performers. Thompson, "not the least bit of an actress . . . dresses superbly, and is happy in the possession of a magnificent figure and a pretty face. . . . knew she possessed attractions and meant to show them off to the best advantage." Pauline Markham was described as a "stately beauty, equally gifted with Miss Thompson in the way of yellow hair and a small, sweet voice." Ada Harland, according to the critic, "is one of the most graceful dancers we have seen for a long time, and we were several times on the verge of applause, but she has dark hair – alas! that it should be so. It obscures her merit." The final principal actress reviewed, Lisa Weber, was remarkable for her lack of beauty. Described as "a peculiar-looking young lady – not exactly pretty, but very arch and captivating" and as a natural blonde, Weber was hailed as the best actress of the troupe (112). As the description of Weber particularly demonstrates, critics struggled to untangle the evaluation of talent from the physical beauty of the Blondes. The two terms seem incommensurate; Harland is denied final approval because she is a brunette, Weber is talented but not pretty, and Thompson is not an actress but does skillfully promote her own attractiveness.

Thompson's relentless self-promotion, the focus on physical appearance, and the growth of imitation troupes seem to have led to a backlash against burlesque. After the Blondes moved uptown to Niblo's Theatre in February 1869, opening *The Forty Thieves*, the hysterical anti-burlesque discourse began. This rhetoric directly references how Lydia Thompson challenged the symbolic boundaries of feminine behavior. According to a February 5, 1869 *Times* editorial, "female face and form carry all [*The Forty Thieves*] honors, and in idiotic parody of masculinity creates its uproarious mirth" (5). Thus, the display of femininity at odds with the performance of masculinity was a further cause for alarm. The *Spirit of the Times*, who had heretofore promoted and supported the British Blondes, joined the attack. On February 13, 1869 the anonymous drama critic argued that for theatrical success

hair and legs only are required, and even the former of these might be dispensed with unless of the lightest golden hue. Brains would be a tiresome encumbrance, and the absence of lungs would be a positive relief, since the only singing that is attempted is so diabolically bad as to wring every sensitive ear that endures it. (416)

This editorial further reduced the Blondes to their body parts; their performances were diabolically bad, but their golden hair and shapely legs could compel audiences. In Olive Logan's angry assessment, "the nude woman of today represents nothing but herself" (*Apropos* 135); thus, her body, not talent, drew the audience. In this way, the Blondes are constructed as only sexual. Without brains or sensitivity they are nothing but bodies.

This sexuality was further viewed as threatening because of the Blondes' and other burlesquers' immigrant status, a growing concern for many mid-nineteenth-century social critics. Marketing Lydia Thompson as a glamorous European entertainer, and naming her troupe the *British* Blondes, the press seized on Thompson's difference as part of her attraction and desirability. However, this discourse was also deployed against her. The *Times* compared burlesque to a contagion, imported from England:

Some dismal folk have predicted destruction to our community from the example of the burlesquers. It is feared that the light hair, the clotheless (sic) and the convulsive symptoms may spread to every home and carry desolation to every hearth. The true remedy may yet be adopted by the Hygienic guardians of the Metropolis; this remedy is quarantine! The infection comes from late importations from England, scarcely a steamer arrives here that does not bear fresh quantities of the gold hair, which once on our shores develop into the true raving, roaring, stamping-mad burlesque! ("Burlesque Mania" 5)

Olive Logan complained that on New York's stage "the greatest rewards are won by a set of brazen-faced, clog-dancing creatures, with dyed yellow hair and padded limbs, who have come here in droves across the ocean" (*Apropos* 135). In May the *Spirit*'s drama critic railed against the "inroads of foreign actors" who, in the case of burlesque, "with their peculiar advantages of undress . . . were good-naturedly accepted," but called for a tariff to protect native actors (192). Burlesquers were talentless immigrant women who had nothing beyond physical display to recommend them and threatened the progress of talented, moral American actors. Burlesque was a plague upon US-American theatre and needed to be stopped before native performers were left morally and financially bankrupt.

Ultimately, it is unsurprising that the British Blondes met with such moral outrage. Archie Gordon's advance publicity stressed their physical appearance and the overwhelming love they inspired in audience members, Thompson and the other Blondes posed for publicity photos in short skirts and flesh-colored tights, and burlesque productions used double-entendre and "naughty" songs for comic effect. As Sinfield warns, a discourse that "aspires to dissidence cannot control meaning either. It is bound to slide into disabling nuances that it fails to anticipate, and it cannot prevent the reactionary inferences" it may engender (*Faultlines* 48). Logan made the link between burlesque and prostitution explicit, explaining that women unable to find work as minor characters at low salaries could "strip [themselves] almost naked and thus be qualified to go upon the stage of two-thirds of our theatres at a salary of one hundred dollars and upwards" (*Apropos* 129) and that once the burlesquers had "stifle[d] conscience, honor, and decency . . . mere money making [was] easy work" (115). The specific references to the transgression of gender norms, immigration, and prostitution demonstrate how deeply embedded in contemporary discourses on sex Lydia Thompson was. Because Lydia Thompson was constructed from within dominant discourse, her subversive power was limited.

Much of the New York anti-burlesque hysteria centered on Alexander Henderson's feud with George Butler, critic for *The. Spirit of the Times*. Under the heading "A Shovel-Nosed Shark in a Sea of Vice" included in "Theatre and Things Theatrical" on May 22, 1869, "at a midnight carousal given at a hotel in this city to his hand-maidens, and, under the influence of cheap champagne," Henderson spoke of the *Spirit*'s anonymous drama critic[9] "in scurrilous terms" and called him a liar, touching off the controversy. As defense, Butler asserted that Henderson had left a trail of "wives" in Canada and Australia where he had previously promoted theatre companies. Butler "suppress[ed] the names of the numerous small actresses who were unfortunate enough to be caught in the web of this natural Mormon" before he joined up with the British Blondes. Butler intimated that Henderson's relationship with the Blondes was as pimp to prostitute; the Blondes were "bound to him by ties unnecessary to mention" and Thompson, "the star [who] beamed softest upon him," gave him half of the net proceeds for each performance because she was under his spell (224). These accusations brought the Blondes' private lives into public view and suggested that the troupe was little more than a singing and dancing brothel.

Henderson threatened to sue the *Spirit* for libel, demanding both a retraction of the previous week's column and the identity of the drama critic. On May 29 editor George Wilkes refused and further demonized Henderson: "the manipulator of the yellow brood," a "merchant in nudity," and "panderer to the grosser passions" did not deserve "the dignity of such consideration." Wilkes claimed that he stood by the drama critic, and hoped that Henderson would be "summarily driven from the city" (232). In that same edition, Butler welcomed Henderson's suit; comparing himself to St. Patrick driving the snakes from Ireland, he promised to rid New York of Henderson and the Blondes (240). That evening Butler went to Niblo's Theatre to confront Henderson in person. According to a letter from Henderson printed in the *New York Times* on May 31, 1869, Butler led Henderson away from the backstage crowd, used "filthy language" against him and the Blondes, and "struck a heavy blow upon [Henderson's] forehead." According to the letter, when a crew member stepped forward in Henderson's defense, Butler pulled a pistol from his pocket but then withdrew. According to the *Times* on June 1 and June 2, 1869, Henderson brought a criminal suit against Butler (2, 4). Butler turned himself in to the police on June 1, 1869, posting a bond of $1,000 for the libel suit and $300 for the assault (4). It seemed as though the personal attack would be settled in court.

The incident, however, was far from over. In the June 5 edition, both Wilkes and Butler apologized for the physical attack on Henderson, but not the sentiment behind it. Wilkes excused his critic as "quite a young man" and the attack on Henderson as "trifling," but gave his approval to the renewed denunciations of burlesque. "For a long while the public gorge has been thickening with disgust at the naked nuisance, and an opportunity generally longed for to drive it from the town"; the feud between Butler and Henderson provided just such an opportunity (248). Butler himself asserted that the assault was "of very small importance" and renewed his promise to "drive the English pest from these shores" (256). Though Butler trivialized the feud, the cultural forces he brought to bear on what seems to be little more than a spitting contest suggests that Thompson and the Blondes threatened US-American feminine ideals. Again using anti-prostitution and anti-immigration discourses to frame the controversy, the press transferred the specifics of the personal feud into a larger cultural debate.

Thompson herself moved quickly to counter the attacks on her husband and troupe. She defended Henderson as her joint partner and then focused on the press attacks on herself, her troupe, and burlesque in general. On June 8, 1869, the *Times* printed her letter:

After so many months of flattering recognition and approval of the class of entertainment over which I preside, it is suddenly discovered, by a certain clique, that the performances are disgusting, vulgar, licentious and degrading, &c. Such attacks, it is too evident, emanate from unscrupulous persons, instigated solely by private malice, with the avowed and published object of injuring me personally in your good opinion, and of driving myself and troupe from the City. (5)

Thompson, never publicity shy, attempted to shift focus from the particulars of the Butler/Henderson controversy onto herself and burlesque. She took the attacks personally, and suggested they were motivated by dislike. The "humble little person" painted herself as a hard-working and talented artist who justified burlesque on the basis of its popularity. Employing a familiar entrepreneurial argument, she suggested that the Blondes were only giving the public what they had asked for. Thompson struggled to insert herself into the feud and focus attention on her performance and personality.

The reaction to Thompson's defense indicates the limits of her discursive agency. Butler and other newspapermen roundly mocked Thompson's letter and support of Henderson. Comparing Henderson to a "dusky warrior" of a "certain tribe in Central Africa" and Thompson to the female slave who "shields his magnanimous person . . . to receive and exhaust the slings and arrows of the enemy," on June 12 Butler asserted that he had not attacked Thompson nor any of her "sister-artistes" but only her manager, who had brought such abuse upon himself. Thus, Butler reframed the feud as a masculine endeavor, moving the concerns of female burlesquers into the background. The *Times'* June 9 response was even more severe. The editorial characterized Thompson's letter as "simply a left-handed manifesto from Mr. Henderson," suggesting that Thompson was unable to write on her own. The two were further disparaged: "to hide behind the skirts of a woman, – if we may use that figure of speech in reference to one who never appears in public with any skirts at all – in times of difficulty, is not usually considered the most dignified method of retreat." Further, the *Times* announced it would no longer print her letters. The *Times* denied that they had acted from personal malice, as it was beneath newspapermen to concern themselves with "persons of Mr. Henderson's stamp" (4). Despite Thompson's attempt at intervention, the press reasserted its own narrative. In the case of the *Times*, Thompson was shut out altogether, as the protests of an unwomanly woman did not fit into the editorial guidelines of such a serious newspaper.

The feud seems to have ended after this exchange, as it is no longer mentioned in either the *Times* or the *Spirit*, though of course this may only indicate that the press stopped reporting on the Blondes, and the *Times* kept its promise not to publish any more of Thompson's letters. The British Blondes left New York in July for their tour of the United States. The entire incident – Henderson's alleged drunken insults against the *Spirit*, the assault on Henderson, Thompson's letter, and the constant editorializing against burlesque – seems to have been part of Thompson's campaign to draw further attention to herself and burlesque. However, Thompson's efforts to assert a different version of events were largely ignored. Her narrative was rejected in favor of the familiar story of the passive but immoral woman controlled by a villainous, exploitive man, a narrative firmly in line with familiar discourses of contamination and prostitution.

The New York leg of the British Blondes' tour demonstrates how Thompson worked within existing discourses in order to construct a public image. Drawing on links between female appearance and female worth as well as the assumption that a woman was valued because men chose her as a romantic partner, Thompson's publicity focused on her attractiveness. However, those same discourses were mobilized against her. Critics who initially approved of Thompsonian burlesque began comparing it to a disease that infected the morals and taste of its audience. The violence that punctuated Thompson's United States tour and the vituperative attacks the Blondes endured demonstrate the resistance to this representation of female sexuality on the US-American stage.

WHO WEARS THE PANTS? THE CROSS-DRESSED WOMAN ON THE NINETEENTH-CENTURY STAGE

The type of entertainment exemplified by Lydia Thompson and the British Blondes was symptomatic of a larger process of hierarchization taking place in US-American theatre. The British Blondes did not invent a new mode of representation, but rather borrowed and changed existing ones, both in terms of their performance content, which followed earlier burlesque models, and their costumes, which drew on a long tradition of breeches roles. Female burlesquers most often appeared cross-dressed or in short pants or tunic and tights, which simultaneously continued and challenged conventional readings of the cross-dressed actress. Though obviously the Blondes' success depended on their "lavish display of person," the cross-dressed burlesquer was not merely sexually appealing. She was also a threat, the "alien sex" that troubled traditional gender categories. The evolution of the breeches role from sexual promise to sexual threat parallels the increasing hierarchization of US-American theatre, as it legitimated some bodies while marginalizing others.

In general, historians argue that in the nineteenth century entertainments and audiences were increasingly split on class and gender lines. In *Highbrow/Lowbrow: the Emergence of Cultural Hierarchy in America*, Lawrence Levine charts the growing split between middle- and working-class audiences, both in terms of their behavior and their amusements. Levine argues that until roughly the middle of the nineteenth century, "the theatre was a microcosm; it housed both the entire spectrum of the population and the complete range of entertainment from tragedy to farce, juggling to ballet, opera to minstrelsy" (56). After mid-century, the discourse of "culture" was deployed in order to distinguish between particular kinds of entertainment and the spectators who consumed them. Levine is careful to note that although "aesthetic values [were] involved in the shaping of high culture" (227), aesthetics must be considered within the social, cultural, and economic context of "the nature of the mores and institutions that accompanied the developing high culture" (228). Thus, by the middle of the nineteenth century, when the British Blondes first toured the United States, an increasingly strict hierarchy relegated their performances to a "low-brow" circuit catering primarily to working-class men and women. Of course, enormously popular performers like the Blondes also attracted middle-class audience members as well.

Though Levine and other historians mark this break by the 1849 Astor Place Riots,[10] the display of female sexuality distinguished "high" and "low" performances as much as the perceived effects of (male) class conflict. The hysteria over the British Blondes and their supposed effect on audiences suggests that the representation of the female body determined whether or not an entertainment was appropriate for women and/or the middle class. As Stallybrass and White point out, the body is a medium through which tensions about class can be exhumed. Describing Ursula, the bawd in *Bartholomew Fair*, they suggest that the highly sexual female body acts as a *"go-between* ... in the symbolic functioning" of a culture (*Politics and Poetics* 65). Like the fictional Ursula, burlesquers mediated between the ideal feminine of the Cult of True Womanhood and transgressive women constructed in discourses of prostitution and feminism.

The increased professionalization of the legitimate theatre was achieved in part by segregating performers into two camps: those who perfected their art through years of training and apprenticeship and performed both classics of the theatrical canon and contemporary masterpieces, and those who sang, danced, and told jokes with very little formal training. Where once all theatre was viewed as suspect and profane, by the nineteenth century a hierarchy was established that distinguished between morally uplifting, educational entertainments and morally bankrupting, spectacular productions. This distinction had little to do with popularity – both legitimate actresses such as Charlotte Cushman and spectacular performers such as Adah Isaacs Menken commanded high salaries and performed for large audiences – and much to do with notions of taste, refinement, and artistic value based on class and appropriate sexuality.

In order to remain at the top of the hierarchy, "legitimate" actresses in the United States had to carefully negotiate between their public personae and private lives.[11] Charlotte Cushman, the first US-American actress to achieve critical and financial success equal to European stars, provides a particularly illuminating example of these kinds of negotiations.[12] First, Cushman described her theatrical career as a sacrifice made to save her family from poverty and destitution, and stressed her beginnings as an opera singer rather than an actress (Merrill *Romeo* 23). In addition, her stories of her early life and family background stressed her family's gentility. Cushman frequently mentioned that her father was descended from Mayflower passengers, focused on her middle-class upbringing and education, and suggested her Christian values had been forged as a member of Ralph Waldo Emerson's famous Unitarian congregation (*ibid*. 18).[13] In this way, Cushman maintained an air of respectability despite her choice of a theatrical career. She always explained that circumstance rather than desire had forced her to make her way on the stage. Though Thompson also stressed her filial responsibility, Cushman continually made family a priority, including her sister, brother, and mother in her theatrical entourage and business dealings.

Second, Cushman presented herself as celibate and chaste, focusing critical attention on her technical virtuosity in morally pure roles and productions and deflecting gossip about her romantic life by remaining a proud spinster. In an age that seemingly prized marriage for women above all else, Cushman framed this choice in moral terms. Biographer Lisa Merrill suggests that Cushman was acutely aware of the accusations of whorishness that dogged all performing women and therefore explained her decision to surround herself with intellectual, female companions rather than marry as a part of her natural distaste for the baser elements of domestic relations (252). Thus, Cushman framed her spinsterhood as a personal choice in line with her own natural chastity. Of course, biographers and theatre historians now tend to read a different narrative. Cushman's wide circles of female friends and intense, long-term relationships with writer Matilda Hays and sculptor Emma Stebbins and niece-in-law Emma Crow suggest to many that Cushman was a lesbian, whether or not her relationships with other women included physical, sexual contact. Seen in this light, Cushman's spinsterhood is even more notable, and her ability to frame her celibacy within the precepts of the Cult of True Womanhood even more remarkable.

Cushman also provides an example of the kind of cross-dressing accepted on the legitimate stage. Though Restoration theatrical cross-dressing seemingly assumes the breeches actress as object of male desire, during the nineteenth century the conventions of the breeches role underwent a significant shift. Legitimate actresses increasingly took on male roles, especially from the Shakespearean canon, in order to prove that their technical skill was on a par with their male counterparts. The burlesquers, on the other hand, appeared cross-dressed for sensational effect. Actresses like Charlotte Cushman appeared in drag not necessarily to titillate their audience but to demonstrate their technical virtuosity. Convincingly playing male characters, which many theatre critics noted with approbation, suggested that these women were legitimate thespians. Cushman played over forty male roles during her long career (Walen "Such a Romeo" 42). In London[14] during the 1845–1846 season she played Romeo to her sister's Juliet, cementing both their reputations. Cushman seems to have successfully disguised her gender during this and other performances. According to *The Illustrated London News* "We have never seen the character better played. In her burst of anger or despair we altogether lost sight of the woman: every feminine characteristic was entirely thrown aside in her powerful interpretation of the *role*" (in Walen "Such a Romeo" 47). Cushman, never noted for her physical attractiveness, seems to have been particularly adept at male roles and did not use them to advertise her (hetero)sexual availability.

On the other hand, Cushman's transvestism cannot be separated from her lesbianism.[15] Biographer Lisa Merrill makes a persuasive case that at least some female audience members were thrilled and excited by the non-traditional (which she reads as lesbian) female Cushman presented onstage. Further, as both Charke and Boutell's case histories make clear, the erotics of the breeches role might appeal equally to male and female spectators.[16] At the very least, cross-dressed female actresses opened a space for feminine/lesbian desire usually foreclosed by the heterosexual narratives of most nineteenth-century plays. Cushman's biography and cross-dressing demonstrate the challenges faced by performing women and queer performers. Though some audience members may have cheered Cushman's cross-dressing for its lesbian erotics or envied her sisterhood of like-minded spinsters, many others undoubtedly viewed her performances as the technical marvels she advertised them to be. That she remained one of the most successful actresses in the United States (her funeral procession was followed by thousands of fans) testifies to her skill at framing her iconoclastic choices within the precepts of the Cult of True Womanhood as well as her theatrical talent.

Citing male sexual norms, either on stage or as an extension of stage performance, does in fact call attention to the construction of gender. According to Kristina Straub, whose work on eighteenth-century cross-dressing has mapped the terms of debate, cross-dressing "gestures toward the performative nature of male sexuality, questioning its 'naturalness' through strategic mimicry" (*Sexual Suspects* 135). In the case of Cushman, as well as Thompson, the cross-dressed actress did not reinforce gender convention, but rather illuminated the history of that conventionality. Cushman's (queer) and Thompson's (monstrous) performances exceeded the bounds of theatrical convention; on-stage as well as off, they refused to participate in the dominant sexual norms that constructed the woman as defining other to the man.

A close reading of two publicity photos, one of Cushman, the other of Thompson, clarifies distinctions between cross-dressed actresses on the legitimate and illegitimate stage. Thompson stands on a rocky path in a flimsy, light-colored tunic, light tights, and high-heeled black leather boots. The tunic stops mid-thigh and is tightly cinched at the waist, leaving her neck, arms, shoulders and a good deal of her chest bare, as well as exposing most of her legs. Her wavy blond hair is encircled with a garland and flows down her back. Thompson stands with one arm at her side and the other at her waist, legs shoulder-width apart, and her head turned three-quarter profile from the camera. Though the photograph is labeled "Lydia

Figure 4.1 Lydia Thompson, challenging the conventions of theatrical cross-dressing, photographed as Ixion (Courtesy of the Library of Congress)

Thompson as Ixion," she seems more to be posing for the camera than playing a role. Sartorial elements – high heeled boots, her own blond hair, the tight waist and exposed bosom – foreground Thompson's femininity. On the other hand, the male name and quasi-Greek masculine attire suggest Thompson's usurpation of masculine identity.

Figure 4.2 Charlotte Cushman, a traditionally styled and virtuoso cross-dressed performer, as Romeo (Courtesy of the Harvard Theatre Collection, The Houghton Library)

The photograph of Charlotte Cushman as Romeo, on the other hand, disguises her gender. Cushman's loose tunic is dark, heavy velvet with long sleeves, high neck, and a skirt that reaches her knees. Cushman wears flat shoes, a floppy hat, and a short wig. A metal belt slung low about her hips holds both a sword at her side and what appears to be a dagger at her crotch, suggestions of phallic power too obvious to ignore. Her legs are crossed, obscuring their shape, and one hand rests at her hip as she leans against a balcony railing in reference to the text. Though Cushman too is clearly posing for the camera, the "period" hat, flat shoes, heavy tunic and sword, as well as the pensive expression on her face, mark her as a theatrical character in a way that Thompson's portrait does not. The marked difference between these two photographs demonstrates the different transvestite conventions of legitimate and illegitimate theatre. In addition, the public believed that Cushman donned male attire in service to her art, while Thompson's costume served the public appetite for sexual display and Thompson's appetite for financial gain. That Cushman was so regarded suggests that she was able to frame her performances within dominant ideology, something the female burlesquers were unable and perhaps unwilling to do.

The cross-dressed female burlesquer may have been particularly disturbing because burlesque had a long history as a *male* entertainment, using travesty for much of its humor and appeal. Traditional burlesque was a theatrical form that claimed its roots in Aristophanes' comedies and was marketed as family entertainment and legitimate theatrical fare. Traditional burlesque consisted of parodies of literary classics; often included topical humor and social satire; and usually featured songs, dances, and the walk-around, borrowed from minstrelsy, where each performer displayed a particular talent for the audience. Traditional burlesque generally employed all-male casts, with men playing both male and female roles (Dressler *Burlesque* 18–23). Burlesque before the British Blondes was already a travesty entertainment; however, the shift from all-male to all-female casts suggests that some of the hysteria greeting Thompson and her troupe was related to women usurping traditional male roles. Thompson's bid to garner attention from the transgression of theatrical norms depended exactly on their currency and force. Like traditional burlesque, Thompsonian burlesque parodied literary classics and familiar myths and included topical references that resonated with theatre audiences, but combined it with the spectacle of cross-dressed and sexually aggressive women.

In the United States both before and after the Civil War, traditional burlesque shared many conventions with minstrel shows, where, according to traditional accounts, Anglo-US-American performers mocked racial stereotypes for comic effect, and included men, often cross-dressed and black-faced, singing and dancing "ethnic" musical numbers.[17] In particular, burlesque and minstrel shows included songs and dances, stereotypes played for comic effect, topical humor, parodies of politicians and political speech-making, and a walk-around, where each performer paraded in front of the audience displaying his particular talent for applause. In the case of Thompsonian burlesque, greater significance attached to the walk-around. Rather than displaying a particular talent, such as spoon-playing and tap-dancing, the British Blondes displayed little more than their bodies. Audiences responded to their physical appearance rather than their theatrical accomplishments, echoing the convention of breeches actresses delivering epilogues in the Restoration theatre. In Thompsonian burlesque as well as Restoration epilogues, these performances were sometimes self-reflexive and ironic, calling attention to the shock of the cross-dressed woman in order to mitigate her threat. In both cases, however, the final image presented to the audience was the cross-dressed woman talking back to the spectators. Thompsonian burlesque combined the traditional elements of parody, song and dance routines, topical humor and the walk-around with the spectacle of scantily clad women.

The British Blondes and their imitators appeared on stage tightly corseted into low-cut bodices that left their arms bare and wore short pants, knickers or short, loose skirts with flesh-colored stockings (Young *Famous Actors* 1075). Though not particularly scandalous to contemporary audiences, Victorians railed against the spectacle of "nude women": female burlesque performers displayed a great deal of skin and wore clothes that drew attention to their legs, bust, and hips at a time when hoop skirts to the floor were the norm. This overt display of female sexuality – in Olive Logan's view, "the disgraceful spectacle of padded legs jigging and wiggling in the insensate follies and indecencies of the hour" (*Before* 586) – challenged bourgeois moral codes by suggesting that women too might enjoy the sensuality of their own bodies.

In addition to appearing in a relative state of undress, burlesquers included songs, dances, and innuendo drawing on masculine sexual mores. For example, *Ixion, or the Man at the Wheel* told the story of a mortal man, Ixion, who seduced several Greek goddesses. Audiences saw Lydia Thompson as Ixion (dressed as a man) flirt with and ultimately seduce Blondes Pauline Markham (Venus) and Alice Logan (Juno). Further, the Blondes performed dances like the hornpipe, a sailors' dance most associated with male performers. Impersonating male attitudes and behavior while highlighting female secondary sexual characteristics, the Blondes (and especially Thompson) presented a blurred image of femininity to theatre audiences, one that upset traditional expectations of burlesque performances, female-to-male crossing, and binary gender presentation.

Lydia Thompson and the British Blondes' usurpation of this previously masculine entertainment rewrote burlesque to place female agency, desire, and ability center stage. This entry into discourse parallels the efforts of nineteenth-century feminists who also struggled to underscore feminine agency and equality. At the same time, the sexuality presented on the burlesque stage seemed to echo nineteenth-century prostitutes' transgressive desire. As I demonstrate below, fashion provides a framework for understanding how all three groups of women struggled to participate in their own discursive representation.

FEMINISM, FASHION, PROSTITUTION, AND PERFORMANCE

The discourses of the Cult of True Womanhood have been used to explain the conventions regulating and influencing nineteenth-century gender behavior. According to feminist historian Carroll Smith-Rosenberg, the Cult of True Womanhood "prescribed a female role bounded by kitchen and nursery, overlaid with piety and purity, and crowned by subservience" (*Disorderly Conduct* 113). This prescription, however, was neither monolithically applied nor rigidly adhered to. Rather, the Cult of True Womanhood is best understood as a discursive construction that enveloped a host of contradictions. Stuart Hall argues that

the dominant culture of a complex society is never a homogeneous structure. It is layered, reflecting different interests within the dominant class (e.g. an aristocratic versus a bourgeois outlook), containing different traces from the past (e.g. religious ideas within a larger secular culture), as well as emergent elements in the present. Subordinate cultures will not be in open conflict with it. They may, for long periods, coexist with it, negotiate the spaces and gaps in it, make inroads into it, "warrening it from within." (Hall et al. in Sinfield *Faultlines* 45)

Specifically, both nineteenth-century feminists and prostitutes contributed discursively to the mid-Victorian understanding of woman as much as the Cult of True Womanhood. Understanding the rhetoric surrounding Lydia Thompson and the British Blondes and their construction as a threat to the feminine ideal includes interrogating the extent of their participation in the discourses of feminists and prostitutes. Sartorially linked to these other monstrous women, the Blondes are discursively linked to them as well.

Nineteenth-century women's movements were reform movements as middle-class women sought to bring about a more equitable society by abolishing existing patterns of behavior. Many of these reform movements focused on moral reform: early feminists directed purity campaigns to eliminate prostitution, formed temperance unions to eradicate drunken-ness, and joined abolitionist groups to end slavery. In conjunction with these moral reform efforts, feminists also engaged in dress reform. According to fashion historian Valerie Steele, feminist dress reformers objected to fashionable dress on three grounds: fashionable dress was unhealthy; fashionable dress was immodest; and fashionable dress was physically and psychologically restrictive (*Fashion* 146). In addition, middle-class women's interest in fashion demonstrated their inferiority to men. Because women were foolish enough to spend excessive time and money following the whims of fashion, the reasoning went, they were too foolish to engage in political or economic affairs. The British *Rational Dress Society's Gazette* warned that

[m]en cannot respect us, or accord us due consideration as long as we behave so foolishly in the matter of our garmenture. If men were to skip about in this style from absurdity to absurdity . . . [t]hey would be on our own level of incapacity and silliness. (in Steele *Fashion* 148)

Thus, feminist dress reformers viewed both feminine fashion itself and feminine interest in fashion as obstacles to overcome on the road to equality; as long as the corset and petticoat remained markers of femininity, women would not enjoy the status and privilege of men.

By linking what women wore with what women did or were able to do, nineteenth-century feminists participated in a cultural belief that what one wears is explicitly tied to who one is.[18] Understanding fashion as a map of social, sexual, and psychic location signals how fashion is necessarily performative; by wearing certain items of clothing, people distinguish who and what they are to others. Identity is written on the surface of the body through gesture, action, and accessory. This use of performative has opened up feminist debates on gender, suggesting that identity is con-structed rather than innate and that a certain agency may be derived through the parodic resignification of norms. In *Bodies that Matter*, Judith Butler argues for a more complicated understanding of gender performativity than her earlier work might have suggested, asserting that she did not think that "one woke in the morning, perused the closet or some more open space for the gender of choice, donned that gender for the day, and then restored the garment to its place at night" (*Bodies* x).

Butler's use of the closet metaphor is telling, however. Though *gender* may not be donned or doffed at will, *clothing* is. Further, outside of postmodernist, poststructuralist theory, most men and women seem to understand clothing as a visible marker of internal identity. Though fashion in everyday terms is usually figured as a form of self-expression rather than a mark of cultural values, the tension over what Victorian women wore suggests that nineteenth-century fashion did in fact bleed into the realm of cultural production. According to Craik, women in particular "wear their bodies through their clothes" (*Face of Fashion* 2). Opening the closet and reaching for pants instead of a skirt does mark gender on the body; choosing the clothes of the opposite sex can be tantamount to choosing the physical and psychic characteristics of that sex. Nineteenth-century women who rejected fashionable feminine apparel, whether they went so far as to wear pants or not, certainly crossed gender boundaries, and their clothing choices were understood not only as personal choices but as bids for social equality.

The extremes of fashion, typified in the 1860s and 1870s by a tightly corseted waist, protruding bustle and an excess of ribbons, bows, and other accessories, was eschewed by the "true woman." Mrs. E. M. King, the Honourable Secretary of the Rational Dress Society, argued that men and women both should dress to "become attractive to the other," but should forgo extreme styles and excessive ornamentation, clothing themselves instead "consistently with honesty, with self-respect, and with purity" (in Steele *Fashion* 149). Like most dress-reformers, King singled out the corset as the most damaging to Victorian women. Urban legends of girls whose tight-lacing had cut their livers in half or squeezed their lungs so tightly that they burst circulated throughout the late Victorian era (*ibid.* 167–70). The corset not only restricted women's activity and possible achievements, it also seemed to threaten their very lives.[19] Further, the corset did not clothe a woman "with purity," rather, it incited lust in the men who saw her and encouraged vanity in women who laced ever tighter in order to achieve a perfectly slender waist. Again, female fashion was a marker of female sexuality. Like the female burlesque performers who highlighted their bosoms and hips through an emphatically narrow waist, bourgeois women dressed to accentuate their breasts and buttocks.

Anti-burlesque hysteria is directly related to tensions over this ideal. Historian Lois Banner argues that the new fitted corset, tight skirt, and bustle that replaced the narrow shoulder line, small waist and dome-like skirt of sentimental fashion were directly influenced by burlesque performers; certainly the new Amazonian silhouette resembled the beautiful burlesquers. Editorials in the press raging against dyed blonde hair and cosmetics also seem to reference the Blondes and other burlesque troops featuring women with blonde hair. Though it is unlikely that fashion was as directly influenced as Banner suggests, given the evidence of a slower, more subtle shift depicted in fashion plates, the burlesque performer did certainly provide images of a more sexualized body to middle-class and working-class women alike. Henry James' "painted, powdered, and enamelled" (in Allen *Horrible Prettiness* 140) matron with dyed blonde hair and shockingly revealing dress directly echoes theatre critics who suggested that the appeal of the British Blondes lay in their legs and light golden hair. Again, the Blondes offered a visible manifestation of an alternative model for thinking femininity.

The overt sexuality of the fashionable late 1860s bourgeois matron astounded conservative reformers, as she seemed to be wearing her sex on her body.[20] Though these extreme fashions would soon be widely accepted, when they first appeared in fashion magazines they were perceived as shocking and new. Following from de Certeau, though dominant norms may prevail for "a more or less lengthy period of time," they are eventually replaced by what had seemed to be improbable threats to their dominance (*Practice* 48). In the specific case of the late Victorian ideal, these fashions were set by the Parisian demi-monde, "in part because it was especially important for them to look attractive, but also because they were much less constrained than most women by the fear of looking immodest or conspicuous" (Steele *Fashion* 131). Parisian couturiers created fashions with this particular class of women in mind, and introduced plunging décolletage, wasp waists, and large bustles to the US-American middle class.[21] When US-American matrons followed fashion, they wore styles initiated by courtesans. According to Steele, "[m]iddle class girls and women adopted styles that had initially been launched by courtesans, actresses and aristocratic ladies; while prostitutes dressed professionally as 'ladies'" (134). Prostitutes had always dressed in order to attract the appreciative attention of potential clients, wearing cosmetics, dying their hair and displaying as much bosom and ankle as they were able.

This erotic display, though eventually incorporated into typical Victorian fashion, was indicative of the gap between an idealized feminine beauty and the earthier sexuality represented by prostitutes, burlesquers, and other sexually suspect women. For conservative Victorians who clung to the domestic ideology of the Cult of True Womanhood, prostitutes represented a false femininity; like the British Blondes, they put on the markers of womanhood in order to entice men. Middle-class men were outwardly terrified by the aggressive sexuality of prostitutes, and strove to differentiate between "fallen" and pure women; even the name of the Cult of True Womanhood seems to reflect the necessity of distinguishing the real from the false. Respectable middle-class matrons employed the devices of prostitutes, blurring the line between true and constructed femininity. When the boundaries of dress expanded to include more attention to detail and adornment than earlier sentimental styles had allowed, it became difficult to distinguish between ladies of fashion and ladies of the evening.

The woman who seemed to reject fashion and femininity altogether blurred gender categories in equally horrifying ways. The specter of the masculine woman – either the feminist who took dress reform to the extreme and adopted male clothes or the prostitute who eroticized the female body with close-fitting pants, hats, and other accoutrements of masculine style – alarmed and aroused outright hostility. This cross-dressed or transvestite female was the extreme to which all feminists and all prostitutes were linked. For middle-class men concerned about maintaining dominance within heterosexual relationships, the cross-dressed feminist suggested lesbianism and the eventual overthrow of traditional domestic arrangements, an assumption still exploited by opponents of feminism. The cross-dressed prostitute, on the other hand, represented the woman so consumed with lust that she took the male prerogative in sexual relationships, thus threatening the power of the phallus even in heterosexual models. In addition, both lesbians and prostitutes impinged on the homosocial roles and spaces of the urban environment. The discursive link between cross-dressing and feminism reveals the extent of the threat such behavior posed to male power. For conservative Victorians, the masculine woman threatened both the domestic ideology which asserted that women and men occupied separate spheres, and the notion that gender identity was innate.[22]

The cross-dressed prostitute was a more familiar figure, at least to some nineteenth-century men, and as a whore she was indicative of the monstrously phallicized female. Prostitutes dressed as men and practiced lesbianism at the request of male clients (Smith-Rosenberg *Disorderly Conduct* 273), female prostitutes dressed as men among the Western gold rush camps (Senelick "Boys" 89), and both male-to-female and female-to-male cross-dressing prostitutes plied their trade on New York City streets in the 1860s (Gilfoyle *City of Eros* 136–37). An 1871 wood engraving printed in the newspaper *The Day's Doings* depicts the London courtesan Catherine Walters, better known as Skittles, astride her horse, brandishing a whip, and wearing a man's top hat with a curling ostrich plume (Nead *Myths of Sexuality* 61–62). The prostitute, like the female burlesquer, used male attire to highlight her sexuality and project an aura of domination. However, this sexuality was also thrillingly masculinized. Not only did the prostitute abandon the prescriptions of the Cult of True Womanhood

and take the initiative in sexual interactions, she traded her body for
money, thereby participating in the economic sphere. As the *Day's
Doings* illustration makes clear, the prostitute's sexuality was ambivalent:
the (phallic) ostrich plume in Skittles' hat both undercuts and draws
attention to its masculine connotations. Further, the whip and dressage
costume is an obvious antecedent for the contemporary dominatrix.

The cross-dressed woman was little more than a shadow figure in
nineteenth-century feminine ideology, despite her discursive use as a trope
for threatening female sexuality and the hysteria cross-dressed burlesquers
engendered. The prostitute, on the other hand, was a more obvious figure
to whom Lydia Thompson was linked, as the final section of this chapter
demonstrates. Examining the construction of the nineteenth-century prostitute contextualizes the accusations flung at Lydia Thompson and the
British Blondes and their rhetorical power to influence how women were
represented on the US-American stage. In general, women were defined as
prostitutes when they regularly exchanged sex for money. The implications
of this exchange significantly threatened class and gender distinctions:
prostitutes entered the public sphere and directly engaged in commerce,
activities regarded as properly belonging to the middle-class male. Further,
prostitutes were discursively divided into two categories: working-class
women who earned all or part of their income through commercial sex
and once respectable women who entered prostitution after seduction and
abandonment by unscrupulous men (Nead *Myths of Sexuality* 95).

Prostitution assumed enormous significance during the nineteenth century. Historians suggest that in both London and New York during the
period from 1850 to 1900, there were more prostitutes per capita than ever
before. Statistics from this period are difficult to gauge, as different definitions of prostitution, a variety of census methods, and the goals and
assumptions of statisticians (ranging from police officers to moral reform
workers) produce widely ranging figures. Prostitutes in the 1870s in
London numbered between 8,000 and 80,000 depending on the source
(Nead, *ibid.* 107), and in New York estimates ranged from 1,200 to 10,000
during the same time period (Hill *Their Sisters' Keepers* 30). Whatever the
actual numbers, prostitution in Victorian urban centers was perceived as a
significant social problem – in fact, "the great social evil" – and concen-
trated attempts were made to regulate and control commercial sex. As
Michel Foucault points out, the Victorians "installed . . . an apparatus for
producing an ever greater quantity of discourses about sex" that defined
how and why a potentially transgressive sexuality could be understood and
regulated (*History 1* 23). Because the prostitute posed a threat to the moral

fabric of Victorian society by troubling traditional constructions of female sexuality, she had to be narratively and discursively contained in order to limit her potential influence on middle-class women, just as Thompson was contained in order to limit her influence on theatre audiences.

Attempts to contain the threat of the Victorian prostitute placed her within a narrative of the fall. Regardless of their initial status – whether they "fell" from a respectable position or were already a member of the lower classes – prostitutes were dangerous women who disregarded properly chaste conduct by trading sex for money. According to Amanda Anderson in *Tainted Souls and Painted Faces: the Rhetoric of Fallenness in Victorian Culture*, the representation of the prostitute as "fallen" follows from Victorian conventional wisdom and scientific studies of prostitutes: "many British writers conceptualized prostitution itself as an extensive economic and social system, into which the fallen woman was entirely absorbed" (49). The narrative of the fall contained prostitutes in the passive, victim role, and attempted to discursively erase their threat to middle-class ideology. Importantly, unlike eighteenth-century narratives of repentant and redeemed prostitutes, once the nineteenth-century woman fell, she was down forever.

Nineteenth-century narratives of prostitution centered on discourses of disease and contamination, discourses that were used to link the burlesquer to the prostitute. The association of contagion and the female body was familiar to Victorian New Yorkers, as prostitutes were blamed for the spread of syphilis and other venereal diseases. For example, French hygienist Alexandre Parent-Duchatelet, whose views on prostitution were widely disseminated throughout England and the United States at mid-century, compared prostitutes to garbage and filth. Venereal disease was viewed as a public health crisis[23] and within the prevailing discourse "the vagina became the source from which the disease sprang"(Spongberg *Feminizing Venereal Disease* 34). Within anti-burlesque rhetoric, even displays of female sexuality might threaten to infect. A November 1868 *New York Times* editorial warned that "[burlesque performances] are immensely damaging to the public taste and terribly ruinous to the public morals" ("A Dangerous Habit" 6). Thus, burlesque was constructed as an infection contaminating the moral, social body.

New Yorkers took steps to protect their city from the contaminating influence of burlesquers. On May 22, 1869, George Wilkes, editor of the sporting and entertainment newspaper *The Spirit of the Times* promised to banish Lydia Thompson and her Blondes from New York City. He framed his promise within the rhetoric of contagion, contamination, and disease:

the Blondes and their form of burlesque were a "flaxen scrofula" imported from the "slums of London," that infected American citizens with something "worse than yellow fever" ("Barbe Bleu" 232). By casting the British Blondes as a contagion, critics linked burlesquers with prostitutes and suggested they would suffer the same dismal fate. Because the Blondes displayed their bodies on stage, they were already "fallen" women, and once fallen they inevitably slid into dissipation and despair. George Wilkes' readers would have been able to associate "flaxen scrofula" with syphilis-ridden prostitutes, and the "slums of London" with illicit and dangerous sexual activity.

Two doctors and moral reformers in particular distributed the narrative of the fall in order to contain transgressive female sexuality. Dr. William Acton in England and Dr. William Sanger in the United States both stressed the seduced and prostituted woman's swift descent into depravity and disease.[24] Acton was clear about women's natural relationship to sexual desire: "I should say that the majority of women (happily for them) are not very much troubled with sexual feeling of any kind. What men are habitually, women are exceptionally" (Acton *Functions* 112). Also, a prostitute "is a woman who gives for money that which she ought to give only for love; who ministers to passion and lust alone, to the exclusion and extinction of all the higher qualities" (*Prostitution* 166). Of course, Acton's assertions do not mean that all Victorians understood female sexuality within this framework; hegemonic control is notoriously difficult to assert. Thompson, for example, provides evidence of a counter-narrative. In their performances, the Blondes "jigged and wriggled" for the audience, welcoming their admiring gaze. More significantly, the romantic exploits of Lydia Thompson and fellow troupe members further suggested their participation in sexual activity outside the bonds of matrimony. George Butler's accusations of Henderson's sexual hold over Lydia Thompson as well as Henderson's own boasts of sexual conquests among the Blondes mark the limits of any dominant ideology.

William Sanger, the foremost US-American social statistician to study prostitutes, used the narrative of the fall to frame and inform his research as well. Sanger's 1862 *The History of Prostitution: Its Extent, Causes, and Effects Throughout the World* glosses prostitution in ancient Greece and Rome, among most European countries, within the Jewish community, and among the "barbarous nations." Sanger then focuses the remainder of his book (by far the largest section) on prostitution in contemporary New York City. He supports his claims with data taken from interviews and surveys of the inmates of various New York rescue missions and charity hospitals, and describes the typical prostitute:

Her step is elastic, her eye bright, she is the "observed of all observers." ... But this life of gay depravity can not last; her mind becomes tainted with the moral miasma in which she lives; her physical powers wane under the trials imposed upon them, and her career in a fashionable house of prostitution comes to an end; she must descend in the ladder of vice ... To-day she may associate with the wealthy of the land; to-morrow none will be too low for her company. To-day she has servants to do her bidding; to-morrow she may be buried in a pauper's coffin and a nameless grave. This is no fancy sketch, but an outline of the course of many women. (453)

Interestingly, Sanger has to recast the prostitute as fallen, imagining her as she is not. The visible prostitute is well-dressed, happy, and rich; Sanger's admonition depends on a future construction of her as diseased and dead. His narrative thus reveals his anxiety over the prostitute's seemingly high status. This same anxiety contributed to hysteria over the burlesque performer. On-stage, dressed in fancy clothes and blithely singing, dancing, and cracking jokes for the amusement of her audience, the burlesquer appeared happy and healthy. Critics needed to separate the burlesquer from her on-stage appearance in order to stress her difference from the true woman. Many commentators, such as Olive Logan, Richard Grant White, and William Dean Howells, imagined the burlesquer as monstrously depraved, fallen from moral grace, and susceptible to loneliness and even death after the audience's interest shifted to another form of amusement. Logan, herself an actress, warned other young women against taking to the stage: "I can advise no honorable, self-respecting woman to turn to the stage for support, with its demoralizing influences, which seem to be growing stronger day by day" (Logan "Leg" 40), lest they sink into a moral abyss from which family, friends, and society will be unable to rescue them. Like Sanger, Logan imagined the burlesquer as already fallen, despite her outward appearance.

Anti-burlesque hysteria co-opted familiar tropes of transgressive womanhood and merged them with Thompson and the British Blondes. Drawing on discourses of feminism, fashion, and prostitution, commentators nominated Lydia Thompson and the British Blondes as a contaminating influence on the Victorian feminine ideal. However, the Cult of True Womanhood was already fraught with internal contradictions as feminists and prostitutes struggled to insert their own experiences and narratives into the dominant domestic ideal. Thompson's narrative marks this struggle, as she battled in the press, on stage, and in the streets to participate in her own discursive representation.

The tensions the British Blondes brought to the US-American stage crystallize in the narrative of the infamous confrontation between Lydia Thompson and *Chicago Times* editor Wilbur Storey. In February 1870 the Blondes appeared for the second time at Crosby's Opera House in Chicago. This time, Storey made it his personal mission to drive Thompson and her troupe from the Chicago stage, penning acerbic editorials in his daily paper. Linking burlesque performance with prostitution, Storey urged all Chicago theatre managers to stop producing and booking burlesque shows and all Chicago citizens to boycott Thompson's shows in particular. Outraged, Thompson retaliated. Accompanied by Henderson, troupe member Pauline Markham, and publicist Archie Gordon, Thompson assaulted Storey in front of his Wabash Avenue home, striking him with a horsewhip. In traditional narratives of the cultural impact of burlesque, this incident defines the transgressive nature of burlesque performance and frames Thompson as an avenging virago who defended herself and her entertainment against charges of immorality. A close reading of this event, however, demonstrates that Thompson was virtually silenced within official discourse: the courts and the press reframed the event in terms of dominant domestic ideology, downplaying Thompson's role in the attack.

Three months earlier Lydia Thompson and the British Blondes had played Crosby's Opera House. As usual, they performed to the packed houses and approving crowds generated by their advance publicity. Both *The Chicago Tribune* and *The Chicago Times* ran similar advertisements for the Blondes' debut – one column wide and about three inches tall – in their theatre sections. The theatre critic for the *Tribune*, "Peregrine Pickle," informed his readers on November 21 that the Blondes would be in town the next day, and noted that their publicity machine had arrived before them (4). On November 28, the *Times* noted their success and had only mild criticism for their performance:

Miss Lydia Thompson and her company of blonds have met with very excellent success during the past week so far as the number of their auditors was concerned. The style of entertainment is already familiar enough and requires no other comment than the mention of the fact that this style seems to please a good many people and that it is very well done by the present company. (5)

Their first visit to Chicago passed uneventfully. After a sold-out three-week run, Thompson and the Blondes booked another visit before continuing on to St. Louis.

The Blondes began their second run in Chicago on February 19, 1870, again appearing at Crosby's Opera House where they performed *Sinbad* and *Ivano* from their New York run at Niblo's Garden. On February 18, the day the British Blondes rolled into town, *The Chicago Times* and editor Wilbur Storey began a series of editorials, first denouncing burlesque in general and then Thompson and her troupe. Like Wilkes and Butler in New York City, Storey was determined to drive all burlesque entertainment out of the city. "Good warning is given to all managers in this regard. Unless . . . they desire to obliterate all dramatic taste, and thus degrade their profession and ruin their business, they cannot put a stop to these vile performances any too soon" ("A Dramatic Prospect" 4). Two days later, Storey called for a boycott of Crosby's Theatre, which "should have been the foremost in the way of exalting dramatic and musical art" but instead must be "recognized only as a variety show and avoided accordingly." For Storey, female burlesque was the only "vile" variety entertainment: Aiken's Museum, which was currently running the "sensational" *Wolves at Bay,* was singled out as the best theatre in Chicago ("The Amusement Question" 4). Thus, burlesque was constructed as the lowest of lowbrow entertainments, and particularly dangerous for middle-class, moral audience members.

Pickle, though critic for the rival paper, joined the anti-Blonde chorus on February 20 in his weekly review, suggesting that burlesque itself was a reprehensible form of entertainment, and that the Blondes degraded it even further. He was especially repulsed by their substitution of physical display for theatrical talent.

In the first place, there is not one of the so-called blonds who can lay any claim to dramatic ability. They condition their success upon their personal charms alone, and of course, they are lavish in the display of those charms, and omit no advantage of posturing and dancing which shall set them off. . . . Gross animalism is the effect produced. (3)

Like other critics, Pickle responded negatively to the Blondes' spectacular bodies, arguing that their success depended on their willingness to dance and sing nearly naked. Pickle went on to characterize the audience at Crosby's as shameless, crude, vulgar, and particularly unfit as family entertainment: "no woman who would preserve her self-respect can go to these performances" (3). Again, burlesque was cast as a demoralizing influence.

On February 23, 1870 Storey upped the ante, linking burlesque with prostitution in his weekly editorial. This signed editorial charged that Thompson and her troupe "made an unnecessary and lewd exhibition of their persons, such as would not probably be tolerated by the police in any bawdy-house" and that their performances were no more than "mere vehicles for the exhibition of coarse women and the use of disreputable language" ("Blondes in a Nutshell" 4). The Chicago anti-burlesque hysteria echoed the themes present in New York eighteen months earlier. Burlesque was an aggressive assault on middle-class morality, the Blondes were no better than prostitutes, and the performance pandered to the lowest theatrical audience.

In Chicago, the actions of Thompson herself, rather than her manager, were at the center of controversy. After the initial press volleys, Thompson took matters into her own hands. No longer willing to rely on letters,[25] she retaliated physically against Storey. Though accounts of Thompson's confrontation with Storey are muddled and contradictory, some events are clear. On the evening of February 24, 1870, Thompson, Henderson, Gordon, and troupe member Pauline Markham assaulted Storey in front of his Wabash Avenue home as he and his wife were getting into a carriage. According to both contemporary and historical commentators, Thompson struck Storey with a whip as Henderson trained a pistol on him. The extent of Gordon and Markham's involvement is disputed; some eyewitnesses claimed Gordon had a pistol as well and Markham struck Storey, while others claimed that the two merely offered moral support. The police were notified, and all four were arrested, released on bail, and then tried for assault.

The attack, arrest, and trial were given major coverage in Chicago papers as commentators tried to contain Thompson within familiar narratives of passivity and incompetence. According to trial transcripts published in the *Chicago Tribune*, eyewitnesses, including Storey himself, changed their stories to implicate Henderson rather than Thompson. Both the *Tribune* and the *Times* criticized Thompson's behavior but laid the blame on Henderson's influence over her. Further, Thompson is missing from the press record. Neither paper published letters or interviews and she is never directly quoted in reports of any of the events. Rather than narrating Thompson as the powerful central figure, commentators placed her in the role of ineffectual, hysterical participant and passive spectator. The significance of Thompson's absence within the archival record cannot be overstated; she was denied participation in her own story.

The *Tribune* editorialized about the controversy as well as published news articles and trial transcripts; it seems clear they seized on the event as a strategy to boost publication and discredit a rival editor. On Saturday, February 26, an editorial entitled "The Vindication of Virtue" criticized both Thompson's and Storey's behavior: "The attempt by Miss Lydia Thompson to gain some éclat and vindicate her reputation by an assault on the editor of the *Chicago Times* lacks the elements which would enlist public sympathy either for the assailant or the assailed." According to the essay, Storey was a hypocrite: though he refused to carry advertisements for the Blondes' performance at the Opera House, the same issue of the paper "gave an elaborate and, we presume, gratuitous whole-page advertisement to the prostitutes of Chicago and their business." Thompson, on the other hand, was wrong to attack Storey as she did. Though the *Tribune*'s editor agreed that a woman might be respected for "assail[ing] a man in public and [using] a rawhide on his person" if she acted "bravely and instinctively," Thompson had attacked Storey with Henderson as pistol-toting back-up, outnumbering and outgunning Storey as well as endangering the lives of innocent passersby (6). Despite the *Tribune*'s outrage at the behavior of the participants, they continued to report on the event. The next two editions of the paper ran full transcripts of the arraignment hearings, under such inflammatory headlines as "The Mysterious Hack – Young Gordon as a Scout – The Signal – The Killed and Wounded." The *Tribune* continued to run advertisements for the Blondes as well, though the ads published after the attack were fully two inches taller than the previous advertisements and Thompson's name appeared in large type-face on the first line of the advertisement. Clearly, the Blondes were taking advantage of the extra publicity as well. Further, although the official news stories downplayed Thompson's role, the revamped advertisements reminded the public that she was a noteworthy figure.

   The Chicago Times covered the event mainly through editorializing, an obvious tactic for controlling the discourse around the event and limiting the spread of alternate versions. A sensationally titled article, "The Raid of the Prostitutes," attempted to "correct the misapprehensions with reference to the attack upon the editor of THE TIMES by a crowd of prostitutes and their attendants" (2). This article laid the blame squarely on Henderson's shoulders, suggesting that it was only his threat to shoot Storey that allowed Thompson access to him. Unwilling to let the story rest, the *Times* followed up with an article the next day, again repeating Storey's version of the events. The repetition of the same story suggests that despite the best efforts of the *Times*, counter-narratives were proliferating. The second article included a reminder of Storey and the *Times*' moral campaign against the insidious Blondes and suggested the Blondes might attack others in order to sell more tickets.

To properly appreciate the dastardly character of this attack, it should be stated that the criticisms of THE TIMES, which offended the blondes, were candid and legitimate, and at first rather lenient, in comparison to the glaring and disreputable character of their entertainment . . . It is possible . . . that this was another of the many disreputable methods this troupe has taken of advertising their degradation. ("A Cowardly Assault" 3)

The suggestion that Thompson instigated a violent feud in order to fill theatre seats illuminates the concern over her attempts to gain public attention. The Blondes' publicity machine was suspect in the eyes of the press, as the events in both New York and Chicago demonstrate. The *Times* did not publish trial transcripts, preferring to present their own version of events.

The transcripts published in the *Tribune* demonstrate the shifting accounts of the assault, and the attempts on the part of Storey and others to downplay Thompson's role. Several eyewitnesses reported that both Thompson and Markham struck Storey very hard many times with a "small cowhide," a "horsewhip" or a "bullwhip" ("The Blondes" 6). According to Horace G. Chase, a passerby who witnessed the attack, "[Storey] was cut on the ear and bleeding, and his face was flushed" ("The Blondes" 6). Many of these witnesses also characterized Storey as a sort of buffoon, who told the crowd he had "whipped" the blondes although he was bruised and bleeding. William Cahill reported that:

Miss Thompson then cut [Storey] across the face – just as he deserved. He stood there flourishing a stick for some time, saying he would clear out the whole lot, but it was not until the policeman came up and he got some arm of the law by his side, that he thought he would be very brave. But there was not very much bravery. He trembled like a sneak and a coward. ("The Blondes" 6)

Eyewitnesses also reported that Storey and Henderson traded insults. Chase testified that Henderson had called Storey "an old reprobate." Storey responded by calling Henderson a pimp and said "and that lady with you is a –!" ("The Blondes" 6). Eyewitnesses also claimed that Henderson only pulled a pistol in order to protect Markham and Thompson; Storey struck or attempted to strike them with his walking stick. Henderson, backed up by Archie Gordon, claimed he pulled the pistol in self-defense. Several eyewitnesses heard Mrs. Storey, who witnessed the attack but of course did not testify in court, asking her husband where his pistol was. According to Henderson and Gordon, Storey reached into his pocket and then Henderson pulled his own gun. Thompson did not testify, and the *Tribune* did not publish her version of events. Official channels were closed to Thompson, and she was unable to assert her narrative in court or in the press.

Though some eyewitnesses maintained that Thompson acted bravely to defend her honor against a weak but antagonistic aggressor, Storey and other eyewitnesses contradicted this narrative. The transcripts of Storey's testimony were published over two days. Storey laid the blame for his injuries on Henderson and the threat of the pistol. He claimed only Thompson and not Markham hit him, and only once, on the nose, not causing much injury or pain. He admitted to striking Henderson – "I guess you see the mark there now" – but denied striking or attempting to strike either of the women and denied calling Henderson a pimp ("The Blondes" 6). Most importantly, Storey dismissed Thompson as a real threat to his person: "She was slashing around. It was of no consequence, for I have no consciousness that she hit me beyond the first time. It may be that she hit me several times, but I did not feel the blows" ("Actresses at the Armory"3). In fact, he claimed not to notice Thompson and Markham much at all, testifying that he "was not conscious of more than one [woman] striking me. I did not look at them very closely. They appeared very much alike, and I probably should not have known one from the other" ("The Blondes" 6). This last claim is particularly fantastic. According to his own editorials, Storey had recently seen Thompson performing at Crosby's. In addition, at the time of the incident, Thompson was one of the most recognizable women in Chicago thanks to her publicity machine. Storey's assertion that he would not be able to distinguish Thompson from other women indicates Storey's desire to remove Thompson from the sequence of events and the rhetorical contortions he employed to do so.

Despite the press and the court's failure to recognize Thompson's full participation in the confrontation, she took credit for the assault. During her subsequent performances and in interviews later in her life, she claimed full responsibility for the act and for Storey's injuries, which she believed included his pride as well as his body. For example, the night after the initial attack, Thompson included references to the fiasco before an audience of 3,000, which, according to the *Tribune*'s report, "convulsed the house with laughter" ("Actresses at the Armory" 3). Her voice silenced in official discourse, Thompson resorted to the stage to assert her narrative. The *Tribune* reported that the February 25 performance included references to the attack, including impromptu nursery rhymes alluding to other editorial battles:

> Storey, Storey, old and hoary
> You had better mind your horses.
> In fighting Hess you'll get in a mess.
> Better stick to your divorces.

and

> Burnside suppressed *The Chicago Times*
> And covered himself with glory.
> But only mistake he ever made
> Was that he didn't hang old Storey.
>
> ("Actresses at the Armory" 3)

Thompson quipped that she felt "like a leaky ship" because she had "been bailed out" of jail ("Actresses at the Armory" 3). Thompson closed the performance by reading a prepared speech explaining her actions. She told the audience that she had been "forced" to attack Storey because "[t]he persistent and personally vindictive assaults on [her] reputation left [her] only one mode of redress." As she had learned in New York, the press refused to take her words seriously and viewed her body as mere spectacular entertainment. The attack was Thompson's attempt to use her body to further her own agenda. Further, Thompson claimed that she had a special duty to confront Storey. Her actions demonstrated that women were able to publicly challenge and face down their accusers, using language that recalls the rallying cries of feminist moral reformers attacking the male double standard: "[t]hey were women whom he attacked. It was by women that he was castigated." According to the *Tribune*, the crowd interrupted her speech several times, cheering wildly ("Actresses at the Armory" 3). At least some were interested in Thompson's representation of herself and her challenge to official discourse.

"Lydia and the Lash" provides a convenient narrative for examining and interrogating the way burlesque was understood, both during the nine-teenth century and now. In popular burlesque histories, such as Bernard Sobel's 1931 *Burleycue* and Irving Zeidman's 1967 *The American Burlesque Show*, "Lydia and the Lash" explains the relationship between burlesque performance and appropriate female behavior. In these narratives, the assault defeats attempts to contain the female burlesquer; instead, she takes control of her image and redeems burlesque performance from the petty moralists who attack both her character and her art form. Sobel, former public relations agent for the Ziegfeld Follies and a self-proclaimed burlesque historian, recounts the confrontation in typically lurid detail: "Miss Thompson drew a rawhide from under her jacket and struck Mr. Story (sic) in the face... The Blows were laid on thick and fast to the number of twenty" (*Burleycue* 18–19). The image of the petite blonde actress uncoiling a whip from underneath her cloak and beating back her larger male antagonist certainly speaks both to fantasies of female sexual dominance and feminist aspirations toward physical equality.

In scholarly histories as well, such as Banner's *American Beauty* (1985), and Allen's *Horrible Prettiness* (1991), the confrontation between Storey and Thompson signals a larger public debate about the contaminating influence of burlesque performance on appropriate middle-class femininity and sexuality. Banner suggests that Thompson was "as energetic and emancipated as she was erotic... In many ways she was the forerunner of both the new woman of the 1890s and the flapper of the 1910s and 1920s" (*American Beauty* 127). Narratives of the scandal thus suggest that the violent act of erotic, emancipated Lydia Thompson was responsible for some of the gains made by late nineteenth- and early twentieth-century feminists. Casting Thompson as an oppressed nineteenth-century woman defending her right to sexual expression, professionalism, and autonomy explicitly links burlesquers with more traditional exponents of women's rights.

This narrative, while compelling, elides the more interesting story of Thompson's attempts to create and disseminate a public persona in order to increase box office receipts and critical acclaim – that is, the story of Thompson's performance as a sexually attractive and aggressive stage beauty. Placing Thompson's feud with Storey in the context of the Blondes' publicity machine and her previous attempts to court controversy suggests that the assault on Storey and the resulting press coverage were as much a part of a campaign to increase Thompson's publicity as the genuine outrage of a "virtuous" woman. And, of course, this tactic worked. Thompson's place in the annals of burlesque history is secured by her scandalous horsewhipping of the hapless *Chicago Times* editor. Ultimately, despite Victorian attempts to contain Thompson's discursive agency, she is most often remembered as a powerful, central figure.

In the case of Lydia Thompson and the British Blondes, strenuous attempts were made to insert them into traditional feminine ideology, either as prostitutes or as feminists. The Blondes defy such easy categorization, however, and so offer an alternative to familiar narratives of female sexuality. As such, they threaten to expose a gap between the ideal woman and the realities of female sexuality. This threat stemmed not only from their stage appearance but also from Thompson's efforts to control her own representation. It is not coincidental that Thompson was embroiled in feuds with newspapermen. When George Wilkes and Wilbur Storey downplayed Lydia Thompson's involvement by shifting the focus to her "pimp" Alexander Henderson, they attempted to strip her of autonomy and agency over her career and public presentation by reviling her within official channels. However, Thompson strove to reinsert herself into these narratives, using letters, interviews, and performances to subvert hegemonic control. From a marginalized position, Thompson spoke directly to the most central debates of Victorian ideology. Nineteenth-century burlesque hysteria, overlapping tensions about theatre, fashion, feminism, and female sexuality, suggest that the threat personified by Lydia Thompson and the British Blondes continues to resonate through contemporary discussions of proper feminine behavior, both on and off stage.

CHAPTER 5

"We Need Status as Actresses!": contemporary prostitution and performance

I did acting in high school, and I've done some improv. That's what this is. You go in and pretend to be someone else. You kind of make the scene up as you go along, and I like to get really creative, telling the guy some wild stories and trying to get him to play along.

(Alex)

The opening scenes of the 1990 movie *Pretty Woman* depict a streetwalker's preparations for work. Vivian (Julia Roberts) dresses for the evening. She takes off her t-shirt and shimmies into a remarkable white and blue dress cut high on the thigh and open on the sides of her torso. She pulls on knee-high stiletto boots fastened together with safety pins and covers her own strawberry blond mane with a short platinum wig and leather motorcycle cap. She lines her hazel eyes with thick kohl, rouges her cheeks, and paints on a full, dark red mouth. The image she confronts in the mirror post-toilette is completely different from her previous wholesome appearance. Vivian makes her way down to the street corner and solicits Edward (Richard Gere). When he asks for her name, she answers jauntily, "It's whatever you want it to be." The movie establishes the performative nature of sex work from the outset, playing on the familiar notion that whores create fantasy characters for their clients who are very different from their real selves and who exists only when the client calls them into being.

This representation of sex work draws on the historical conflation of actresses and prostitutes elaborated in previous chapters. The contemporary prostitutes' rights movement and popular, mass media depictions of prostitution both actively reference this history. When activist and sex worker Carol Leigh, aka the Scarlot Harlot, reminds her fellow prostitutes that they "need status as actresses," she demands legitimacy for sex workers by recalling the historical elision between actresses and whores. When Hollywood movies such as *Pretty Woman* feature prostitutes dressing for a night out, they participate in the discursive construction of the prostitute as an actress. When Madison, Wisconsin, escorts refer to acting and

improvisation classes in high school as good preparation for their interactions with clients, they situate prostitution within theatrical frameworks.
In the contemporary moment, then, as in earlier periods, prostitution is
generally understood to correspond with acting. Importantly, theatrical
metaphors offer agency to sex workers. Performance is a strategy that allows
working prostitutes to take up the whore position and offer alternative
narratives of female sexuality and experience. "Status as actresses" offers sex
workers a position outside of conventional discourses of the prostitute as
victim or slut.

Prostitutes' rights activists are eager to claim parallels between sex work
and theatre because of the esteem and status awarded actresses in the
twenty-first century. Currently, actresses and actors are generally regarded
as superior craftspersons who provide entertainment, information, and
cultural uplift through their performances. Though actresses were frequently reviled throughout the seventeenth, eighteenth, and nineteenth
centuries, as previous chapters have detailed, by the beginning of the
twentieth century actors and actresses began to occupy a privileged position
in American mass culture. The turn toward realism cemented the legitimacy of theatre, as technical innovations and new acting styles replaced
outmoded models. Producer/directors such as Augustin Daly, Steele
Mackaye, and David Belasco astonished late nineteenth- and early
twentieth-century theatre audiences with technical advances that produced
remarkably realistic effects. Realistic acting styles developed to comple-
ment technical innovation. Early twentieth-century actor training developed realism; Stanislavski's teachings for the Moscow Art Theatre were
first publicized in the United States in the 1910s and 1920s and by the 1930s
the American Method, based on Stanislavski's principles, was the paradigmatic acting program. American audiences throughout the first half of the
twentieth century responded enthusiastically to realistic acting: Method
movie stars like Marlon Brando and James Dean were both popularly and
critically recognized as "serious" actors. Currently, most film and television
acting is a recognizable extension of Stanislavskian Method acting, and
American realism is most often taught in undergraduate and Master of
Fine Arts acting programs. Realism reconceived theatre as an exact mirror
to daily life, suggesting that drama was not merely an art form but also a
mode for studying real human interaction.

This paradigm shift accounts in part for the easy transfer between acting
and prostitution. Realistic acting, as opposed to earlier acting styles and
avant-garde techniques, offers a reasonable model for the kinds of performance that some sex workers enact. Because realistic acting is understood to

be based on life experience, it seems to be an acting style that even those without formal training may adopt. Many prostitutes try to convince their clients that they feel emotion and pleasure while working: according to research conducted by Janet Lever and Deanne Dolnick, call girls in particular present the "illusion of intimacy" with their clients by drawing on life experiences in order to feign emotion ("Clients and Call Girls" 86). Realism's paradigmatic status cements claims that prostitution is "like" acting as it is most commonly understood.

In the twentieth century, actors and actresses were not only regarded as artists, but also as valuable citizens. According to Stanislavski scholar Jean Benedetti, the Stanislavski System and its counterpart the American Method were "rooted in the conviction that the theatre is a moral instrument whose function is to...ennoble the mind and uplift the spirit." Realism was the "best method of achieving this end" (*Stanislavski* 11), as it was based on the direct observation of daily life. Franklin Roosevelt's Works Project Administration (WPA) included out-of-work actors who contributed to American morale-building during the Depression; governmental fascination with all things Hollywood has continued through the present moment, as television, stage and motion picture actors are frequent guests at the White House and share the podium with politicians, publicizing their pet causes. In Great Britain, of course, actors are held in equally high esteem. In 1895 Henry Irving became the first performer in English history to be knighted; Sean Connery, most famous for his role as British Secret Service agent James Bond, was knighted in 1999. The public acclaim for both the extraordinary talent and citizenship of actors helps explain why sex workers claim parity between their profession and theatre.

Twentieth-century actors are stars as well as talented craftspersons. As film, radio, and later television dominated mass media production in the twentieth century, the actors appearing in these media became familiar faces and voices to the American public. In *Stars*, media scholar Richard Dyer suggests that the lifestyle of stars "combines the spectacular with the everyday, the special with the ordinary, and is seen as an articulation of basic American/western values" (35). Within Dyer's framework, stars are regular people who have parlayed a particular talent into a luxurious lifestyle; they embody the American dream. Where once "actress" articulated "prostitute," it now means "star," another reason contemporary prostitutes enthusiastically identify with actresses. Not coincidentally, the myth of the small-town girl who finds glamour and wealth in Hollywood at the expense of her wholesome values is thematically similar to the myth of the small-town girl who finds glamour, wealth, and degradation through prostitution. Both narratives stress the upward mobility offered by a pretty face, attractive figure, and ability to convincingly impersonate someone other than oneself. By exploiting similarities between actresses and prostitutes, contemporary sex workers borrow some of the glamour and status offered stars.

In this chapter, I explore the implications of thinking of prostitution as performance. Much of the evidence for my claims in this chapter comes from interviews conducted with Madison, Wisconsin, escorts and their managers. Between September and November 1996, I interviewed about a dozen area sex workers.[1] I contacted several agencies listed in the local paper, and conducted interviews over the phone, in agency offices, at a local mall, at bars and restaurants, and in sex workers' homes. My sample is admittedly small; there are only a handful of agencies in Madison, and many girls[2] refused to be interviewed. I spoke to most interview subjects only once, but I did develop a lengthy relationship with some of the employees of one escort service, Exploits, Unlimited. Kevin, Exploits' manager, acted as a sort of informant. I had several conversations with Kevin as well as with his employees. He encouraged his employees to talk with me and included me in staff meetings. I gained an in-depth knowledge of this particular agency because of my varied interactions with Kevin and his employees: our exchanges included both formal interviews and more casual conversations. Most of the girls I talked to were students at the University of Wisconsin-Madison and worried about anonymity and privacy; the managers, on the other hand, worried about possible legal repercussions. In order to help all interview subjects feel safe, I took very few notes during the interviews and tape-recorded nothing. I wrote up the interviews from memory immediately after talking to the escorts and agency owners. Necessarily then, the conversations contained within this chapter are reconstructed, though I have attempted to retain individual girls' vernacular.[3]

My research in previous chapters only involved historical subjects and my ethical responsibility to the archival and secondary sources I deployed were limited to scholarly considerations of context and citation. However, my limited ethnography raises more pressing ethical questions. Human subject research is a fraught topic in the contemporary academy; those debates inform my approach to the ethnographic data. Though all the girls and managers were aware of my position as a Ph.D. candidate at the University of Wisconsin-Madison and knew that our conversations might become part of this project, many interactions were deeply personal. Therefore, I feel a strong responsibility to accurately record their impressions and experiences[4] while examining my own motives and methods.

Michel Foucault's notion of confession is a useful model for considering my interpretation and use of these narratives. Foucault suggests that the Western, Christian framework of confession, where "[t]he truth did not reside solely in the subject who, by confessing, would reveal it wholly formed" but also in "the one who assimilated and recorded it" (*History I* 66) informs all exchanges between interview subject and ethnographer. In my case,[5] I understand my interactions with Madison sex workers as a performance as well, where I played the role of hip, scholarly feminist researcher, and entered equally into a theatricalized space where normalcy and transgression postured for central position.

The contemporary prostitutes' rights movement draws parallels between acting and prostitution in order to further a political agenda. Madison escorts, on the other hand, are not activists. Their narratives thus illuminate how performance can be a strategy used to speak from the whore position. Importantly, like the historical women I discuss, Madison escorts are not consciously trying to reshape definitions of female sexuality, but rather make sense of their own experience. Their stories demonstrate how some sex workers can use acting theory on a more personal, emotional level. Though in many ways the Madison sample parallels the experience of urban professionals, important differences remain. What was most significant about the ways these sex workers talked about their lives is that they almost never identified themselves as prostitutes. They were "escorts" or "strippers," not whores. They went on "dates" or "kept appointments" rather than solicited prostitution. They saw "clients" or "guys," not tricks or johns. On one hand, their refusal of the prostitution label necessitated rhetorical contortions. On the other, it is an accurate reflection of how they viewed their work. In this way, they denied a discourse which labels prostitutes as deviant "bad girls," a discourse which does not adequately explain their experience. In addition, they viewed their prostitution as part-time, short-term employment. They were making extra money, not embarking on a career in the sex industry nor living the kinds of lives represented in the mass media as constitutive of prostitution. This refusal to name their work prostitution is a linguistic distancing technique, which I read as a further performance: they performed normalcy and banality in the interviews, a strategy that separated their experiences from prostitution qua prostitution.

Like West, Boutell, Charke, Leeson, and Thompson, contemporary prostitutes struggle to separate themselves from negative and oppressive ideologies of female sexuality. By claiming parallels with acting, contemporary sex workers attempt to influence their discursive representations, and detach the prostitute from her construction as pathetic victim or predatory nymphomaniac. In this chapter, I explain how contemporary sex workers understand prostitution as performance. First, I describe contemporary representations of prostitution, available in mass media depictions and in feminist discourse. I argue that the Madison escorts use these representations in order to structure their own narratives: they sometimes dress, talk, and behave in ways parallel to mainstream depictions of prostitution. In particular, the availability of performance metaphors in both mass media and feminist portrayals of prostitution has enabled the Madison, Wisconsin, escorts to use those metaphors themselves. Next, I turn to a discussion of how and why the Madison sample uses acting techniques in order to negotiate agency. When whoring becomes an act, sex workers are able to understand and reconcile traditional concepts of femininity and sexuality with their experience as working prostitutes. They can inhabit the whore position and speak from within it, reinscribing familiar narratives with their own experience.

WHORES IN DISCOURSE: CONTEMPORARY REPRESENTATIONS
OF PROSTITUTION

The Madison sex workers' unwillingness to identify themselves as prostitutes may be based in part on the difference – both real and perceived – between their lives and experiences and existing discourses about prostitution. Indeed, Madison sex workers do not fit neatly into traditional understandings of prostitution. In the past decade a number of anthologies collecting sex workers' writings and experiences have been published. Though these anthologies by no means construct an essential prostitute, and in fact are often committed to recognizing difference among sex workers, some commonalties exist between most published accounts of sex workers' experience.[6] In short, most of the narratives in most anthologies are from the perspective of urban, professional, older, experienced, outspoken prostitutes. The differences between their views on whoring, and the views of the girls I interviewed, provide a unique perspective on the negotiation of sex work, personal sexuality, performance, and self-identity, one not found in most other published accounts.

Not only were the Madison workers different from professional, activist prostitutes, but also from mass media representations of prostitutes. In the documentary *The Celluloid Closet*, Richard Dyer suggests that film tells men and women who they are and how they can behave. Though he is speaking specifically about gays and lesbians, his claims about how the media cements identity are valid for sex workers as well. Prostitutes are familiar figures in

Hollywood cinema and on television; contemporary sex workers both model and contrast their behavior with these representations. As the popular fiction and theatre of the seventeenth, eighteenth, and nineteenth centuries represented cultural debates about female sexuality, so does film in the early twenty-first century. Therefore, examining media representations of prostitution provides insight into how contemporary sex workers situate their own experience vis-à-vis dominant discourses of prostitution.

When sex workers perform prostitution, they are citing behaviors that allow them to be read as women and prostitutes. They construct their identity as sex workers from a variety of cultural sources, including the mass media. Annette Kuhn points out that

one of the major theoretical contributions of the women's movement has been its insistence on the significance of cultural factors, in particular in the form of socially dominant representations of women and the ideological category "women" and in delimiting and defining what has been called the "sex/gender system." (*Women's Pictures* 4)

Careful attention to media representations of women offers a critique of the construction of normative femininity. In addition, the mass media provide models for how women should act within a patriarchal, capitalist society. In the specific example of prostitution, the mass media offer several primers on how to be – and be read as – a prostitute.

Historically, media depictions of prostitutes follow stereotypic patterns, as demonstrated in previous chapters. These representations have sedimented in two competing but often overlapping constructions of the prostitute: the pathetic victim of male lust and financial deprivation, plying her trade under the control of a brutal pimp in dangerous conditions; or the sexual deviant, corrupting and contaminating middle-class morality and the body of the client along with her own. In the modern version of the latter construction, as Priscilla Alexander points out, the prostitute is assumed to be a sexually abused, drug-addicted runaway, infecting her middle-class clients with AIDS and other sexually transmitted diseases through her indiscriminate sexual contact and drug use ("Feminism" 186, 211–18). Certainly, this image of the prostitute is typified and strengthened through representative made-for-television and theatrical movies about prostitution such as the paradigmatic *Dawn: Portrait of a Teenage Runaway* (1976) through *Kiss of the Dragon* (2001). In these films and others like them, the prostitute dies by murder, disease, or drug overdose. Other films focus on the prostitute's rescue by a loving client or sympathetic acquaintance: the Oscar-winning *Klute* (1971) is the paradigm here.

In films such as *L.A. Confidential* (1997) and *From Hell* (2001), for example, prostitute characters are reformed and rescued by strong men who are, not coincidentally, police officers. In these narratives, the prostitutes are generous and open-hearted, and often naïve or at least uninformed about other options available to them.

On television, prostitutes are often used to denote gritty urban realism, providing colorful background in most police shows; *NYPD Blue* often includes prostitutes being led through central booking or waiting to make bail. Soap operas and sitcoms also use prostitutes to add excitement. For example, from 1998 to 2000, Patty D'Arbanville played Selena, *Guiding Light*'s resident ex-hooker. Frequently, she remembered encounters with clients, other prostitutes, and mob figures shot in hazy soft focus to a pulsing "Latin" soundtrack. Ultimately, Selena left town in order to protect her family and friends from both the Mob and the shame of her past. Prostitutes are also used humorously. An episode of NBC's Emmy-nominated *Just Shoot Me*, broadcast during the May 1999 sweeps period when rates are set for advertisers, recycled a familiar plot: successful photographer Elliot, depressed over his failed romance with magazine writer Maya, was set up with a seemingly perfect woman. Of course, she was actually an expensive escort whose services were purchased by Elliot's well-meaning co-workers; typical sit-com hilarity ensued. Network television produces a variety of prostitution discourses, most of which conform to traditional victim or "hooker with a heart of gold" narratives.

Prostitution is also a favored topic for both network and cable news programming, which frequently run documentary programs about the lives of prostitutes and their clients. Though the HBO 2000 documentary *America Undercover: Hookers and Johns* is the extreme to which these programs can be compared, its tropes are similar to other sex work documentaries. In *Hookers and Johns*, viewers see numerous women topless and even naked, view several instances of intercourse, and, in a scene that could be barely referenced in most network television programs, watch three men perform cunnilingus at a "gentlemen's club." These scenes are certainly titillating, but they also mark the sex workers as degraded and vulnerable, a position underscored by the documentary's featured subjects and narrative arc. The majority of the prostitutes featured are young, African-American streetwalkers, often heavily tattooed and pierced and dressed in tawdry, revealing clothing. They talk freely about oral sex, venereal disease, their own drug use, and their clients' sexual tastes. These confessions are supplemented by scenes of streetwalkers soliciting clients and engaging in various sexual activities, primarily fellatio and intercourse from behind, in cars and deserted alleyways. The camera also catches them between clients, where the women sigh, slump against telephone poles and bus stops, painfully adjust their clothing, and hobble down the street crippled by their stiletto heels. Though the explicitness of *Hookers and Johns* sets it apart from similar programming on network TV, like those programs it insists on the conventional discourse of victimization.[7] As these representative film and television programs indicate, prostitutes are pathetic, drug-addicted cripples; victims who are either rescued by the love of a good man or conveniently die in the final reel; or unimportant, unnamed extras who provide visual spectacle but never intrude on the main plot. These tropes influence the discursive construction of the prostitute, and condition popular understanding of the sex industry.

These mass media depictions influence working prostitutes as well. As the narratives of the Madison sample demonstrate, prostitutes are ordinary women who can be assumed to partake in popular culture as frequently and avidly as their non-prostitute friends and neighbors. The frequency with which many sex workers cite theatrical metaphors, for example, suggests that prostitutes are aware of their circulation in the mass media. In addition, some Madison call girls and managers seem to specifically model themselves on representative sex workers. For example, I asked Kevin, Exploits' owner, if he had ever read *Mayflower Madam*, as some of his business tactics seemed to be lifted from Barrows' memoirs. Though he had never read the book, he admitted he had rented the television movie before opening Exploits in order to "pick up some pointers." He seemed pleased that I'd recognized his savvy use of the media, and his reliance on entertainment media for information demonstrates the power popular culture exerts on everyday behavior and actions.

Few sex workers reference popular culture as explicitly as Kevin, though it is generally accepted by media scholars that the media influence behavior and identity.[8] For the Madison sex workers, media representations of prostitution seemed to support their belief that their experiences differed from traditional understandings of prostitution. None of the Madison escorts were drug-addicted streetwalkers, none of them had been arrested, none of them were desperate and diseased: the victim scenarios presented in television and movies did not mesh with their biographies. On the other hand, the fairy tale scenario, presented in *Pretty Woman* and other stories where prostitutes are rescued from degradation by the love of a wealthy client, seemed equally foreign. Though many enjoyed close relationships with particular clients, none had any illusions about those relationships nor any desire to leave prostitution for a more traditional relationship with those clients. At the same time, the clothing, personae, and attitudes adopted by the Madison sex workers seemed to reference popular culture depictions of the prostitute. The girls were friendly, sexy, and dressed provocatively, just like whores on television and in the movies. Thus, sex workers identify both with and against mass media representations of prostitution.

Though most media depictions of prostitution rely on either rescue or punishment narratives, some filmmakers have offered portraits of prostitution that take into account feminist debates about agency, performance, and choice. In the 1980s and 1990s, when the prostitutes' rights movement in the United States began to garner feminist and scholarly attention, two films, *Pretty Woman* and *Working Girls*, provided two different portraits of prostitution. *Pretty Woman* follows a fairy tale structure and ends with the prostitute heroine's rescue by her handsome, rich client; starring Richard Gere and Julia Roberts (who was nominated for an Academy Award in the role), directed by Garry Marshall, and released by Disney's Touchstone division, it was 1990's highest grossing motion picture. *Working Girls* employs a cinema verité style and depicts one day in a New York City brothel. Written and directed by feminist filmmaker Lizzie Borden and released in 1986 by Miramax Films, it enjoyed modest critical acclaim and attracted an art house audience. Though the two films differ in style, audience, and politics, they both engage debates about the agency of the prostitute. Interestingly, *Pretty Woman*, the more mainstream of the films, suggests more strongly that prostitution offers financial and sexual freedom, despite its Cinderella ending. *Working Girls*, its materialist feminist pedigree notwithstanding, asserts that the autonomy offered by prostitution is illusory. The two films ultimately provide partially traditional representations of prostitution, demonstrating that although debates about prostitution were registered by both Hollywood and independent cinema in the 1980s and 1990s, the victim scenario remained the guiding principle.

Pretty Woman seems to follow a traditional narrative of prostitution. Vivian Ward, the stereotypic hooker with a heart of gold, and Edward Lewis, the wealthy and emotionally frozen client who buys her service as a "beck and call girl" for a week, fall in love and ride off into the sunset. Along the way, Vivian acquires the attitude, manners, and wardrobe of an upper-middle-class socialite and Edward recovers his ability to love and be loved. The sex work in *Pretty Woman* is as much a fairy tale as the love story: one critic commented that Vivian is a nice girl "unsullied by the mechanics of prostitution" (Doherty *Pretty Woman* 40). Ultimately, *Pretty*

Woman, in the film's own vernacular, is a "Cinder-fuckin'-ella" story of mutual rescue and redemption.

When *Pretty Woman* was released, feminist critics scrambled to account for its phenomenal box office success in light of its retrograde sexual politics. Many explained its pull by referencing the romance's fairy tale structure. Recycling Cinderella, *Pretty Woman* updated the most enduring fairy tale in Western culture and tapped into a powerful cultural myth of gender relations. For example, Karol Kelley argued that *Pretty Woman* "uses current fashions and artifacts and ignores the older sexual taboos" to give the film a modern and progressive appearance, though it "does not illustrate any major changes in gender expectations and is unaffected by any form of feminist ideology" ("Modern Cinderella" 88). Other critics argued that *Pretty Woman* glorified patriarchal capitalism. From the opening line "No matter what they say, it's all about money" to the silver limousine conveying Edward on his rescue mission as well as the second-act Rodeo Drive power-shopping sequence, the film represents economic privilege as the key to happiness. The visual pleasure offered by luxurious surroundings, physically attractive stars, and designer clothing coupled with the romance narrative seem to explain the film's success. However, regardless of the specific mode of analysis, feminist critics agreed that "in one fell swoop, *Pretty Woman* did away with every advance for women's rights made in the last ten years" (Cooks, Orbe, Bruess "Fairy Tale Theme" 86).

Though most feminist critics decried the conservative portrayal of gender relations offered by the text, they tended to focus on its fairy tale and consumer narratives, eliding its representation of prostitution.[9] However, another reading of the film is available, one that insists that *Pretty Woman*'s representation of prostitution complicates feminist critiques of the text. Though in many ways Vivian is a stereotypic Hollywood hooker and the film aggressively reinscribes normative heterosexuality, the film confounds easy explanation. Edward rescues Vivian from the dangers of street walking, but the text displays an ambivalence about the benefits of that rescue. Vivian has a strong and mutually protective relationship with her roommate and fellow prostitute, Kit deLuca (Laura San Giacomo) that suggests her life before Edward was not entirely without pleasure. In addition, Vivian has to modify her behavior in order to please Edward: he constantly orders her to stop fidgeting; demands that she spit out her gum; disapproves of her "street" language and behavior; and generally quells her exuberance. A resistant reader might assume that Vivian's sacrifice of her freedoms is not worth the traditional marriage that closes the narrative.

Most importantly, Vivian's transformation from whore to lady decreases her ability to control sexually difficult situations. When Vivian and Edward attend a polo match, Edward tells his lawyer, Philip Stuckey (Jason Alexander), that Vivian is a prostitute. Stuckey propositions Vivian and suggests he could introduce her to other rich clients. After the polo match, Vivian is furious with Edward. She asks why he made her get dressed up – she is wearing a demure sundress complete with hat and gloves – if he was going to tell everyone she was a hooker. Vivian further explains that "in my own clothes, when some guy like Stuckey comes up to me, I can handle it. I'm prepared." As a prostitute, Vivian can determine her inter-actions with men. As (Edward's) lady, she is more readily victimized. The film thus suggests the power a prostitute might wield in sexual transactions, a power denied to more traditionally defined women.

Kit deLuca dodges incorporation and is a source of narrative tension. Kit is sharply contrasted with Vivian: she prostitutes herself in order to feed her cocaine habit and seems more emotionally connected to the pimps, drug dealers, and other streetwalkers than Vivian is. Though in many ways the text suggests that Kit is a traditional prostitute victim, Kit is more assertive and independent than Vivian. For example, Kit repeats the mantra "we say who, we say what, we say how much" at crucial points in the narrative, reminding Vivian and the audience that their bodies are their own to control. When Kit goes to the Beverly Wilshire Hotel where Vivian is staying with Edward, she remains unimpressed with its luxury and refuses to modify her behavior. Kit revels in her ability to shock. Waiting for Vivian at the front desk, she notices an elderly couple staring at her in horror. Kit leans over and breathes wetly on the desk. Turning to the couple, she announces "Fifty bucks, grandpa. For seventy-five, the wife can watch." Kit thus suggests that the middle-class morality that condemns prostitution is hypocritical and outmoded. Further, Kit demonstrates the transgressive sexual potential of prostitution; the text's deployment of her character foils the fairy tale narrative's insistence on monogamy, morality, and marriage.

Lizzie Borden's *Working Girls* takes a much less glamorous view of prostitution than *Pretty Woman*. The narrative follows Molly (Louise Smith) during her last day working for greedy brothel madam Lucy (Ellen McElduff). The text relies on Marx rather than myth for its narrative structure: Borden's film is a treatise on capitalist oppression of the laboring class that ends with Molly lecturing Lucy on surplus value. *Working Girls* depicts a typical day in the sex industry and includes all of Molly's client transactions and several conversations between Molly and the other employees. The rates, house rules for behavior, and contraceptive methods are all explained in detail. The apartment brothel, where the majority of the narrative takes place, is peopled with a variety of women. Molly seems to be the requisite non-stereotypical whore; she was educated at Yale and holds degrees in philosophy and English literature. The other workers are all particular prostitute types: Gina is a smart, professional call girl who has worked for several years and may one day open a business of her own; April is a drug user and part-time dealer who is aging ungracefully; Dawn is a tough and trashy college student who started out in street prostitution; Debbie is a striking African-American whose race limits her client base; and Mary is a single mother driven to prostitution by economic need. The clients also represent a variety of men: Bob is a shy accountant with a taste for Kama Sutra poses; Joseph is an elderly gentleman with a penchant for light domination; Dan likes to role-play elaborate scenarios; John wishes Molly was his girlfriend. By presenting a range of sex workers and clients, *Working Girls* suggests that prostitution straddles several economic, emotional, and intellectual worlds, an assumption in line with the contemporary prostitutes' rights movement.

Molly is a popular prostitute, and the film suggests her success is based partly on her ability to play different roles with different clients. Most notably, Molly's "real" sexual identity is lesbian. The film opens on Molly and her partner, an African-American with a pre-teen daughter, waking up and going to work in the morning. At work, however, Molly plays straight. Though Gina knows that she is a lesbian, the other employees do not. In fact, Mary refuses to enact lesbian sex with Molly at a client's request. Molly assures Mary that it will be easy, and that they will both receive a $100 tip. Mary still demurs, telling Molly that she's always been afraid of lesbians. Molly laughs, and tells her not to worry. "I don't look like a lesbian, do I?" "No," Mary giggles, and the two have sex with each other and the client.

Molly also performs other specific identities with clients. For example, Dan insists on elaborate fantasy scenarios. He explains to Molly that she is a blind virgin whose sight will be restored by sexual intercourse with him in his role as her doctor. Molly complies, and Dan reaches orgasm as she sees for the first time. Dan is so pleased with her performance that he tips her and makes another appointment for the following week. Bob and Joseph also want Molly to perform. As a prelude to intercourse, Bob and Molly assume several erotic poses in front of the mirror. With Joseph, Molly ties him to the bed and berates him as a bad boy who wants to fuck his mother. These examples demonstrate the technical demands placed on prostitutes by clients looking for a fantasy experience.

In addition to these interactions, *Working Girls* acknowledges performance in other ways. Molly arrives for work in loose black pants and a
sweater. Once in the apartment she changes into a short blue dress,
pantyhose, and high heels. She applies make-up and styles her hair. In
between appointments, Molly is relaxed, bored, and detached. She eats
lunch, visits the drugstore for extra condoms, and participates in complaints about Lucy's mercenary business tactics and ridiculous love life.
When a client comes into the apartment, however, her demeanor changes.
She smiles and feigns interest in the client's work, asking questions that
demonstrate her intelligence and friendliness. At several points in the film
she displays her frustration with a particular client or Lucy, and then
immediately regains her cheerfulness when again interacting with them.
These shifts between modes of behavior foreground the theatricality of sex
work and insist on prostitution as a performance.

Borden's text is explicitly feminist and the film is careful to break down
stereotypes of victimized, nymphomaniac prostitutes. The title itself references an understanding of prostitution as labor and the discussions
between employees about work conditions, the whore stigma, and the
fantastic demands of clients all point to the agenda of the contemporary
prostitutes' rights movement. However, despite this progressive portrayal,
Working Girls does reinscribe some traditional notions of prostitution.
Though the girls are choosing sex work, the film suggests that capitalistic
patriarchy is to blame for the continued existence of the sex industry. In
many ways, *Working Girls* repeats and enlarges on earlier texts, such as
Mrs. Warren's Profession, that argue for a Marxist interpretation of sex work.
Like Kitty Warren, the girls are oppressed by economics rather than male
lust or their own psychological demons. Further, the film does not address the
sexual freedom potentially available from sex work nor the transgressive
sexuality represented by the prostitute. Despite its insistence that the
girls are not easily reduced to familiar stereotypes, *Working Girls* does not
acknowledge the pro-sex feminist position on prostitution and ultimately
presents Molly as oppressed and desiring escape. In this way, *Working Girls* is
at least as traditional as the more mainstream *Pretty Woman*.

The mass media offers a variety of representations of the prostitute,
many of which specifically reference performance as an enduring trope.
These films and television programs depict a variety of sex workers –
streetwalkers, call girls, drug addicts, educated feminists – and tend to
rely on familiar narratives of victimization. Though most popular representations of prostitution reinscribe stereotypes, even mainstream films
may acknowledge the liberatory possibilities inherent in sex work. Ultimately,

the discursive construction of the prostitute as actress is supported by popular culture representations of the sex industry. The circulation of theatrical metaphors in films such as *Pretty Woman* and *Working Girls* concretize understandings of prostitution as performance. In this way, even the most conventional texts may participate in the politics of the prostitutes' rights movement, affirming the opportunity for agency available in sex work within otherwise conservative narratives.

Feminism also offers contradictory representations of prostitution. Historically, feminist inquiries into the nature and causes of prostitution – not to mention its eradication – have ignored the voices and lived experiences of prostitutes. Priscilla Alexander, co-editor of the immensely influential *Sex Work* (first published in 1987 and re-edited and re-published in 1998), accused "some self-described feminists [of silencing] sex workers who did not agree to portray themselves as victims" (Alexander "Feminism" 17). Sex workers have addressed this silence by publishing books, essays, and news-paper and magazine articles that present their perspective. *Sex Work*, Wendy Chapkis' *Live Sex Acts: Women Performing Erotic Labor*, Shannon Bell's *Whore Carnival*, the Jill Nagle-edited *Whores and Other Feminists*, and Carol Queen's *Real Live Nude Girl* have provided a public forum for prostitutes to tell their own stories. The popular press has also included many prostitutes' stories – nearly every major women's magazine has run a feature article on prostitution in the last year – although often for titillation as much as education and political outreach.

Many prostitutes use these publications to vent frustration with feminist movements. As working prostitute and NOW member Teri Goodson discovered, her "efforts to build bridges" within that feminist coalition were not as successful as she had hoped. In her experience, NOW was primarily concerned with eradicating prostitution, "'rescuing' the women whom they often reduce to being nothing but helpless toys for men" ("Prostitute Joins NOW" 249). Many feminist organizations replicate the whore stigma, reducing prostitutes to victims in need of rescue from both demanding pimps and clients, and the false consciousness that lets them believe they have control over their sexual encounters. Even, and perhaps especially, within the feminist movement, prostitutes still strive to define themselves outside of a stereotypical victim position.

The stereotyping and silencing of prostitutes by feminists is rooted in the foundations of the US women's movement. Early encounters between prostitutes and feminists typically unfolded as feminist projects to remove prostitutes from their homes and workplaces.[10] Evangelizing methods included offering Bibles and other religious tracts to streetwalkers and entering brothels early on Sunday mornings to pray and sing hymns (Hill *Sisters' Keepers* 18–20). New York City female moral reformers conducted dozens of purity campaigns directed at both ridding the streets of prostitutes and denouncing the men who patronized them. For example, the 1835 New York Moral Reform Society's resolution demanded that "the condemnation of the guilty of our sex remain entire; but let not *the most guilty of the two* – the deliberate destroyer of female innocence – be afforded even an 'apron of fig leaves,' to conceal the blackness of his crimes" (in Hill *Sisters' Keepers* 66). By condemning both the prostitutes who plied their trade on the city streets and in the brothel houses *and* the men who supported and even encouraged prostitution, these reform movements attempted to shift focus from the prostitute toward her client: however, their agendas clearly marked the prostitute as a powerless victim.

In the United States during the Progressive era, prostitution again assumed centrality, and reform movements again focused on removing the prostitute from a position of influence. For example, Jane Addams argued that women had maintained their "superior chastity" because they were safe within the domestic confines of the middle-class home, and worried that under new urban pressures "the old restraints may give way" (in Connelly *Response to Prostitution* 36). Thus, feminist progressives stigmatized prostitutes as victims and contaminants. Throughout the nineteenth and early twentieth centuries, reform movements were populated primarily by upper-middle class women intent on bringing bourgeois, Christian morality to the working classes, often ignoring the desires, sentiments, and material constraints of the prostitutes they were attempting to rescue.

Contemporary feminist debates on prostitution often reinscribe nineteenth- and early twentieth-century views of the prostitute. Radical or cultural feminism (associated with anti-pornography feminists such as Andrea Dworkin, Catharine MacKinnon, and Kathleen Barry) focuses on the prevalence of violence against women and the association between prostitution, pornography, and violence. From this foundation, radical feminism draws the conclusion that pornography and prostitution must be completely abolished. Within a radical feminist system, there is no space for female sexual agency nor female heterosexual desire for everyday women or especially prostitutes. Within this system, where "rape is . . . the defining paradigm of sexuality" (Dworkin *Pornography* 62), women are only victims, an assumption firmly in line with the agendas of most early reform movements.

Some prostitutes and pornographic actresses support and enlarge on radical feminist critiques. For example, Linda Marchiano, who appeared under the name Linda Lovelace in *Deep Throat* and other 1970s pornographic movies, described the psychological and physical torture she suffered during filming in *Ordeal* (1980) and *Out of Bondage* (1986). In lectures and essays, Catherine MacKinnon repeatedly cites Marchiano's example, arguing that women are unwilling to face the truth about pornography and prostitution because they know similar torture "could happen to them at any time, and nothing would be done about it" (*Feminism Unmodified* 11–12). MacKinnon uses Marchiano's specific experience to further the agenda of radical feminists. Marchiano's voice is heard, albeit in ways that support existing notions of prostitution and oppression.

The organization Women Hurt in Systems of Prostitution Engaged in Revolt (WHISPER), founded by a group of former prostitutes opposed to the contemporary prostitutes' rights movement, outlines a radical feminist critique of prostitution and pornography.

We, the women of WHISPER, reject the lie that women freely choose prostitution from a whole array of economic alternatives that exist under civil equity . . . We reject the lie that turning tricks is sexual pleasure or agency for women. We reject the lie that women can and do become wealthy in systems of prostitution. We reject the lie that women control and are empowered in systems of prostitution. We reject the false divisions imposed by society which differentiate between pornography, peep shows, live sex shows, and prostitution as it is commonly defined. . . . We reject the false hierarchy imposed on women by men which claims that "call girls" are inherently better off than "street walkers" . . . . We oppose current and proposed legislation . . . which treat the institution of prostitution as an "urban blight" or eyesore that needs to be hidden from view yet kept available to men. . . . We want the state to stop arresting prostitutes and to start enforcing laws against men who traffic in women's bodies for profit and pleasure. (Wynter "WHISPER" 269–70)

WHISPER, like nineteenth-century reform movements, focuses on the sexual double standard that oppresses women. WHISPER, Marchiano, and other former sex workers participate in the construction of the prostitute as victim. Though they construct and influence narratives of prostitution, they represent themselves as having little agency when working within the sex industry.

Many pro-sex or sex radical feminists take a combative position against radical anti-pornography feminists. Arguing that radical feminists reinscribe the whore stigma by casting prostitutes as victims, pro-sex feminists insist on the agency offered by sex work. For these feminists, prostitution is a viable career choice, offering financial rewards and sexual expression. Wendy Chapkis, in *Live Sex Acts*, argues that pro-sex feminism suggests that pornography and prostitution (as well as other non-traditional sexualities) provide potentially liberatory outlets for sexual expression and experimentation. Sex radical feminists such as Pat Califa, Susie Bright, Carol Queen, and Camille Paglia, assert that pornography and prostitution cannot, and in fact should not, be eradicated, given their ubiquity in Western society and their ability to provide economic independence for women and sexual expression for all. Pro-sex feminism further asserts that sexual relations exist on a "terrain of struggle" (Chapkis *Live* 26) that reflects not only patriarchal and oppressive power relations between men and women, but also the opportunity to subvert and co-opt those power relations.[11] Margo St. James, founder of Call Off Your Old Tired Ethics (COYOTE), one of the first prostitutes' rights organizations, insists that "[t]he whore has power. She is in charge, setting the terms for the sexual exchange and the financial exchange" ("The Reclamation of Whores" 82). Therefore, although the prostitute may be seen as the most oppressed female within a structure that systematically oppresses all women, she may also be seen as a sexual subject, subverting and challenging male sexual and economic dominance.

Pro-sex feminists validate their position by including sex worker's narratives. *Sex Work* contains the largest collection of prostitutes' writings, and covers a broad demographic range, including streetwalkers, massage parlor workers, call girls, and pornographic actresses and models. Though many of these women affirm that sex work is a liberatory experience, most are aware that the industry can both negatively and positively affect a woman's self-esteem and sexual identity. Sunny Carter, who worked as a prostitute in order to provide her son with medical treatment for his cystic fibrosis, ends her narrative with:

[p]rostitution has served me very well, indeed. It was a most useful tool. I have no regrets, no shame, no remorse. Instead, I look back on my prostitution experience with a sense of pride and accomplishment. I did it, I'm glad I did it, and I applaud those who do it now. Here's to the Ladies of the Night – Carry on! Save your money, make wise investments, and above all else – *love yourself.* ("A Most Useful Tool" 165)

Carter's exhortation to "love yourself" indicates she is aware of the potentially damaging effects of sex work. The anthology also includes narratives of women who believe they were coerced into sex work and damaged by their experience: Cecelia Wardlaw was a heroin addict regularly beaten by her pimp; Rosie Summers worked long hours in a massage parlor because she didn't believe she could get a regular job. Pro-sex feminists' willingness to include disparate voices and experiences sets them apart from anti-pornography feminists in important ways. Whereas anti-pornography feminists only include narratives that support their position (as when Catherine MacKinnon recounts Linda Marchiano's experiences) and in fact deny the validity of alternative accounts of prostitution by labeling them "false consciousness," most pro-sex feminist organizations encompass multiple perspectives. By including a variety of experience – both negative and positive, as well as from women of color and working-class women – the pro-sex feminist agenda allows more opportunity for prostitutes to represent their own experiences.

Debates on prostitution and pornography have divided feminists; the so-called sex wars are one of the most contentious issues facing millennial feminism. Though the two poles of the prostitution debate are radically different, one important assumption underlies both positions. Prostitution is the extreme to which all female sexual experience is compared and contrasted. For the anti-pornography feminists, the prostitution system informs gender relations between men and women, reinscribing a hierarchy that posits male sexual dominance as natural and legitimizes rape and violence against women. For pro-sex feminists, on the other hand, the fear of the whore stigma keeps women from naming and acting upon their sexual needs. The sex wars, then, occupy a central position within contemporary feminism, suggesting that examining prostitution as performance may yield a deeper understanding of female sexuality and the way it is represented and expressed.

PERFORMING PROSTITUTION: ACTING AND AGENCY

The polarities of the prostitution debate ignore the in-between space many prostitutes inhabit: the financial independence and sexual experimentation sex work offers contrast sharply with the physical and psychic dangers it engenders. For many, performance offers a way to control the sex work experience. The theatrical metaphor is particularly apt for understanding and describing commercial sex. According to Michael Kirby, "[t]o act means to feign, to simulate, to represent, to impersonate" ("Acting" 154). Prostitutes, according to this definition, are "acting" as they work. Prostitutes sometimes feign passion, simulate desire, represent sexuality, and impersonate a fantasy lover. Prostitution is about the creation of illusion, and the power the creator of that illusion holds over his/her audience.[12] These metaphors suggest that performance offers agency for the prostitute. Sex workers deploy "performance" in multiple ways: they ally themselves with stars in order to glamorize and legitimize their activities; they distance themselves from negative representations of prostitution; normalize their participation in the sex industry; and separate their "real selves" from the commercial sexual transaction.

Though the prostitutes' rights movement is explicitly concerned with raising the status of sex workers by reversing the conflation of the actress/whore, their agenda is not mine. Instead, I focus on how sex workers use performance to intervene in their own representations and negotiate agency. As early chapters demonstrate, the whore stigma is deployed by the dominant culture to minimize women's influence in the public sphere. For instance, my reconsideration of Betty Boutell suggests that historians' partial accounts deny female agency and sexual subjectivity to the first generation of English actresses, and to Boutell in particular. In much the same way, contemporary prostitutes use performance to negotiate agency both within the broader political arena and their personal lives. "Status as actresses" offers sex workers a metaphor to describe their work that moves beyond the whore stigma and the victimization it entails; as part of a political agenda, as in the prostitutes' rights movement or as a strategy for negotiating between multiple identities and experiences, as in the Madison sample, "performance" mitigates the whore stigma and opens up the whore position.

Many sex workers make specific links between acting and prostitution. Claudette, a professional New York call girl working for Sydney Biddle Barrows, described her job: "Now, every night is like a drama, and it's always different – different characters, different backdrops, and different scripts. Sitting in my living room, waiting for the phone to ring, I feel like a star in her dressing room" (Barrows *Mayflower Madam* 98). Claudette's rose-colored description of prostitution clearly frames her work as theatre, though the glamour[13] referenced by this understanding may seem hyperbolic or naïve.

Acts of performance help maintain the boundaries between self and role, but those boundaries are not impermeable. Carrie talked about the usefulness of performing for clients.

The less I like a guy, the more I lie. I usually tell them I'm a college student. But if I know I don't want to see a guy again, I tell him I'm a nurse, and that I'm older or younger than I am, or that I have a boyfriend, or that I'm from Chicago. With a regular you have to stick to the truth, or you'll get caught lying.

Carrie "lied," or in my theoretical construct, acted as though she was someone she was not. She used this performance to keep herself safe and separate from clients she disliked. However, she recognized that this performance had inherent dangers; she could be caught in a lie when a disliked client became a regular.

In "Acting and Not-Acting," Michael Kirby suggests a performance continuum[14] that delineates between different kinds of theatrical performances from performance art to realistic theatre; he terms the final phase of the continuum complex acting. Because Kirby insists that complex acting requires skill and technique, he argues that it is not applicable to performance in daily life and instead applies only to theatrical performances in a traditional sense. Though demarcations between everyday performance and theatrical performance are important, Kirby's continuum does apply to the ways prostitutes situate sex work as acting. Prostitutes are certainly complex actors; their work requires great skill and technique. Most call girls, massage parlor workers, and even streetwalkers are tipped in addition to the set fee. The more they convince their client that the experience was fantastic, the higher that tip will be. Therefore, they must master the skills to assure their clients the sex was pleasurable and meaningful. Prostitutes control their body movements and their voices to elicit a response from johns not unlike the catharsis Aristotle deemed necessary for successful theatrical production. Their interactions are as skilled and technical as actors called upon to play Lady Macbeth six nights a week and twice on Wednesday. An actor may not always feel as though she is a power-hungry woman leading her husband down a path of destruction, but she must make her audience believe she is, just as a sex worker may not always feel like having sex with a client, but she must make him think she does.

In many situations, sex workers are aware that they are putting on an act for a client and discuss it in those terms. For example, Alex compared sex work to the improvisation and acting classes she'd taken in high school: "you . . . pretend to be someone else." She tried to "get [the client] to play along," requesting his complicity in prostitution as performance. Other Madison escorts, however, were less specific and less conscious of performance techniques. Prostitutes are stereotypically viewed as hyper-feminine, hyper-sexual creatures. Of course, in real life, they are often average men and women. When working, they make adjustments in their appearance and behavior in order to appeal to the client; they perform a specific sexual identity. For example, Amanda told me "I have a velvet bodysuit with holes on the side. Sometimes I like to really slut out for work. It's so not me, you know?" Amanda wore "sexy" clothes when working, presenting a front and playing a character, though she did not seem to deliberately make acting choices or think of prostitution in theatrical terms.

My understanding of the Madison sample is enriched by sociological studies of the workplace, such as Arlie Russell Hochschild's 1983 *The Managed Heart: Commercialization of Human Feeling*. Hochschild studied flight attendants' strategies, defining "emotional labor" as "the management of feeling to create publicly observable facial and bodily display; emotional labor is sold for a wage, therefore, it has *exchange value*" (7). Drawing on Stanislavski's theories of acting, Hochschild divides emotional labor into two categories, surface acting and deep acting. "In surface acting we deceive others about what we really feel, but we do not deceive ourselves" (33). Deep acting is more complex, and its emotional costs are therefore higher. In deep acting, "display is a natural result of working feeling; the actor does not try to seem happy or sad but rather expresses spontaneously . . . a real feeling that has been self-induced" (35). Sex workers employ both surface and deep acting with their clients.

Cherri, Private Entertainments' top booker, seemed to almost exclusively use surface acting with her clients. She was very businesslike as she described a typical appointment, and stressed her indifference to her clients.

Usually, the guy is really excited before I even get there. I walk in the door, unbutton my blouse, and drop it on the floor. Guaranteed hard-on. I hand him the contract, and while he looks it over, I get out my massage oil and put on some music. Then I tell him to get undressed. They like that, me being in charge . . .

So then I start oiling them up, telling them they're sexy, and that I'm wet, and stuff, and then I tell them to jack off. Usually I take off my bra then. I keep talking to them, telling them that they're doing a good job, and that I like their cock. Then I tell them to come on my tits. Then I leave. They almost always tip me, and they almost always call back.

Cherri's encounters seemed to close down the possibility of emotional involvement, and she rarely had sexual intercourse with her clients. She reported that she had several regulars, but denied the kind of personal relationships that marked some of the Escorts employees' experience. Instead, Cherri seemed to specialize in quick, businesslike but (at least for her clients) sexually exciting transactions. This may be because Private Entertainments bills itself as a strip service, rather than an escort service, and discourages sexual contact.

Deep acting, on the other hand, accesses real emotion; Hochschild argues that deep actors must employ emotion memory, a concept she attributes to Stanislavski.[15] Deep acting therefore relies on a conscious recognition of the self and the memories and previous emotions of the actor (*Managed Heart* 40–42). According to Hochschild, deep actors recall events similar to the current situation and transfer the attendant emotion, imagining how others might act in similar situations, and/or reframing the events as part of a more manageable narrative. Hochschild includes the testimony of a flight attendant who used deep acting in order to handle difficult passengers: "I try to remember that if he's drinking too much, he's probably scared of flying. I think to myself, 'he's like a little child.' Really that's what he is. And when I see him that way, I don't get mad that he's yelling at me. He's like a child yelling at me then" (55). The Madison escorts also employed deep acting in order to enjoy having sex with certain clients. Kristeen regularly saw Steven, a paraplegic who had lost the use of his legs in a car accident.

He's nice enough, but I don't really like having sex with him – it's just oral stuff, and it's really weird helping him out of the chair and into bed. And it really freaks me out that he can't feel anything, but still have sex. But he doesn't know I'm weirded out. Sometimes I pretend that he's a Vietnam vet who was injured defending his country and I'm the wife he left behind. My dad was in Vietnam . . . I pretend it's something like that, not just a drunk-driving accident. And I always fake lots of orgasms with him, but tell him they're real, so he'll feel better about everything. I mean I don't want him to feel worse than he already does, you know?

Deep acting allows sex workers to reframe the sometimes degrading and often discomforting commercial exchange as pleasant or even ennobling.

In some cases, deep acting may not adequately explain the desire a sex worker feels for a client. Most of the girls working at Exploits, Unlimited had regular clients and had emotional attachments to these men. These relationships seemed important to the escorts, suggesting that what began as deep acting could become real feeling. The Exploits employees spoke freely and at length about their regular clients and seemed to use these relationships to define their experience with prostitution. For that reason, I include several anecdotes about regular clients here. Lesley had visited Doug regularly for about four months before I began the interviews, and continued this relationship throughout the interview period. As her comments attest, her involvement with Doug carried over into her personal life.

Doug is really nice. He's tall, about 23 years old, an engineering student, and kind of fat. He just broke up with his girlfriend. I go over, and the money is always just waiting on the dresser for me. We talk for awhile, and then we have sex. It's good sex. I usually come. We usually talk some more. He likes just really basic stuff. When I first started going, he was really shy, but he's getting more adventurous. One time he bought spray whip cream to put on my breasts. He was real cute about the whole thing.

I asked Lesley how she felt about Doug.

Sometimes it's a little weird. I see him every week, sometimes twice, and I usually stay for about two hours. We talk a lot, about school, and our friends, and what we did on the weekend. And sometimes when I'm with Jerry [her boyfriend] I think about Doug, and try things I've done with him.

Carrie had a lengthy relationship with Paul, similar in some ways to Lesley's relationship with Doug. She saw him at least once a week, often for several hours. She told me they had "amazing" sex, and spent time together eating pizza, drinking wine, and listening to country music. She did not charge him for the extra time and in fact gave him her beeper number so he could contact her directly and bypass the agency – and its fee. Carrie's relationship with Paul was very complicated, and crossed the boundaries between the typical whore/john exchange.

I know Paul wants me to just be his girlfriend, and I sometimes think about dating him. And since I'm not seeing anyone right now, it's like I *am* his girlfriend. We talk about school, what I'm studying, his job, our families, everything. But when I borrowed money from him for my tuition last semester, I paid him back in cash. He wanted me to just see him three times for free. I couldn't do it. It was too weird. If I'd seen him for free it would have been like we were dating, and I couldn't ask him for money the next time. But I *need* him as a client, because it's really steady money, so I had to see three other guys and pay him back out of that.

Kristeen has been seeing Jim for over a year. The two of them have a very comfortable relationship, and talk about their personal lives.

Jim is great. He's a really good kisser, he likes to kiss a lot. And I'm the only one he comes with. Like, when I'm having my period, sometimes he'll see someone else, but he only comes with me. And he always gets a hotel room, usually with a Jacuzzi and some wine. The calls take a long time, and I've spent the night twice. He has my pager number. Kevin doesn't like that. And he knows all about Kevin [Kristeen is dating Kevin, Exploits' owner] and we've talked about that situation. Jim's older, and sometimes I think we should just date, but I have Kevin, and he has a girlfriend. He's my favorite call. And he's a big tipper.

The emphasis the girls placed on these relationships suggests that these interactions were part of their performance of normalcy. Lesley, Carrie, and Kristeen – as well as Amanda and Alex – had regular clients in whom they took a personal interest. These clients allowed the escorts to reframe their commercial sex within traditional romantic narratives.

The relationships Lesley, Carrie, and Kristeen have with their regular clients clearly cross the line between business and pleasure, though in most cases the girls remained aware of the financial component of the relationship: Jim is both a good kisser and a big tipper. With these men the girls presumably are more honest and less conscious of acting out a certain type of femininity. What may have started as deep acting – the escorts tried to find things in common with regular clients, tried to fully embody the role of girlfriend and confidant, tried to make the business transaction as personal as possible – soon became an intimate relationship. The relationships Madison escorts had with regular clients parallels more professional call girls' experience; for example, Lever and Dolnick report that one informant told them "[y]ou cannot know someone that long without it being a real relationship," and that many claimed to be genuinely interested in their regular clients' lives ("Clients and Call Girls" 98). In fact, the Madison escorts' amateur status may have led them to be particularly intimate with their clients. Their insistence that they were not prostitutes suggests that they may have attempted to cast their commercial relationships within a more traditional, heterosexual model.

The Madison escorts' experience provides a rich convergence between perform*ative* models of identity (as elaborated by Judith Butler), and more voluntaristic models of perform*ance* (as in Erving Goffman's sociology of role-playing). With their clients and in their more properly "private" lives, Madison sex workers perform specific, often contradictory, identities. They often perform a hyper-femininity in order to please the client. In their private lives, they perform "normal" femininity in order to keep their sex work a secret. In important and analytically irreducible ways, these dual performances are self-conscious. The norms of femininity sex workers parodically cite in willful self-conscious performance, however, are often the same ones they *un*self-consciously cite in other aspects of their lives.

Erving Goffman's 1959 *The Presentation of Self in Everyday Life* is the seminal text for understanding daily interactions as conscious role-playing. Goffman argues that individuals adopt certain roles, behaviors, and attitudes in order to convince others of their trustworthiness, competence, and character (14). He is careful, however, to point to the limits of such an understanding:

The claim that all the world's a stage is sufficiently commonplace for readers to be familiar with its limitations and tolerant of its presentation, knowing that at any time they will easily be able to demonstrate to themselves that it is not to be taken too seriously. (254)

Regardless of his self-imposed limits, Goffman's use of the theatrical metaphor provides specific models for analyzing performance in everyday life.

Theories of performativity further complicate and enrich my interrogation of performance and prostitution. Judith Butler defines performativity "not as a singular or deliberate 'act,' but, rather, as the reiterative and citational practice by which discourse produces the effects that it names" (*Bodies* 2), a definition that owes much to J. L. Austin's speech act theory. Austin claims there are two different kinds of speech: constative speech is language that describes reality and merely states something, while performative speech is language that performs an action and calls a set of conditions into being. Further, in the performative utterance, both parties must recognize that a set of conditions has been called into being.

An example from my conversations with Kevin demonstrates how the link between "performance" and "performativity" becomes evident in practice. I met Kevin at his downtown Madison office. He began our conversation by describing the contract system with which he operated, and the security those contracts provided.

I tell the girls that the contract protects both them and the guy. This way, nobody can be arrested. And if they don't want to have sex with the guy, or there's something they don't want to do, all they have to do is refer to the contract. The guy's not paying for sex, he's paying for their time only. That's clear.

I asked Kevin if the girls usually had sex on their dates. "Well," he said, "they're not paying for sex. But that's what they expect. And 99 percent of the time, that's what happens." Both client and escort knew what to expect, but the specific language of the contract protected them from the sordidness of paying and being paid for sex.

The contracts themselves (which three of the four agencies I contacted used) served a performative function. The contracts had a series of propositions that the clients and escorts initialed and accepted at the beginning of the transaction. The contracts basically affirmed that the client was paying for the escort's time only and that no promise of sexual contact had been exchanged for money. Accepting the contract thus determined that no acts of prostitution were about to occur, even though, according to Kevin, "99 percent of the time" his employees had sex with clients after receiving a fee. Though under most definitions, prostitution *was* occurring between client and escort, the contract (following Austin) performatively called into being a set of conditions under which the transaction was not prostitution. In fact, the ubiquity of the contracts seemed to prop up the girls' claims that they were not whores, but simply escorts, masseuses, or strippers.

One of the key aspects in Goffman's performance in everyday life is his distinction between front and back. The front[16] is divided into two areas, setting and personal front. The setting includes furniture, décor, and physical layout, and in this case may refer to the way an escort sets up or appropriates an apartment or hotel room for her purposes. Goffman defines personal front as "insignia of office or rank; clothing; sex, age, and racial characteristics; size and looks; posture; speech patterns; facial expressions; bodily gestures; and the like" (*Presentation* 23–24). All of the agency owners presented a front of banality by emphasizing the legal and even culturally sanctioned aspects of their work. They met me in their offices, in their homes, and in a local shopping mall. They used legal and economic discourse to convince me that their agencies were mainstream rather than criminal. Through the office setting, his casual tone, and his discussion of legality, Kevin presented a front designed to convince me that his business practices were unremarkable, and that he was an honest, legal businessman.

The girls also manipulated front, echoing their managers' concerns and separating themselves from their work. I spoke with Kristeen from Exploits several times for this project. The first time I saw her she was wearing a sweater and jeans; I was struck by how plain and normal-looking she was. The next time I met her at a local bar after she'd finished a call. She was wearing a tight leather skirt with a slit up the front, white lace thigh-high stockings, black high-heeled pumps, and a white silk blouse. Her face was expertly made up. I commented on the difference in her appearance and she responded:

The guy is paying you $150 an hour, and you better look sexy. Plus, I just saw this guy in a hotel, and I have to walk through the lobby and look like I belong there, not like I'm there to do business. So I think a lot about what I wear, trying to look sexy and not trashy. I have a lot of clothes I almost never wear unless I'm going out on a date that I bought for work.

Kristeen, like other sex workers, recognized that creating the proper front would help her do her job, though of course she did not explicitly discuss it in those terms. Front also helps sex workers control how they are read and therefore treated by clients and others. Kristeen had to balance looking "sexy" with looking "trashy." Her front established her character for the client as well as for the hotel staff who might have been suspicious of a women in, say, a mini-skirt, halter, and fishnets. The front Kristeen presented was "classy," which protected her from harassment by clients and others. Clothing and behavior, then, helps sex workers think of themselves as playing a role as well as shielding them from negative judgments.

Though in early interviews, I only saw the escorts' and agency owners' front, my relationship with some of them eventually became more personal.

In Goffman's terms, I was allowed into the back. According to Goffman, the back is private space, "where the impression fostered by the performance is knowingly contradicted as a matter of course" (*Presentation* 112). As private space, the back is rarely accessible by audience members, and according to Goffman, all pretense is dropped. In the back, according to Goffman's model, sex workers are able to stop performing for the client and act as they please. Sex workers in the back may denigrate the clients they just professed to love or at least desire. For example, many of the girls at Exploits visited Greg. They talked about how he often gave them gifts – picture frames, candlesticks, photo albums – they considered tacky. They showed me some particularly kitschy presents they kept at the Exploits office. They considered Greg a pathetic, lonely, emotionally needy man, but they always gratefully accepted his gifts and averred that they never mocked him to his face. I imagine they were both kind and sexually forthcoming with Greg: according to the records Kevin kept on computer, he scheduled one or two appointments per week.

Though Goffman insists that performance is limited to the front and that the back region is a space for "true" exchange, this delineation is too simple. Individuals still perform in the back, albeit in different ways than for an audience. The difference lies in the degree of self-consciousness present in the actors. In front of clients, sex workers know they are acting. Among themselves, they seem less aware. Many of the Madison escorts seemed to gloss over some of the contradictions in their narratives.[17] For example, Amanda offered this anecdote when I asked her what (if any) problems she encountered while working as an escort.

They take a long time. I have to take a shower beforehand, get all dressed up, and then go. I usually take a shower with the guy, and have sex with him in the shower. They really like that. Then I have to take a shower when I get home. It's kind of a pain trying to explain to my roommates why I have wet hair all the time.

Amanda's complaint about her work was mostly limited to the inconvenience of several showers a day. Her description, however, does not address why she needed to take a shower both before and after a call, or why she asked her clients to shower before having sex with them. It is easy to interpret her remarks as an expression of ambivalence about her work, or to assume that she feels "dirty" because she works as a prostitute. On the other hand, this story was easily told and Amanda did not seem to recognize that she might have been expressing a deeper conflict. I interpret Amanda's remarks as an example of the unselfconscious acting that takes place in the back. She did not realize that possible alternative interpretations of her remarks were available, and so did not seem to be confessing anything particularly shattering.

The shift between front and back presses especially in the girls' discussion of sexual satisfaction. Through our conversations, it became clear that an important part of managing sex work and escaping the whore stigma was the conversations about the different sexual experiences the girls had with clients. In the back, they freely discussed themselves and the clients, interrogating their own emotional and physical responses. Gary was a very frequent client, and all of the girls had seen him at least once. Their discussions about Gary reveal how they discussed their interactions. Though I did not speak to Gary directly,[18] the girls reported that Gary wanted them to enjoy their time with him; he wanted them to have orgasms, and he wanted them to like him. Ashlee talked about Gary.

Gary just cracks me up. He's always saying like "Baby, we should go to the Sexual Olympics in Miami. You just come and come. Baby, you've never felt like this before, have you? Do you come with the other guys? It's just me, right? You love my big cock." I don't come with him – I don't come with anybody. He must think I'm some kind of machine – twenty minutes and I come five times? But he's *so* sure. . . .

Ashlee was able to convince Gary that she enjoyed sex with him; she pretended to be a multi-orgasmic sexual dynamo, which she emphatically was not. Alex was another of Gary's favorites. When I was at the Exploits office for a staff meeting, Gary called to schedule an appointment. Kevin put Alex on the phone, and she began giggling and flirting with him. Kevin remarked that her whole personality had changed (Alex had been very businesslike at the staff meeting): "Listen to that crap. He's eating it up." Clearly, Alex shifted into the role of giggly flirt in order to please Gary, a role very different from the one she had adopted during the staff meeting. Alex worked to convince Gary she liked him and was pleased to talk to him between appointments. Of course, she hung up the phone and berated Kevin for making her talk to a client off the clock.

Sexual satisfaction may have been easier to perform when that behavior was recited. Often, the girls used scenarios familiar from pornographic movies or other typical fantasies. Carrie talked about seeing a semi-regular client who requested she visit him dressed in garter belt, stockings, and bra covered by a raincoat. Another client wanted her to tell stories of being caught masturbating at a local nude beach while performing oral sex (she wryly noted the inherent difficulty of combining conversation and fellatio). Alex told me about another specific fantasy: being with two girls at once. As Alex explained it, she and Kristeen (her regular partner) performed scenes straight from male porn. Alex played the role of experienced lesbian, and Kristeen was the naïve virgin who really wanted a man; the client watched and then joined in to "finish the job." Like Charke's use of theatrical scenes and Leeson's reliance on the tropes of sentimental fiction, the Madison escorts cited familiar scenarios with their clients, using them to construct a specific identity. This parodic resignification, then, resisted the experience the client had purchased. Following from Butler, citation offers a measure of agency for sex workers. Recycling heterosexual convention, the Madison sample resisted and denied those conventions: Alex insisted she was not a lesbian. Repetition, when self-consciously enacted, allows prostitutes to negotiate the ways their bodies and sex are read. First acting and then narrativizing according to familiar tropes suggest that sex workers reframe and reinterpret experience, a performance that helps mitigate the potential difficulties of their work. Carrie reported strongly disliking her raincoat client, but played along with his fantasies because he was a big tipper.

Of course, sex workers consciously cite norms of femininity they unconsciously cite every day to construct subjectivity and self. Resignification is only a matter of degree, as repetition forms the subject. According to Butler, the performance of sex and gender is "one of the norms by which the 'one' becomes viable at all, that which qualifies a body for life within the domain of cultural intelligibility" (*Bodies* 2). It is the history of the norms, their previously established "feminine" or "masculine" nature that can give them weight in the discourse between prostitute and client. When a prostitute plays a specifically feminine role, she draws upon all her learned notions of femininity. Though a performance of gender and self may seem like an isolated act, Butler argues that it purposely hides the fact that it is a reiteration of previous conventions, and that each performance has a history, albeit hidden, that affects both the current performance, and the formation of the subject (12). When working girls consciously cite cultural norms, they are only deliberately doing that which they do every day in order to construct a subjectivity.

The way the girls perform femininity is complex, and points toward how all women (and men) perform gender. The cramped arena of the prostitution exchange illuminates how performativity "works." The self-conscious performance of sexuality is different from unconscious reiteration of the cultural codes that determine sexuality in Western society. When these girls cite a certain norm in order to present a hyper-feminine identity, they are only choosing to cite that norm which is automatically cited in their daily lives. Though she never talked about sex work in Butlerian terms, Kristeen cited and reiterated feminine cultural norms when she was working – she tried to look sexy, not trashy. Like Alex's portrayal of a "butch" lesbian, Kristeen modeled her appearance on what she assumed her clients would find sexy.

Madison sex workers switch from performed femininity to normalcy constantly as they move between work and private lives, and noted the difficulty of maintaining boundaries. This difficulty is hardly surprising, as they had to perform both banality and hyper-sexuality, switching from one frame of reference to another as they fit their appointments between boyfriends, classes, parties, and homework. The girls also wanted to blend in with their peers, keep their sex work hidden, and appear normal and average. For example, Alex reported sometimes feeling uncomfortable in her women's studies classes. When the other students railed against the oppression of the pornography and prostitution industries, Alex maintained an uncomfortable silence.

I've taken some women's studies courses. They're cool. But when everybody starts talking about prostitution and porn, I just have sit there, or else go along... They're talking about how these women are *victims*, but I'm thinking about how much I really like Gary, and how much fun it is to get all dressed up and make $150 for sex. And I like sex, and I like having sex with Gary, and, you know, *most* of them.

Alex was required to perform a version of feminism that opposed her own experience as a sex worker in order to seem like her classmates.

Most of the girls limited their complaints to the inconvenience of having to hide their sex work from their peers. However, they also worried that their "real life" would become too available to the clients. Amanda talked to me about her relationship with Eric, one of her regulars. He offered to give her a car if she spent the weekend with him. Amanda needed a car, but she didn't want to take one from a client, as she was afraid it would give him too much control over her. And, she worried about spending too much time with Eric: "It's too much time, you know? I can't be horny for a whole weekend. And I can't talk to him for that long either, cause there's stuff I don't want to have to get into." Amanda balked at spending an entire weekend as a prostitute. It seems she needed to be able to limit her contact with her clients in order to mitigate her identity as a prostitute. Further, the performance of hyper-feminine sexuality is difficult to maintain for long periods of time.

One of Kevin's employees, Ashlee, was particularly disturbed by her experience with prostitution. I met her the first day I interviewed Kevin, when she returned from a call to drop off her money. First, she told me that she liked her work, and triumphantly showed me the $145 (including a sizable tip) she had just made. But as we continued talking, her confusion and despair became obvious. Peppered with nervous giggles, Ashlee told me she really needed the money, that her phone had been turned off, and that she had started working for Kevin out of pure financial need. Finally, she began to sob.

Sometimes when I'm with my boyfriend, I just want to kill him. I look at him, and I feel like I'm doing all this stuff for him, and he's doing nothing for me. I never come with him. I never come when I'm working. I only come when I'm by myself. Maybe there's something wrong with me.

Working in prostitution, Ashlee reached a crisis point in terms of her sexual identity and desires. When sex became a job, she started to question her sex life with her boyfriend, and became angry, frustrated, and sad. Kevin told me a few weeks later that Ashlee had quit working at Exploits in order to spend more time with her boyfriend and try to have a baby. I was relieved she'd quit working; it seemed clear that she was not able to fit prostitution into her life. By attempting to re-embody traditional notions of femininity, I think Ashlee was trying to leave prostitution behind, though I wondered if substituting parenthood with a potentially flawed partner was much of a solution. Ashlee's experience suggests that for some women, performance is not enough. The whore position is too constricting, and the potential for sexual liberation and financial independence is not attainable by all women.

Carrie told me that working as a prostitute (she was the only girl who identified herself as such) was "messing with her desire." When she had sex on her own time, she rarely used condoms, in order to make it different from work. In addition, she told me

I have trouble sometimes having one night stands. I start thinking about how to turn him on, I want him to like me, and so I do stuff I've done at work. It can get confusing, because I sometimes can't tell if I'm having a good time, or just pretending, and so I have a good time. And, when I go to a party or a bar, I know, I feel like, I can get any man in the room, because I'm a hooker. It makes me feel confident – if some guy blows me off, I just tell myself other guys are paying me.

In their personal relationships, Madison sex workers struggled with whether or not to tell friends and lovers about their part-time jobs. Most had a friend in whom they confided, and Lesley told her boyfriend a watered-down version of her job description. But for the most part, they keep their identities as part-time prostitutes a secret, even denying it to themselves. The performance of hyper-sexuality at work and normality at home was the strategy that made sex work possible. They gained confidence and financial independence through sex work but at the same time resisted identifying themselves as whores because of their internalized representation of the prostitute as weak, dirty, oppressed, and shameful.

Switching from (performed) normalcy to (performed) hyper-sexuality, literally lying to friends and family about the time spent working and the origin of the money received, trying to separate the emotional attachment to regular clients from the business transaction, all converge to make these co-ed call girls skillful cultural actors, albeit out of necessity. As cultural actors they specifically and self-consciously perform normative (and constructed) sexual orientations within the boundaries of culture. They know they are putting on a performance, and that performance resists the "reality" of the sex the client believes he has purchased. In this way, then, prostitutes negotiate a degree of agency through the performance of femininity. The performance strategies these women deploy give them a measure of control and anonymity; their real selves are exempt from the sexual transaction.

In the contemporary moment, the assumption that an actress is a whore has shifted to a preoccupation with demonstrating that a whore is an actress. The prostitutes' rights movement demands "status as actresses" in order to legitimate sex work. This political motive attends to the performative aspects of gender and sexual identity. Prostitutes' narratives offer a fertile site for investigating how female sexuality is constructed and represented. More importantly, theatrical metaphors offer strategies to open up the whore position. Self-consciously performing femininity, sex workers reconcile traditional representations and discourses of prostitution with their own experiences and identities. As the Madison narratives make clear, feminism has sometimes elided the voices and lived experience of many contemporary sex workers. Insisting on either oppressive or liberatory analyses of the sex industry, feminism has ignored the ambivalences that make up most prostitutes' experience: as Tracy Quan asserts, "[t]o embrace the identity of prostitute is to embrace a multitude of contradictions" (in Bell *Reading* 109). As I suggest in the afterpiece, those contradictions are captured and reflected in new technologies and new articulations of the whore position.

CHAPTER 6

Afterpiece: millennial prostitution

"I don't know," I blubbered. "I think I'm in love with one of my clients and I just had this mind-blowing weekend with Randy and he hasn't called me and I didn't realize how much I cared about Matt until last night. . . . I don't know what or who I want anymore."

(Quan *Diary*)

In her 1999–2000 bi-weekly diary entries in Salon.com, working prostitute and activist Tracy Quan detailed the adventures of her alter ego, "millennial call girl" Nancy Chan. In the serial, Chan struggled to define herself in relation to her clients, her friends, the prostitutes' rights movement, her non-paying lovers, and her past as a love-starved and money-hungry first-generation Asian-Canadian. Originally available only on the Internet, *Diary of a Manhattan Call Girl* specifically engages with prostitutes' attempts to position themselves within existing discourses of female sexuality, feminism, and ideals of femininity. Through this autobiography, Quan performed a particular version of the prostitute, one whose inflection of traditional narratives of prostitution depends on specifically "millennial" conditions of technology, culture, and social identity.

Millennial discourses of the prostitute/actress produce multiple representations, rendering visible a proliferation of meanings attached to contemporary prostitution and its performative aspects. In the contemporary period, prostitution is as ubiquitous as it seemed to nineteenth-century reformers who promised that anyone who "walk[ed] certain streets of London, Glasgow, or Edinburgh" would know "without troubling his head with statistics . . . what a multitudinous amazonian army the devil keeps in constant field service, for advancing his own ends" (Miller *Prostitution* 5). A century and a half later, prostitution is equally visible; however, one important difference distinguishes the Victorian prostitute from her contemporary US-American counterpart. Sex workers, both actual and fictional, are obvious not on street corners but in television, film, and print media. Visibility politics preoccupy media scholars, theatrical performers, and political activists. Gay playwright and activist Harvey Fierstein, for instance, argues in the documentary *The Celluloid Closet* for "visibility at all costs." For Fierstein and others who position themselves similarly, stereotypic and even oppressive representation is better than no representation at all. Although the prostitutes' rights movement, even in its most politicized and strenuous form, is not neatly analogous to other identity-based movements – homosexuality and race, for example, are permanent categories lived through a web of biological, social, and economic experiences where prostitution is a job chosen or rejected relatively freely – questions of visibility, stereotype, and representation do concern some working prostitutes and activists. If one goal of the prostitutes' rights movement is to mitigate the whore stigma, then negative representations of the prostitute (as victim, predator, nymphomaniac) should be regarded with apprehension. As Peggy Phelan wryly notes, "[i]f representational visibility equals power, then almost-naked young white women should be running Western culture" (*Unmarked* 10). The proliferate visibility of prostitutes and the prostitutes' rights movement does not necessarily translate into the political power of the movement nor agency on the part of individual prostitutes.

The increased visibility of prostitution in late twentieth- and early twenty-first-century media does, however, suggest that the meanings now attached to the sex industry are dispersed through multiple sites of articulation. These multiple sites insure that "prostitution" is more fluid than in previous centuries. Two sites of discursive production, Quan's *Diary of a Manhattan Call Girl* and Whorenet,[1] a bulletin board and website maintained by the Whores' Activist Network (WAN), a coalition of prostitutes' rights organizations, enable a different kind of prostitute visibility.

AUTOBIOGRAPHY ON THE INTERNET: TRACY QUAN AND THE WHORES' ACTIVIST NETWORK

As the previous chapter makes clear, most mass media representations of prostitution are in line with traditional narratives of victimization; sex workers are exploited for ratings and shock value. In other mass media sites, however, representations supporting the prostitutes' rights movement are more evident. The Internet allows multiple representations of prostitution: sex work is both commercial and community building. Prostitutes are of course visible on many websites: a cursory glance at the Internet confirms that pornography accounts for a great deal of all online commerce. Though few commercial sex sites mention the prostitutes' rights movement, some activist groups have also created websites in order to publicize their activities. As members of a particularly marginalized and vilified group, prostitutes' rights activists, like other silenced or minority factions, have used the Internet for community building, information sharing, and political action.

Many contemporary theoretical interrogations of the Internet suggest that its importance as a communications medium lies in its facilitation of community building. In *Web.Studies: Rewiring Media Studies for the Digital Age*, David Gauntlett discusses two kinds of Internet communities. The first, people sending electronic text to each other create community through the exchange of both personal and practical information. Some communities are short-lived, existing for a single chat-room session. Others grow and develop over time, as when like-minded individuals frequent list-serves, bulletin boards, or theme websites, contributing to an evolving dialogue about issues endemic to that community. Gauntlett contrasts this individual, text-based notion of Internet community with "communities that develop amongst similarly themed websites and their creators . . . the more websites there are, the more complex the community webs may be" (14). Some sex workers have used the Internet to build community. Tracy Quan published autobiographical fiction that spoke to many about the powers and pleasures of prostitution, reinflecting traditional narratives for a large body of readers. In different ways, WAN also used the Internet for community building, providing information on the prostitutes' rights movement, support groups for prostitutes, advertisements for escorts, and forums for discussion and action.

Salon.com employs prostitutes' rights activist Tracy Quan, founding member of Prostitutes of New York (PONY), as an expert on commercial sex, feminism, and female sexuality. From June 1999 through January 2000, Quan also penned *Diary of a Manhattan Call Girl*, a bi-weekly serial detailing the adventures of Nancy Chan. Chan, an exclusive, expensive, and successful call girl clearly modeled on Quan's own personality and experience, charted her love affairs with stockbroker Matt and personal trainer Randy, her busy schedule of client appointments, her chaotic relationships with co-workers and friends, her entanglements with the IRS and former madams, and her reluctant entry into the prostitutes' rights movement. The narrative ended with Chan simultaneously accepting Matt's marriage proposal and pledging greater involvement with the international prostitutes' rights movement. Quan has expanded the *Diary* into a novel for Three Rivers Press, a division of Random House. Her narrative participates in the tradition of women occupying the whore position to offer alternate accounts of female sexuality and experience.

Figure 6.1 Nancy Chan, Millennial Prostitute (Courtesy of Tim Bower for Salon.com)

Diary of a Manhattan Call Girl, despite its status as a work of fiction, is clearly modeled on Quan's own life story. Like Nancy, Quan is a first generation Asian-Canadian who began working as an escort in New York City as a teenager. Quan eventually went into business for herself, eschewing the traditional escort service or massage parlor for greater financial and sexual autonomy. Like Nancy, she was recruited as a woman of color by the prostitutes' rights movement. After struggling with the movement's hierarchy that limited involvement from streetwalkers and ethnic minorities, she became a leading voice for PONY and other groups. The first-person style of the *Diary* furthers notions of authenticity in the text; the voice is distinct and compelling, and accounts of sex, shopping, and relationship turmoil resonate with the concerns of many third-wave feminist readers. Nancy's struggle to reconcile prostitution and romance presents a version of the prostitute that seems real, familiar, and legitimate.

Diary of a Manhattan Call Girl's initial publication in Salon was enabled by Salon's identity as an edgy, hip Internet content site. Founded in 1995 by David Talbot, Salon includes regular daily sections on news, politics, technology and business, parenting, arts and entertainment, sex, books, celebrities, and comics. Though Salon was initially a free site, in 2003 they moved to a subscriber-only format, with "premium" content available for a yearly fee. David Horowitz, Tina Brown, Andrew Leonard, Greil Marcus, and Ariana Huffington contribute regular columns and its original features and stories are supplemented by wire services. In general, Salon positions itself as a sort of highbrow *USA Today* for Internet users. Though it includes politically and socially conservative columnists, Salon generally takes a liberal position on governmental, moral, and political issues.

Quan's *Diary of a Manhattan Call Girl* complemented Salon.com's identity as an entertaining, politically conscious, technologically aware content site. Quan name-dropped New York City art galleries, restaurants, hair salons, and bars presumably familiar to Salon's hip, urbane readers, and Nancy was abreast of current trends in clothing, accessories, cosmetics, and stock trading. Salon's prostitute seemed like a regular gal, albeit a little hipper, a little sexier, and a little smarter than many of her readers. For example, Nancy and her best friend, Jasmine, shopped for Manolo Blahnik shoes and Fendi baguette purses, had painful Brazilian bikini waxes, attended receptions at the New York Museum of Metropolitan Art, traded Internet stocks, and lunched at sidewalk cafés. (Pop culture junkies will no doubt notice similarities between Nancy and Jasmine and the characters on HBO's *Sex and the City*.)

What sets *Diary of a Manhattan Call Girl* apart from similar narratives of single New Yorkers is its prostitute main characters. Quan's alter ego offered recognizably political musings on her assumed sexual passivity and insatiability as an Asian woman and her position as a woman of color within the prostitutes' rights movement. Feminists have long insisted on the relevance of women's personal experiences to their political identifications and activities; Quan's inclusion of personal detail counters the clichéd images of sex workers offered by other mass media. Of course, *Diary of a Manhattan Call Girl* also includes explicit enumeration of Nancy's sexual relationships with both clients and lovers. Importantly, on Salon.com, the political juxtaposes with the prurient. I suggest that this juncture benefits both the website and the prostitutes' rights movement; the political and sexual articulation of prostitution parallels Salon's identity as a millennial magazine, perfect for readers who want and need a bit more from their daily news. For example, Quan has considerable clout within the prostitutes' rights movement; she has published several essays in feminist anthologies about prostitution and appeared on numerous television talk shows. She also writes freely and with first-hand knowledge of the pleasures and perils of the sex industry. Nancy's erotic adventures and political consciousness enhance Salon's position as a content site for the smart, sexy media consumer while Quan trades on Salon's identity as an edgy, hip, Internet content site to lend credibility and respectability to her description of prostitution. Quan occupies a whore position enabled by Internet technology.

The Internet also allows more concrete responses to traditional notions of prostitution, through websites by and about sex workers. The WAN website, for example, existed as a portal to information about the Network: links to traditional porn sites; information about the prostitutes' rights movement; bulletin boards; biographies and photographs of working prostitutes; online companies where books, clothing, and other memorabilia could be purchased; and academic articles about prostitution were all accessible from WAN's homepage. The prostitute made visible by WAN suggests that she is a member of a wide-ranging community that includes fellow sex workers, clients, and academic feminists. Importantly, the WAN website was accessible on search engines alongside more traditional cybersex and online escort service sites. This seems particularly relevant to understandings of how the prostitutes' rights movement has used the Internet to increase its visibility; political webpages are as available as more traditional sex sites. Following from Gauntlett, the community created by the juxtaposition of these websites complicates narratives of "cybersex."

That said, the WAN website design was fairly schizophrenic, combining sexual spectacle with prosaic text. The background included the silhouette of a slender, long-haired, bosomy woman with remarkably erect nipples.

Links to original content were labeled with moist, dark red lips and the page was outlined in a shade of vaginal pink. Link descriptions included both teasing banter: "slick, glossy"; "just for you"; and "where active folks can share" and drier verbiage: "forum for racism, classism, and sexism"; "informative"; and "we do your reading for you." These links included bulletin boards with information for beginning sex workers and clients, news about decriminalization efforts in the United States and around the world, photos of working prostitutes, information on the documentary WAN produced, and a book review section. A box on the left side of the screen included links to several regional and national prostitutes' rights groups, including PONY, COYOTE, and WHISPER. Finally, the bottom of the page included links to cybersex sites and Internet sites selling sex paraphernalia. The WAN site presented a variety of information, ranging from sex for sale to information on the prostitutes' rights movement. This range is key to understanding the possible impact of the WAN website on discursive representations of prostitution; Internet technology enables the visibility of several kinds of prostitutes accessible from a single portal. Working within existing discourses of Internet sex, commercialism, and political expression, WAN provided alternate content accessible to those surfing the Web for sex. In short, the Internet allows new narratives of prostitution. Community juxtaposes victimization and nymphomania. This new focus, while certainly not replacing traditional narratives nor solving the problems of exploitation, does suggest other strategies for negotiating agency. Though performance remains an important component of prostitution, technology has opened the whore position even further.

Mae West, Elizabeth Boutell, Margaret Leeson, Charlotte Charke, Lydia Thompson, and contemporary sex workers intervene in their discursive representation through the performance of both prostitution and femininity. Using performance – both on stage and off – as a framework for self-representation, these women expanded definitions of acceptable female sexuality. At the same time, their efforts were resisted and restricted by the whore stigma. Boutell, Leeson, Charke, Thompson, West, and other performing women of their respective generations were dogged by accusations of whorishness that curbed their impact. These women were viewed in their own time as outsiders who threatened to pervert the moral and social order with their aggressive display of female sexuality. Further, their experience warned other women against acknowledging or asserting either sexual desire or, perhaps more saliently, their desire for financial autonomy and class legitimacy. The whore stigma, familiar to contemporary feminists as a strategy for circumscribing the sexual behavior of all women, was publicly applied in order to limit their transgressive potential. The enduring link between acting and prostitution overlaps other tensions about the place of women in the public sphere, the (il)legitimacy of the theatrical profession, appropriate modes for representing female experience, and struggles over women's attempts to separate their intellectual and emotional labor from their physical appearance. Thus, the trope of the actress/whore expatiates other discursive constraints on the intellectual and sexual autonomy of all women.

The contemporary prostitutes' rights movement has reversed the trope of the actress/whore in order to insist that prostitutes are "like" actresses, a strategy that reframes the discourse in order to allow for a negotiation of agency. Claiming parallels with performing women who have been designated whores, contemporary prostitutes insist on the technical skill inherent in sex work and demand that it be acknowledged as legitimate labor. At the same time, performance metaphors offer working prostitutes a variety of strategies that both mitigate the whore stigma and physically and emotionally protect them on the job. In interviews, their own writings, and pro-sex feminist accounts of the sex industry, sex workers struggle to intervene in their narrative representation in much the same way as the historical women. New technologies, however, suggest new strategies for mitigating the whore stigma, and new ways to occupy the whore position.

Notes

CHAPTER I

1 I use the word whore self-consciously and deliberately. Contemporary prostitutes' rights activists have reclaimed the word "whore" in order to minimize that
label's negative connotations, blurring the boundaries between "good" and
"bad" women. This rhetorical tactic is in line with other marginalized groups'
projects to reclaim language, such as lesbian and gay rights groups use of the
word "queer." Thus, the re-articulation of "whore" offers historians a new way
to understand accusations and labels of prostitution in previous historical
moments.

2 Of course, some film and television personalities might add much to a continued
examination of the trope of the actress/prostitute: Marlene Dietrich's cross-dressing
and lesbianism; Louise Brooks' scandalous European films and notorious promiscuity; Elizabeth Taylor's congressionally indicted and papally banned affair with
Richard Burton all suggest parallels to Boutell, Charke, and Thompson.

3 For preliminary discussions of the sexual scrutiny facing male actors see
Atchison, Fraser, and Lowman, "Men who buy sex: Preliminary Findings of
an Exploratory Study"; Barish, *The Anti-Theatrical Prejudice*; Campbell,
"Invisible Men: Making Visible Male Clients of Female Prostitutes in
Merseyside"; Harbin, "Monty Woolley: the Public and Private Man from
Saratoga Springs"; Roach, *The Player's Passion*; Senelick, *The Changing Room*;
Strand, "'My Noble Spartacus': Edwin Forrest and Masculinity on the
Nineteenth-Century Stage"; and Straub, *Sexual Suspects*. For more on contem-
porary male prostitution, I offer this representative sample of current and
foundational work: Boles and Ellison, "Out of CASH"; Boyer, "Male
Prostitution and Homosexual Identity"; Brown and Minichiello, "Research
Directions in Male Sex Work"; Dixon and Dixon, "She-Male Prostitutes:
Who are they, What do they do, and Why do they do it?"; Gibson, *Male
Order: Life Stories from Boys who Sell Sex*; Knox, "Negotiations and
Relationships among Male Sex Workers and Clients in Liverpool, Merseyside,
United Kingdom"; Lloyd, *For Money or Love: Boy Prostitution in America*; Skee,
"Tricks of the Trade"; and West, *Homosexual Prostitution*.

4 An enormous amount of feminist research has focused on third-world prostitution, debating its cultural meaning in terms of colonialism, imperialism,
agency, and race. Very little of this research focuses on the performative aspects
of sex work taken nearly for granted in US and European studies; third-world

prostitution is generally figured as more degrading, dangerous, and exploitative than Western prostitution for obvious economic reasons. However, in recent years, some feminist scholars have argued that presuming third-world women to have little agency replicates imperialist frameworks of figuring and describing the Other. Studies of third-world prostitution include Alexander's "Feminism, Sex Workers, and Human Rights"; Bindman, "An International Perspective on Slavery in the Sex Industry"; Bindman and Doezema, *Redefining Prostitution as Sex Work on the International Agenda*; Cabezas, "Discourses of Prostitution: the Case of Cuba"; Davidson, *Prostitution, Power and Freedom*; Davis, *Prostitution: An International Handbook on Trends, Problems, and Policies*; Kempadoo, "The Migrant Tightrope: Experiences from the Caribbean"; McClintock, "Screwing the System: Sex Work, Race, and the Law"; Montgomery, "Children, Prostitution, and Identity: a Case Study from a Tourist Resort in Thailand"; Murray, *No Money, No Honey: a Study of Street Traders and Prostitutes in Jakarta*; Patullo, *Last Resorts: the Cost of Tourism in the Caribbean*; Slamah, "Transgenders and Sex Work in Malaysia"; Truong, *Sex, Money, and Morality: Prostitution and Tourism in Southeast Asia*; and Watenabe, "From Thailand to Japan: Migrant Sex Workers as Autonomous Subjects."

5 For more on micro-narratives see Allen, *Horrible Prettiness*; Foucault, "Nietzsche, Genealogy, History"; Ginzburg, "Microhistory: Two or Three Things I Know About It"; Mittell, "Invisible Footage: Industry on Parade and Television Historiography"; and Trouillot, *Silencing the Past: Power and the Production of History*.

6 This discursive representation of prostitution had material effects in the nineteenth century. Prostitutes were conceived as "fallen" women who necessarily died alone and diseased soon after their initial seduction. In the twentieth century as well, *Camille* continues to resonate. Films often feature the whore with the heart of gold who sacrifices her own happiness and often her life for her respectable friends and lovers: *Half Moon Street*, *The Razor's Edge*, and *The Hustler* all have doomed prostitutes at their center. Prostitutes' rights activists decry the stereotyping of contemporary sex workers as abused, drug-addicted women at the mercy of their pimps and street violence, a discursive representation that is rooted in the tragic women of the nineteenth-century courtesan play.

7 Though feminist critic Pamela Robertson suggests that *Sex* is the story of the "self-sacrifice of a Bowery prostitute unwilling to ruin the man she loves by exposing him to her past" (*Guilty Pleasures* 30), the ending is better interpreted as Margy's choice to leave boring Connecticut for new adventures.

8 For various interpretations and discussions of Mae West and her impact on US-American culture and sexuality, see Curry, *Too Much of a Good Thing: Mae West as Cultural Icon*; Ells and Musgrove, *Mae West*; Hamilton, *When I'm Bad, I'm Better: Mae West, Sex, and American Entertainment*; Leider, *Becoming Mae West*; Leonard, *Mae West: Empress of Sex*; Robertson, *Guilty Pleasures: Feminist Camp from Mae West to Madonna*; and Tuska, *The Films of Mae West*.

9 In fact, West's figure was criticized by some of the reviewers of *Sex*; they deemed her too heavy to convincingly play a flapper. It seems West took that criticism

seriously, and rarely appeared in contemporary dress in her subsequent productions.

10 Interestingly, critics compared *Sex* to a disease, echoing earlier criticisms of Thompsonian burlesque. For example, *The New York Daily Mirror*, on April 30, 1926 railed that "[t]his production is not fit for the police. It comes rather in the province of our Health Department. It is a sore spot in the midst of city that needs disinfecting"; and the May 8, 1926 *New Yorker* complained that the audience was left "as sick as whenever they were when close by anything indescribably filthy." For more on contamination and its metaphoric link to prostitution, see "Breeches, burlesque, and Blondes" below.

11 Some facts about Mae West are difficult to pin down. Her own 1959 biography *Goodness had Nothing to Do with It* has long been accepted as factual; however, many of her claims there are obviously hyperbolic at best. Historians and biographers have variously reported the number of *Sex*'s performances as 339, 356, 375, and 385.

12 West's arrest for *Sex* is generally attributed to anxiety surrounded the preview performances of *The Drag*, a play about New York City homosexuals. Though West did not appear in *The Drag*, she wrote and directed the play, and participated in pre-show publicity. For an in-depth discussion of *The Drag*, see Hamilton, *The Queen of Camp: Mae West, Sex, and Popular Culture* and "Mae West Live: *Sex, The Drag*, and 1920s Broadway."

13 For more on West and censorship, see Curry, *Too Much of a Good Thing*.

14 One of West's strengths as a performer and celebrity was her remarkable control over both her career and her personal life. Beginning in the 1920s, West vigorously rewrote her life. Her 1959 biography, *Goodness Had Nothing to Do with It*, finessed details of her impoverished upbringing, exaggerated her early vaudeville successes, claimed credit for saving Paramount Pictures from bankruptcy, and suggested that her 1926 play was the first time "sex" was used to denote sexual activity in addition to gender difference. Her narrative stressed her independence and autonomy, asserting that she had never needed a man. (For example, she denied her 1911 marriage to Frank Wallace immediately after its celebration until 1937 when Wallace sued her for support. However, in the 1960s and 1970s she often remarked in interviews that she had never been married [Hamilton *Queen* 15].) This narrative control, while admirable for a woman born at the turn of the twentieth century and subject to repressive ideologies of female sexuality and passivity, ultimately worked against West. At the end of life, she seemed not a flesh-and-blood woman with natural desires and fears but a legend created out of half-truths and illusion. She was a drag queen: not a "real" woman, but someone merely playing at and with femininity.

CHAPTER 2

1 Both contemporary and modern historians define Restoration England by sexual activity. The *Memoirs of Count Grammont*, recollections of Charles II's

first French ambassador, offer one such view: "At court all was happiness and pleasure, refinement and splendour such as may be called forth only by a prince of gentle and noble character. Beauties sought only to be enchanting, men tried to please and everyone made the most of their natural gifts. Some of them distinguished themselves by the grace of their dancing, some in the magnificence of their appearance and some by their wit, but most of them by their love affairs and very few of them by their faithfulness" (in Bloch *Sexual Life in England* 235).

2 For more on Charles II's effeminacy, see Ketchum, "Setting and Self-Presentation in the Restoration and Early Eighteenth Century"; McKeon, "Historicizing Patriarchy: the Emergence of Gender Difference in England, 1660–1760"; Parker, *Nell Gwyn*; and Weber, "Charles II, George Pines, and Mr. Dorimant: the Politics of Sexual Power in Restoration England" and "Carolinean Sexuality and the Restoration Stage: Reconstructing the Royal Phallus in *Sodom.*"

3 Of course, male actors were sexually suspect as well. The link between homosexuality and male actors is as pervasive as the collapse of actress into whore. Kristina Straub argues that men who put their bodies on display for profit could not hope to earn the same kind of respect accorded to other professional men who used their minds. Because of the emphasis on display, the actor's "personal exhibitionism placed him at odds with the increasingly dominant image of masculinity defined as a spectating subject, rather than a specularized object" (*Sexual Suspects* 258).

4 Conversely, entries on male actors tend to focus more on their business dealings and professional projects. Of course, male actors were more likely to hold shares, own property, and gain admiration from Pepys and other contemporaries for their elocutionary skill rather than their dimples and ankles: the variety of source material on male actors is obviously richer. Still, Restoration theatre studies is a concrete example of the way histories, especially the histories of women, are written.

5 Mark Poster, in *Cultural History and Postmodernity*, argues that Stone commits the serious error of attributing twentieth-century motivations and explanations to early modern societies: "reasons and causes are provided, and these reasons erase differences between the present and the past, linking the two in a chain of continuity" (29). Though *The Family, Sex, and Marriage* is under-theorized and Stone is under-reflexive, he is invaluable as cultural historian's whipping boy. Whatever other value Stone's tome holds for historians, it has certainly provided a necessary and easy target for revisionists; without this text, many other texts could not exist.

6 Stone largely ignores this majority category of Englishmen and women based on the "nature of the surviving evidence" (*Family, Sex, and Marriage* 12). Most of the anecdotes he uses to demonstrate his thesis come from aristocratic and upper-middle-class households, as those members of society were more likely and better equipped to document their lives. According to his research, only the literate and articulate upper class left records of their existence.

7 For further discussion of romantic love during the seventeenth century, see MacFarlane, *The Family Life of Ralph Josselin; a Seventeenth-Century Clergyman: an Essay in Historical Anthropology*; Harris, "Marriage, Sixteenth-Century Style: Elizabeth Stafford and the Third Duke of Norfolk"; *Some Account of the Life of Rachel Wriothestey, Lady Russell*, ed. Mary Berry; Newcastle, *Poems and Fancies*; Hull, *Chaste, Silent and Obedient: English Books for Women, 1475–1640*; and Houlbrooke, *English Family Life, 1576–1716: an Anthology from Diaries*. And, one needs no further confirmation of the representation of English romantic love pre-1780 than William Shakespeare's body of work: *As You Like It, A Midsummer Night's Dream, The Winter's Tale, Hamlet, The Tempest* and of course *Romeo and Juliet* all attest to the affects of love, passion, and desire, providing in most cases both a female and male perspective.

8 Obviously, I have not discussed lesbian sexuality; even less information exists about Restoration female same-sex desire. Despite my omission, I do not mean to suggest that lesbianism was non-existent during the Restoration, and in the following chapter I more fully consider early female homosexuality.

9 These studies include but are not limited to Milhous, *Thomas Betterton and the Management of Lincoln's Inn Fields, 1695–1708*; Kenny, *British Theatre and Other Arts, 1660–1800;* Styan, *Restoration Comedy in Performance*; Boswell, *The Restoration Court Stage 1660–1702*; Van Lennep et al. *The History of the London Stage, 1660–1800*, vol. I; and Highfill, Burnim, and Langhans, eds., *A Biographical Dictionary of Actors, Actresses, Musicians, Dancers, etc. in London, 1660–1800*. Primary sources include Betterton, *The History of the English Stage from the Restauration to the Present Time, Including the Lives, Characters and Amours of the most Eminent Actors and Actresses*; Pepys *Dairy*; Cibber, *An Apology for the Life of Mr. Colley Cibber, Comedian*; and Downes, *Roscius Anglicanus.*

10 John Downes gives Killigrew's original actors, sworn in October 6, 1660, as Charles Hart, Theophilus Bird, Robert and William Shatterel, Micheal Mohun, Mr. Lacy, Mr. Burt, Mr. Cartwright, Mr. Clun, Marmaduke Watson, Mr. Hancock, Mr. Kynaston, Mr. Wintersel, Mr. Bateman, Mr. Baxter, and Mr. Blagden (Milhous and Hume *Roscius* 4–6). Killigrew's women included Katherine Mitchell Corey, Anne Marshall, Mrs. Eastland, Elisabeth Farley Weaver, Rebecca Marshall and Margaret Rutter, all sworn in March 1661. Mary Knepp, Margaret Hughes, Mrs. Uphill, Elizabeth Davenport [Boutell], Nell Gwyn, Mrs. James, Mrs. Verjuice, and Mrs. Reeves all joined within the next few years (Downes *Roscius* 8–9).

11 Davenant hired Thomas Betterton as his principal actor, along with Thomas Sheppy, Mr. Lovel, Mr. Lilliston, Mr. Underhill, Mr. Turner, Mr. Dixon, Robert Nokes in early October 1660. Edward Kynaston, James Nokes, Mr. Angel, William Betterton, Mr. Mosely and Mr. Floid played women's roles (Downes *Roscius* 44). Between 1661 and 1562 six actresses were sworn in as members of Davenant's company: Hester Davenport, Moll Davis, Mary Saunderson (Betterton), Jane Long, Ann Gibbs, Mrs. Holden, Mrs. Norris, and Mrs. Jennings (Downes *Roscius* 49–50). Davenant's company continued to

attract new talent. William Montfort, Percival Verbruggen, Susannah Montfort Verbruggen, Colley Cibber, Elizabeth Barry and Ann Bracegirdle all acted with the Duke's Company to great success and public acclaim.

12 For discussions of the character of Restoration audiences, see Roberts, *The Ladies: Female Patronage of Restoration Drama 1660–1700*; Gill, *Interpreting Ladies: Women, Wit and Morality in the Restoration Comedy of Manners*; Nicoll, *History of English Drama 1*; and Avery, "The Restoration Audience." Roberts' study in particular is notable for its largely unsupported claims, based primarily on Samuel Pepys' accounts of his wife Elizabeth's play-going habits.

13 Deborah C. Payne suggests that professionalization and objectification are "mutually defining terms" ("Reified Object" 17). Both discourses reduce the actress, either to a theatrical worker who performs the tasks demanded by the profession, or to an object of male desire. Instead, in order to include agency in the biographies of Restoration actresses, she suggests considering the two traditional narratives in tandem, rather than separating them, as feminist critics have traditionally done. According to Payne, professionalization and object-ification both diminished and amplified the actress, making her a "nouveau aristocrat of an emergent visual culture that rewards a captivating performance more than the reorganization of the British navy" (35).

14 *The History of the English Stage*, though compiled and probably written by Edmund Curll, is presumed to be Thomas Betterton's memoirs of his life in the theatre, and includes biographies of many prominent actresses and actors. Tradition generally confers authorship on Betterton and I have followed that convention here.

15 Elizabeth Boutell's name is variously spelled "Boutel," "Bowtall" and "Bowtell," the latter spelling verified by Judith Milhous as the official spelling on at least some of the legal documents pertaining to her marriage and will in Suffolk. However, most historians have agreed on "Boutell," and I follow this convention except when directly quoting a primary source.

16 According to *The London Stage*, an incomplete compilation of London theat-rical production since 1660, Boutell was on the King's Company roster as early as 1662 (van Lennep *History* 32). Milhous believes that Boutell, then known as Elizabeth Davenport, joined the company in 1662 or 1663 ("Elizabeth" 125). *The London Stage* lists "Boutell" as early as 1662 because its editors work from John Downes' *Roscius Anglicanus*, another incomplete but contemporary record of King's Company casts. Downes often interchanged actresses' married and maiden names indiscriminately (Milhous "Elizabeth" 125).

17 Actual cross-dressing is recorded in Restoration and eighteenth-century England. As in Restoration dramatic narratives, female-to-male cross-dressing is generally understood as demanded by exceptional circumstances and adopted only as a temporary expedient, though many narratives (see Charke below) disprove this assumption. For more on seventeenth-century transvest-itism, see Dekker and van de Pol, *The Tradition of Female Transvestism in Early Modern Europe* and Keeble, *The Cultural Identity of Seventeenth-Century Woman*, 243–51.

CHAPTER 3

1 For many theatre scholars, performative writing moves away from both J. L. Austin's speech-act theory and from strict autobiographical writing to new understandings of how and why to write about performance. Peggy Phelan defines performative writing as "different from personal criticism or autobiographical essay, although it owes a lot to both genres . . . . Rather than describing the performance event in 'direct signification,' a task I believe to be impossible and not terrifically interesting, I want this writing to enact the affect force of the performance event again, as it plays itself out in an ongoing temporality made vivid by the psychic process" (*Mourning* 11–12). For Phelan and others, performative writing transforms events through writing so that they may be re-experienced and re-understood. Though I recognize the importance of theorizing performative writing, I suggest that the performances Leeson and Charke enact through their autobiographies have more to do with the constitution of the self than the reconstitution of a particular object or event. For a cogent summary of the links between performance, language, performativity, and theatre, see Carlson's *Performance: a Critical Introduction*, pp. 56–75. For definitions of performative writing, see Phelan's *Mourning Sex*, and Pollock's "Performing Writings."

2 Many of Charke's critics and biographers point to her varied careers as further evidence of performance: she played the role of merchant and servant in ways similar to her role-playing on stage. For more on Charke's other occupations, see Philip Baruth's "Who is Charlotte Charke?" Charles Peavy's "The Chimerical Career of Charlotte Charke" and Robert Rehder's introduction to *A Narrative of the Life of Mrs. Charlotte Charke.*

3 Castle suggests that masquerade was linked to traditional English public festival: "[t]he classic features of the masquerade – sartorial exchange, masking, collective verbal and physical license – were traditional carnival motifs and hint, if at first obscurely, at a historical connection with . . . 'festivals of misrule' popular throughout Europe in the early modern period" (*Masquerade* 11). Further, as Castle points out, masquerade has strong links to theatre. Inigo Jones created detailed and fantastic allegories while William Shakespeare included masques in plays like *The Tempest*. Castle argues, however, that theatrical and court masking were elite activities and had little bearing on the public balls (19–20). Castle develops her theory of masquerade from Bakhtinian carnival, which may account for her dismissal of its theatrical origins. Even so, masquerade is clearly based on and draws from performance traditions and conventions.

4 Obviously, the relative influence of conduct manuals is difficult to gauge; regardless, conduct manuals are an important normative representation to which many responded.

5 Of course, "feminist" is anachronistic. I use it as I use "lesbian," to signal a continuity of specific practices, beliefs, and ideals between modern definitions and historical understandings.

6 Women's autobiography was an important area of English studies by the middle 1990s, although many foundational texts, such as Felicity Nussbaum's *The Autobiographical Subject* and Sidonie Smith's *A Poetics of Women's Autobiography*, point out the "fundamental resistance to valuing women's experience" (Smith *Poetics* 11) evidenced by a canonical focus on men's autobiography until recent feminist incursions into the academy. "Life-writing," generally understood to be a broader category than autobiography, includes "versions that have been excluded because of the gender, class or ethnicity of its authors and/or the forms in which they took up their telling" (Barros and Smith *Life-Writing* 21) and includes letters, diaries, and journals as well as more traditional autobiographies. "Life-writing," too, seems to emphasize how women used writing to material effect. For more on life-writing, see Barros and Smith, *Life-Writings by British Women, 1660–1850*, Coleman, Lewis and Kowalick, *Representations of the Self from Renaissance to Romanticism*; Folkenflik, *The Culture of Autobiography*; Nussbaum, *The Autobiographical Subject*; Spacks, *Imagining a Self*; and Sidonie Smith, *A Poetics of Women's Autobiography*.

7 A tremendous amount has been written about eighteenth-century women writers. See Turner, *Living by the Pen: Women Writers in the Eighteenth Century* and Jones, *Women and Literature in Britain 1700–1800* for representative discussions.

8 Importantly, Charke wrote her own biography; Woffington's was written by others. It is therefore unsurprising that the image Charke presents of herself is less focused on sexual behavior and more on professionalism, autonomy, and community. Even so, Charke was undoubtedly writing against her audience's expectations (Wanko "Eighteenth-Century Actress" 85) and as her opening pages and table of contents make clear, she teases those readers with the suggestion that she will ultimately detail her sexual adventures.

9 Though Leeson lived and worked primarily in Dublin, much of the research on eighteenth-century British prostitution focuses on London. For the most part, what was true for London was likely also true for other British cities. First, most prostitution research and reform took place in London; research suggests there was not much difference, except in scale, between London and, say, Manchester, Edinburgh, or Dublin (see Henderson's *Disorderly Women*). Second, eighteenth-century novelists and poets wrote of the "city, which in eighteenth-century England meant London" (Radner "Youthful Harlot's Curse" 59), equating all city experience with what happened in London. Third, and most importantly, Leeson herself noted no real difference between prostitution in London and Dublin, or between Dublin and English resort towns (although she vows several times that her own countrymen are kinder and more generous than the English). As a woman who lived and worked in a variety of locations, her testimony seems most persuasively to indicate that prostitution was experienced similarly throughout the British Isles.

10 Both Kathryn Norberg and Vivien Jones point out that in the 1790s, when Leeson published her memoir, understandings of prostitution and the

prostitute were undergoing significant shifts. The shift from victim to villain-ess, which in the nineteenth century resulted in legislation such as The Contagious Disease Acts, has its roots in late eighteenth-century discourse. The "great social evil" (which I discuss in the following chapter) is prefigured in the "turbulent, reformist and repressive 1790s" (Jones "Placing" 203), and the shift from sentimental to contagion narratives of prostitution was under-way by the time *Memoirs* reached its audience. For this reason, I suggest, Leeson was especially careful to frame her story in older, conventional ways.

11 Simply going to work, however, was not enough to ensure that women became respectable. Women who worked were linked with prostitutes: working in public occupations such as millinery made them susceptible to the seductions of both a more luxurious lifestyle and the clients who might offer it (Jones "Placing" 207–08). Middle-class women could only remain moral if they remained unemployed, a cruel double-bind.

12 Boswell, for example, insists that the streetwalkers he engages are miserable (Radner "Youthful Harlot's Curse" 59), and the focus on penitence suggests that contemporaries believed prostitutes had much for which to feel guilty.

13 After Richard Charke abandoned her and then died (about 1737), Charke was single until her second marriage. In May 1746, she married John Sacheverell. Very little is known of Sacheverell, and Charke, obviously, did not use his name for most of her life. The dissolution of the marriage is unclear, but Sacheverall is unnamed in the narrative and figures even less than Richard Charke. Fidelis Morgan suggests that Sacheverell was possibly an imposter hoping to be associated with the "famous and wealthy Dr Sacheverell of St Andrew's Holburn," or a bigamist; either way, Morgan asserts that Charke went to great lengths to erase any record of this (admittedly mysterious) marriage (*Well-Known Troublemaker* 207).

14 By the mid-1730s, four unlicensed theatres were operating in London. As historian Vincent J. Liesenfeld recounts, opposition to the proliferation of London theatres, as well as to the plays produced there, came from several quarters. Sir Robert Walpole, George II's chief minister, was concerned that theatrical satire was often dangerously close to treason, and might incite an already uneasy populace to riot and revolution. In addition to political oppos-ition to the theatres, the church was still opposed to theatre-going in general: Jeremy Collier's notorious *Short View of Immorality and Profaneness of the English Stage* (1698) was still in circulation, and the theatre performers and audiences were frequently chastised from the pulpit. Finally, London mer-chants and tradesmen "tended to disapprove of playhouses" (Liesenfeld *Licensing Act* 3), as they often signaled an increase in prostitution, violence, and petty theft. The legislation in place was not sufficient to combat the threats to both London business and the monarchy represented by unlicensed theatres and unlicensed productions. In May 1737, Walpole read *The Golden Rump* to Parliament as evidence of the need to censor dramatic performances. *The Golden Rump* shocked Parliament into recognition of "the necessity of putting a check to the representation of such horrid effusions of treason and

blasphemy" (Coxe in Liesenfeld *Licensing Act* 129). The Licensing Act of 1737 was "the model censorship device in modern Western society" (Liesenfeld *Licensing Act* 3). For working actors, it was much more. The Licensing Act did more than censor plays; it set the boundaries for authorized theatres to the City of Westminster, where Drury Lane and Covent Garden were located. For more on the Licensing Act of 1737, see Vincent J. Liesenfeld's excellent and comprehensive study, *The Licensing Act of 1737*. Also, Philip E. Baruth's "Who is Charlotte Charke?" (*Introducing Charlotte Charke: Actress, Author, Enigma*) explains the Act in specific reference to Charke's career.

15 Scott Cutler Shershow argues that eighteenth-century puppet theatre was a powerful, satiric weapon, rather than the children's entertainment it is now, and that Charke presented "in miniature the complex dynamics of class, gender, and culture which her whole difficult career can otherwise be seen to illuminate" (*Puppets* 54).

16 There are as many as eight extant portraits of Charke. The women and girls presented all have similarly high foreheads, large eyes, and "sweet" mouths. Robert Folkenflik, however, has questioned the accuracy of some of these portraits, arguing that in fact the most widely circulated image of Charke is taken from Francois Nivelon's 1737 *The Rudiments of Genteel Behaviour*. He suggests that a little-known print in the archives of the Garrick Club provides the most likely image of Charke; I have included it here. For more on the theoretical and historiographic importance of identifying Charke's images, see Folkenflik's essay "Charlotte Charke: Images and Afterimages" in the Baruth collection *Introducing Charlotte Charke: Actress, Author, Enigma*.

17 Many critics make much of Charke's on- and off-stage mimicry of her father. Marsden discusses the Cibbers' penchant for autobiography in "Charlotte Charke and the Cibbers: Private Life as Public Spectacle" (*Introducing Charlotte Charke: Actress, Author, Enigma*), arguing that both Charke and her brother Theophilus write to assert their version of the family dynamic and to claim some of their father's prominence as actor, manager, and writer as their own. Straub, on the other hand, suggests that Charke's on-stage assumption of Cibber's fop roles and her autobiographical mimicry are "unsettling representation[s] of a daughter aping a father whose masculinity is already becoming questionable within dominant gender ideology" (*Sexual Suspects* 139). By choosing such a flawed model of masculinity, then, Charke's impersonations are more rather than less challenging to conventional understandings of the male/female binary.

18 Her estrangement from Cibber, which many critics point to as a leading motivation in Charke's decision to publish her *Narrative*, may be tied to these particular roles. Morgan and others suggest that an undated letter (which might also refer to Charke's marriage to the faithless Richard Charke) refers to her association with Fielding and the kind of roles she played for him: "Why do you not dissociate yourself from that worthless scoundrel . . . . You will never be any good while you adhere to him, and you most certainly will not receive what otherwise you might from your father" (in Morgan *Well-Known Troublemaker* 87).

19 Charke's theatrical cross-dressing also differs from the career of Charlotte Cushman, which I discuss in more detail in the following chapter. Cushman and other nineteenth-century actresses seem to have played male roles at least in part to demonstrate their technical virtuosity, a concern which does not seem to motivate Charke. Though Cushman's biographies are filled with comparisons of her performances to her male counterparts, Charke does not compare herself to Richard Yeates in the same roles.

20 Though Straub admits that Charke might have been passionately viewed by both male and female audiences, she argues that the cross-dressed actress, even one so contradictory as Charke, was ultimately contained. Following her argument, eighteenth-century audiences take pleasure in gender confusion only "when that confusion is 'for sale' as a theatrical commodity, an obviously artificial construction" (*Sexual Suspects* 131).

21 Susanna Cibber was charged with dressing as a man in order to facilitate her affair with William Sloper, and Peg Woffington supposedly seduced away a former lover's innocent fiancée. For more on the indiscretions of these and other breeches actresses, see Pat Rogers' "The Breeches Part" and Kristina Straub's *Sexual Suspects*, especially pp. 129–30.

22 Baruth makes a similar argument in "Who is Charlotte Charke?" See especially pp. 46–49.

23 Ironically, as several later critics have pointed out, Morgan undercuts her case through her misreading of Charke's text. Morgan insists that Charke and Mrs. Brown did not sleep together, because "[Charke] 'consulted my pillow what was best to be done. And communicated my thoughts to my friend.' If she had slept with her friend she needn't have wasted any time discussing the matter with the pillow first!" (*Well-Known Troublemaker* 205). As subsequent editions make clear, the text in question actually reads "I consulted on my Pillow what was best to be done, and communicated my Thoughts to my Friend" (121), which Baruth glosses as meaning either that the two shared a bed and Charke thought it over herself before discussing it with her friend, or that the two did not share a bed, as Morgan asserts. Baruth further suggests that "[b]y putting a period between Charke's 'Pillow' and her 'Friend,' Morgan enacts typographically the same sort of need to assert a heterosexual norm that she demonstrates in her approach to Charke's life as a whole" (50).

24 More has been written on Charke's sexual orientation than any other feature of her life or *Narrative*. See Baruth, "Who is Charlotte Charke?" (especially pp. 46–52); Kahn, "Teaching Charlotte Charke: Feminism, Pedagogy, and the Construction of Self"; Mackie, "Desperate Measures: the Narratives of the Life of Mrs. Charlotte Charke"; Nussbaum, "Afterword: Charke's 'Variety of Wretchedness'"; and Straub's *Sexual Suspects* (especially pp. 135–39).

25 Many critics have noted Charke's use of the sentimental heroine trope, particularly Sidonie Smith and Patricia Meyers Spacks. The mid-eighteenth-century sentimental novel featured "adventurous heroines [who] reform their errant ways or bring their lives into congruence with cultural expectations" (Nussbaum "Afterword" 231). Smith suggests that the *Narrative* most strongly

expresses Charke's desire to reconnect with her father and return to a socially sanctioned feminine role (*Poetics* 104). Though Charke is clearly writing at least in part to regain her father's affection, the *Narrative* refuses to cast Charke as truly penitent. She is too angry with her oldest sister, whom she blames for her estrangement from her family. Too, Charke was treated warmly by some family members. The *Narrative* includes anecdotes about the support she received from her other sisters and her brother, and expresses genuine affection for her nieces. Within the family, Charke played both outcast and beloved.

CHAPTER 4

1 "The British Blondes" is a bit of a misnomer. The troupe was officially called the Lydia Thompson Troupe in advertisements and press notices during their first season in the United States. In about February 1869, newspapers such as *The Spirit of the Times* and *The New York Times* began referring to the troupe as "the Blondes" or the "British Blondes," presumably in order to highlight their physical features and émigré status. Historians tend to refer to the troupe as "The British Blondes"; I have continued this practice here.

2 In *Ziegfeld Girl: Image and Icon in Culture and Cinema*, Mizejewski uses "persona" to refer to the identity created through performances, public appearances, photographs, and publicity announcements. In the case of Thompson, this distinction is particularly important, as her biography is incomplete and contradictory and so much publicity was generated on her behalf. Thus when I speak of "Lydia Thompson," I borrow Mizejewski's understanding of persona.

3 Though Wood's Museum and Metropolitan Theatre produced full-fledged theatrical entertainments, it was not exactly a "legitimate" theatre. Wood's was modeled after Barnum's successful synthesis of educational lectures, theatrical entertainment, and displays of human freaks. The first theatrical artist, the singer Maggie Mitchell, shared the bill with "Siamese twins; Sophie Gantz, the baby woman; giants and giantesses, dwarfs, fat boys, automatons, wax figures statuary, mechanical works of art and everything that could be suggested to the management" according to an advertisement in *The New York Times* in the week preceding the opening. Thompson and her troupe also shared billing with these "human curiosities," though after her first week's success, advertisements focused solely on the production of *Ixion*, with descriptions of Thompson, Harland, and Markham replacing mentions of giants, dwarfs, and Siamese twins.

4 Though Allen's *Horrible Prettiness: Burlesque and American Culture* is an excellent cultural history of burlesque, his research is often undocumented and incomplete. See my "They Never Raided Minsky's: Popular Memory and the Performance of History" in *Performance Research* 7 (2002).

5 Sanger's claim is inflammatory at best. According to his reckoning, of the 6000 women working in prostitution in New York in the 1850s, 1500 died and were replaced each year. Clearly, this claim defies all logic, as Margaret Wood Hill

demonstrates in *Their Sister's Keepers* (see pp. 60–61). Rather, it seems that Sanger depended on existing narratives so strongly that he could not conceive of any other end to a career in prostitution than wide-scale death.

6 For a further discussion of traditional burlesque, and the implications of the shift from an all-male to an all-female form, see Dressler, "Burlesque as a Cultural Phenomenon."

7 It is impossible to gauge how much actual control Thompson exerted over her career, especially in regards to her burlesque shows. The Blondes followed burlesque tradition, and reworked existing material to incorporate local gossip, political issues, and even the weather of the city in which they were performing. For example, the troupe's first show, *Ixion*, was an older burlesque reworked to fit the Blondes' performance style. However, contemporary critics held Thompson responsible for the content of her performances, Thompson claimed credit, and historians also tend to regard Thompson as author of her performances (see Young *Famous Actors*).

8 For the biographies of Thompson, see Allen *Horrible Prettiness* 5, Young *Famous Actors* 1075–1076, Zeidman *American Burlesque Show* 25–27, Sobel *Burleycue* 24–25, and especially Gänzl, *Lydia Thompson, Queen of Burlesque*.

9 The "anonymous drama critic" had actually died three days before Henderson made his remarks; his name is lost to the historical record. Butler defended his dead colleague's name and opinions, and entered into a feud with Henderson himself.

10 Levine, following academic tradition, uses the New York City Astor Place Riot as a turning point in the hierarchization of culture. Fans of native actor Edwin Forrest and Englishman William Charles Macready converged on the Astor Place Opera House on May 10, 1849. Inflamed by class rhetoric and anti-European sentiment, the rioters destroyed property and human life; twenty-two people were killed and one hundred and fifty wounded. Though the Astor Place Riot certainly demonstrates that the utopic theatrical microcosm revered by Levine was illusory and short-lived, I suggest here that the representation of female sexuality factors equally in the split between respectable and unruly audiences and entertainments. For a fuller discussion of the riot, see both Levine, *Highbrow/Lowbrow* (pp. 63–69) and Allen, *Horrible Prettiness* (pp. 58–77).

11 Tracy C. Davis' *Actresses as Working Women* describes how Victorian actresses occupied an "equivocal" position in society; as wage earners they differed significantly from middle-class women who did not work outside the home and their often lavish or at least middle-class lifestyles set them apart from working-class working women (xi). Davis' research, though conducted only in Great Britain and focusing primarily on the years 1870–1890, provides a basis for claims about how all Victorian actresses may have been viewed. Davis portrays Victorian actresses as women limited by gendered expectations about the kinds of roles they could play, the kinds of private and public lives they should lead, and the kinds of sexuality they might embody on stage. At the same time, "women could make as much money as men in the Victorian

theatre" (24), as salaries usually reflected box office draw. Though the financial and critical rewards for women could be excellent, the opportunities for those rewards were limited. A surplus of young, ambitious women meant that the labor pool was virtually unlimited; few actresses were able to develop lasting careers in the theatre based on their talent and skill. Rather, "the system took them in regularly when youthful and spat them out permanently when mature" (49). Even on the legitimate stage, young and beautiful women were favored over older women with experience. In addition, Davis is careful to note that actresses had to work harder than actors – engaging in charitable activity and maintaining domestic stability –in order to reap the financial and social rewards increasingly associated with the theatrical profession (5). Davis does admit that despite the constraints placed on actresses' reputations and prospects, their philanthropic activities, bourgeois morality, and professional advancement increased the legitimacy of the theatrical profession as a whole (100). In addition to working as actresses, Victorian women also took part in theatre production. For example, actress and playwright Anna Cora Mowatt and novelist Frances Hodgson Burnett both enjoyed considerable success as playwrights; Mowatt's *Fashion* (1845) was one of the most financially successful and widely produced plays of the late nineteenth century. In addition, several women worked at least briefly as theatre managers and producers, and several female critics regularly contributed to entertainment papers. See T. Davis for a further discussion of women's involvement.

12 For biographies of Cushman, see Clapp, *Reminiscences of a Dramatic Critic with an Essay on the Art of Henry Irving*; Faber, *Love and Rivalry: Three Exceptional Pairs of Sisters*; Leach, *Bright Particular Star: the Life and Times of Charlotte Cushman*; Merrill, *When Romeo Was a Woman: Charlotte Cushman and her Circle of Female Spectators*; Stebbins, *Charlotte Cushman: her Letters and Memories of her Life*; Walen " 'Such a Romeo We Never Ventured Hope For': Charlotte Cushman"; and Winter, *The Wallet of Time.*

13 Merrill and others have established that Cushman exaggerated her family's genteel roots and purposely left out portions of her biography, especially regarding her parent's marriage and grandmother's life story in order to present a solidly middle-class front.

14 Interestingly, Cushman was not hailed for her talent in the United States until *after* she had made a successful European tour. Success abroad, before the supposedly more discriminating British audiences, was a prerequisite for US-American success.

15 For a full queer reading of Cushman's theatrical cross-dressing, see Walen " 'Such a Romeo' ; and Merrill, *Romeo*. For other examples of queer scholarship on theatrical cross-dressing, see Schanke and Marra, eds., *Passing Performances: Queer Readings of Leading Players in American Theater History*; Epstein and Straub, eds., *Body Guards: the Cultural Politics of Gender Ambiguity*; Garber, *Vested Interests: Cross-Dressing and Cultural Anxiety*; Ferris, *Crossing the Stage: Controversies on Cross-Dressing*; and Senelick, *The Changing Room.*

16 Of course, Thompson was also a subject of lesbian desire. In Chicago in 1870, the press reported on one of Thompson's overzealous female fans. This "Lesbian attacker" stalked Thompson, and was eventually arrested. For more, see Gänzl *Lydia Thompson* 140.

17 Garber notes that female impersonation in minstrel shows was divided into two types: the low, comic "Funny Old Gal" and the romantic "wench." Further, men playing wench roles were the highest paid members of the minstrel company and their impersonations were generally considered to be true depictions of femininity (Garber *Vested Interests* 276), critiqued in the same vein as Cushman's portrayal of Shakespearean heroes. These male-to-female transvestite figures were double-cross-dressers: men playing women, white playing black. Following from Garber, the transvestite figure of the minstrel show troped tensions about the increasingly blurred racial and gender categories of post Civil War America. Though the parallels between racial performance in minstrel shows and the Blondes' displacement of immigrant tensions might be a fruitful avenue of exploration, it is beyond the scope of this chapter. For more on the specifics of minstrelsy, see Lott, *Love and Theft.*

18 Fashion historians tend to view fashion as a language or sign system, one that reveals the "contours of the psyche" (Finkelstein *Fashion* 6). This "language" can be interpreted by anyone who trains him/herself in the codes of contemporary fashion, and provides psychological insights about the wearer – according to critic Alison Lurie "the woman in the sensible grey wool suit and the frilly pink blouse is a serious, hard-working mouse with a frivolous and feminine soul" (*Language of Clothes* 245). Although Lurie's assessment of one woman's clothing and therefore her psyche may seem a bit pat, many other fashion and social theorists discuss fashion in terms of semiotics. Lévi-Strauss in *The Savage Mind* and Barthes in *The Fashion System* both argue that a culture reveals itself through its clothing. In *Fashion and Eroticism* Steele determines that fashion demonstrates erotic interest, revealing a society's foci on specific secondary sexual characteristics, a point that Hollander echoes in *Sex and Suits*. According to many theorists, fashion designates wealth and class, sexuality and sexual difference, mood and personality.

19 The US-American phrenologist Orson S. Fowler argued in the 1850s that the corset "caused" sickly and degenerate children, spontaneous abortion, sterility, immorality, hysteria, and insanity (in Steele *Fashion* 40). In addition, cancer, tuberculosis, scoliosis, depression, epilepsy, deformities of the internal organs, and reproductive diseases were all attributed to corsetry. However, Steele argues persuasively that the hysteria over corsetry reflects as much a twentieth-century abhorrence of the idea of tight-lacing as a Victorian phenomenon. Demonstrating that most corsets from the 1850s to 1900 lace closed at twenty to twenty-five inches, and that "the size alone . . . does not indicate how tightly they might have been laced" when worn on a daily basis (*Fashion* 163), Steele disputes the claim that most women and girls laced to approximately seventeen inches and that many laced even tighter. In addition, Steele points out that the correspondence in *The Englishwoman's Domestic Magazine*, often cited to

prove that Victorian women laced to the point of medical danger, reads more like fetish correspondence than documentary evidence (177–85). Contemporary tight-lacing fetishists such as the corset designer Mr. Pearl, regularly tight-lace to about twenty-three inches, with no reported ill-effects (Steele *Fetish* 81–89).

20 Some historians argue that the fashions of the 1860s to 1870s are connected to "the nascent efforts towards [women's] social and even political emancipation" (Burn *Age of Equipoise* 26). These fashions do seem bolder than their immediate predecessors, and the new ideal woman literally took up more space. Her tall body, accented with large hats, parasols, and walking sticks and clothed in a trained skirt with bustle protruding behind presented an imposing figure in the drawing room or on the street. However, most fashion historians have rejected this argument, suggesting that late Victorian fashionable dress was primarily ostentatious and restrictive rather than powerful and freeing.

21 Of course, working-class women also followed this fashion when they were able. Steele points out that although a standardized uniform of loose-fitting dresses with aprons and small caps was adopted by domestic servants and factory workers alike while at their places of employment, some photographic and other evidence exists of working-class women in fashionable dress while on holiday or engaging in leisure activities (*Fashion* 75).

22 Such ideas persisted despite the fact that few women actually wore pants. Amelia Bloomer's 1851 invention was quickly discarded, and in fact barely resembled male dress at all. In a tunic reaching well below the knees that covered loose pants gathered at the ankle, wearers looked more like a romanticized version of a dairy-maid than a businessman. Most women who regularly cross-dressed were in lesbian relationships and wore male clothing in order to hide their biological sex. These women faced serious repercussions if their cross-dressing was discovered, as demonstrated by the example of Lucy Allen Slater, who lived as the Reverend Joseph Lobdell, married a woman, and lived a quiet country life until her 1880s discovery sent her to a mental institution (Smith-Rosenberg *Disorderly Conduct* 272–73). Of course, some female celebrities such as the French novelist Aurore Dudevant, who lived and wrote as George Sand, also cross-dressed. However, it is important to note that although Sand was often reviled for both her unconventional sexuality and feminist views, she was emphatically heterosexual, with well-publicized love affairs with Alfred de Musset and Frédéric Chopin.

23 Much scholarly work has been done regarding the nineteenth-century construction of the prostitute as diseased, especially in the context of the British Contagious Disease Acts of the 1860s to 1880s. See Mahood, *The Magdalenes: Prostitution in the Nineteenth Century*; Poovey, *Uneven Developments: the Ideological Work of Gender in Mid-Victorian England*; Spongberg, *Feminizing Venereal Disease*; and especially Walkowitz, *Prostitution and Victorian Society: Women, Class, and the State*. For a discussion of venereal disease in the US, see Haller and Haller, *The Physician and Sexuality in Victorian America*.

24 In *Child-Loving: the Erotic Child and Victorian Culture*, James Kincaid questions the wisdom of using Acton, or any one doctor, as representative of social views on female sexuality and prostitution. Kincaid's excellent argument aside, I will be treating Acton and Sanger as representative. Acton's and Sanger's works are the two most widely cited and circulated texts on Victorian prostitution; for that reason these two social historians are discussed almost exclusively in this chapter. For other contemporary accounts of prostitution, see Greg, "Prostitution"; Hooker, *Womanhood: Its Sanctities and Fidelities*; Logan, *The Great Social Evil: Its Causes, Extent, Results, and Remedies*; Judge, *Our Fallen Sisters. The Great Social Evil. Prostitution: Its Cause, Effect, So Called Use, Decided Abuse, and Only Cure or Remedy*; Blackwell, *Essays in Medical Sociology*; and Chapman, *The New Godiva and Other Studies in Social Questions* (1885). Further, though these contemporaries differ from Acton in detail and sometimes focus, the crux of the argument – that prostitution must be eradicated lest it destroy the middle class – remains the same.

25 In *Horrible Prettiness*, Allen quotes one of Thompson's letters to the *Chicago Times*, reprinted in the broadside "The Play of the Period: the Blondes and Their Accusers," an undated and unpublished manuscript located only in the New York Public Library's Performing Arts Collection. However, no letters from Thompson appear in any of the Chicago papers in February 1870 and I have been unable to verify Allen's claim.

CHAPTER 5

1 For this study, I interviewed a dozen sex workers – five escort agency owners and eight escorts. All of the names of clients, sex workers, and agencies have been changed for privacy. Kevin owns Exploits, Unlimited, and I spoke with seven of his girls: Lesley, Kristeen, Ashlee, Amanda, Alex, Jodi, and Carrie. Darrell and Dwayne run Private Entertainment and allowed me to interview Cherri, their top booker. I spoke to Meshella, the owner of Luxuries, and Bonnie, who runs a strip service.

2 The term "sex worker" is the preferred term of the contemporary prostitutes' rights movement, as it insists on the labor involved in prostitution. "Girls," which I also use to refer to the women whom I interviewed, is not meant to imply youth or immaturity on the part of the sex workers, but is how they refer to themselves and how they were referred to by their managers.

3 I was originally concerned about my ethnographic method and the legitimacy of my findings. Practicing ethnographer and anthropologist Jack Kugelmass, who oversaw the early stages of this project, assured me that my methods were in fact valid. Examples of similar ethnographic studies include Kugelmass' *Masked Culture: the Greenwich Village Halloween Parade* and Duneier's *Sidewalk*.

4 In general I choose to believe the escorts, and rejected the "false consciousness" arguments some anti-pornography feminists deploy. Most of the Madison call girls with whom I spoke enjoyed their work; this reflects the testimony of many

published professional call girls as well. Although the idea that prostitutes enjoy their work is often considered the last great myth of female sexuality, all of the escorts I interviewed claimed to receive sexual satisfaction from at least some of their clients. Certainly casual, impersonal sex with often unattractive strangers is not satisfying in every case, but denying the pleasure potential in sex work denies the sexual autonomy of sex workers.

5 See my contribution to the anthology *Jane Sexes it Up: Feminist Confessions of Desire*, ed. Merri Lisa Johnson.

6 For example, most of the sex workers who contributed to Delacoste and Alexander's *Sex Work* are women living on the West Coast who worked in the sex industry for at least five years – many of them for over a decade. The Madison call girls are obviously located in the Midwest and none of them had been working for more than a year at the time of the interviews. The contributors in Nagle's *Whores and Other Feminists* are all actively involved in the prostitutes' rights movements, identify as feminists, and are vocal about their time working in the sex industry. The Madison call girls are not interested in legalizing prostitution or advocating for social change, and they aggressively keep their work secret. The commentators in Chapkis' *Live Sex Acts* are generally also older, professional sex workers from Amsterdam and urban centers in the United States. None of the women with whom I spoke was over thirty.

7 *Hookers and Johns* is also misleading in its representation of prostitution. In the United States, streetwalkers are estimated to be less than 10 percent of all prostitutes (Alexander "Prostitution" 218); *Hookers and Johns* presents them as the dominant type of prostitution. This kind of portrayal of prostitution is blamed by many prostitutes' rights activists for the continued stereotyping of prostitution that results in the whore stigma.

8 See D'Acci, *Defining Women*; Doty, *Making Things Perfectly Queer*; Douglas, *Where the Girls Are*; Fiske, *Television Culture*; Giroux, *Disturbing Pleasures*; Gray, *Watching Race*; Grossberg, *Dancing in Spite of Myself*; Inness, *Tough Girls*; Leibman, *Living Room Lectures*; Morrison, *Playing in the Dark*; and Wiegman, *American Anatomies* for further discussion of mass media representation and identity.

9 See Caputi, "*Sleeping with the Enemy* as *Pretty Woman* Part II?"; Cooks, Orbe, and Bruess "The Fairy Tale Theme in Popular Culture: a Semiotic Analysis of *Pretty Woman*"; Greenberg, "Rescrewed: *Pretty Woman*'s Co-opted Feminism"; Kelley, "A Modern Cinderella"; Lapsley and Westlake, "From *Casablanca* to *Pretty Woman*: the Politics of Romance"; and Miner, "No Matter what they Say, It's all about Money."

10 Additional information on US prostitution and the female moral reform movement during the progressive era may be found in Bland, *Banishing the Beast*; Cohen, *The Murder of Helen Jewett*; Connelly, *The Response to Prostitution in the Progressive Era*; Gilfoyle, *City of Eros*; Hill, *Their Sisters' Keepers*; Kishtainy, *The Prostitute in Progressive Literature*; Peiss, *Cheap Amusements*; Rosen, *The Lost Sisterhood* and *The Mamie Papers*; and Stansell, *City of Women*.

11 Hill and Chapkis represent only the tip of the iceberg of contemporary prostitution analyses and histories. See Nagle, *Whores and Other Feminists*; Barry, *Female Sexual Slavery*; Laurie Bell, *Good Girls/Bad Girls*; Dworkin, *Intercourse* and *Pornography*; MacKinnon, *Feminism Unmodified* and Alexander, "Prostitution: *Still* a Difficult Issue for Feminists" for further discussion of the different sides of the prostitution/pornography debate.

12 Of course, other occupations demand feigning, simulating, representing, and impersonating. The salience of acting models for prostitution is that other occupations may require performance in the course of the job while prostitutes are only performing. Further, the historical conflation of the actress and the prostitute demands a more careful consideration of performance by prostitutes than is necessary for other occupations and professions.

13 Claudette's narrative, like most of the examples in this chapter, draws upon one scenario of prostitution: middle-class, romanticized, and glamorous. Most of the women whose narratives have been collected in anthologies, and all the women I interviewed, are call girls. Their clients usually contact them, either through a madam or pimp and visit them in hotel rooms, apartments or more rarely brothels and massage parlors. The transactions usually last one hour or more and the women are usually paid upwards of one hundred dollars for their services. This scenario ignores other commercial sexual transactions, most notably the streetwalker performing quick sex acts for little pay. The romantic notion of the high-priced call girl is the one most frequently written about and also the scenario most frequently represented in fiction, plays, and film. However, the availability of this scenario should not suggest that it is the only model of prostitution. Nor do I intend to suggest that theories about performance and the negotiation of agency can be applied wholesale to all prostitutes' experience. Certainly, claims about performance break down in the face of the realities of street prostitution and third-world sex tourism; even in the call-girl scenario these claims are tempered by individual prostitutes' experience. For a cogent discussion on the limits of agency in the prostitution exchange, see Julia O'Connell Davidson's *Prostitution, Power and Freedom*.

14 Another important step in Kirby's continuum is the "symbolized matrix," which bridges not-acting and complex acting. Here, a "performer does not act and yet his or her costume represents something or someone" ("Acting and Not-Acting" 155). In performance, this happens when an actor wears cowboy boots and a hat but doesn't play a cowboy. His costume might suggest a certain rugged, outdoor quality to the audience. Or, in real life, a woman might wear four-inch heels, a short skirt, and garter belt. She may not be a prostitute, but it is likely that in some cases she might be mistaken for one.

15 Hochschild plays relatively fast and loose with Stanislavski's system of acting and its American off-shoot, Method acting. Her definition of "emotion memory" owes as much to Lee Strasberg and the Actor's Studio as to Konstantin Stanislavski. Though her definitions display a certain misconception about acting theory, that misconception has little bearing on the usefulness of deep acting in an analysis of performance and prostitution.

16 Goffman complicates his notion of personal front in *Relations in Public*, describing "territories of the self." These territories are personal space; the stall or temporary space like a bench or theatre seat; use space, or the area in front of an individual s/he uses in his/her work, such as a streetwalker's corner; the sheath or body covering of clothes and skin; possessional territory, or an individual's objects; informational preserve, or the set of facts the individual believes to be true about him/herself; and conversational preserve, of the decision to talk to other people (29–41). MacCannell has also expanded Goffman's definitions of front and back space in "Staged Authenticity."

17 While it was important to listen to what the Madison sample told me, and to treat their narratives with respect; and important to assume a supportive listening position, I cannot deny that some of their narratives were ambivalent. For all their professed enjoyment of their work, many told stories, like Amanda's, that hinted at deeper conflicts.

18 My research did not include any interviews with clients. Of course, many of them are undoubtedly aware that the prostitute is feigning interest, and the Madison escorts reported that some men were unconcerned about their pleasure. However, for the most part, the Madison escorts engaged in extensive foreplay with their clients, some reported having regular orgasms, and all agreed that most men needed to believe they were sexually satisfied. Clients in the Madison sample were, according to both escorts and managers, usually married men in their forties employed in white collar jobs, though Exploits also supplied escorts to students (particularly foreign students) at the University of Wisconsin-Madison. This client profile is supported by larger and more empirical studies; see "The Client: a Social, Psychological, and Behavioral Look at the Unseen Patron of Prostitution," "Invisible Men: Making Visible Male Clients of Female Prostitutes in Merseyside," "Men who Buy Sex: Preliminary Findings of an Exploratory Study," and "Negotiations and Relationships among Male Sex Workers and Clients in Liverpool, Merseyside, United Kingdom" collected in *Prostitution: On Whores, Hustlers, and Johns*, eds. Elias et al.

CHAPTER 6

1 The WAN website no longer exists. Its project has been taken up by similar sites, such as PENET run by Carol Leigh, and Blackstockings.com, operated by Seattle sex workers. Neither of these sites, however, so cogently combines different representations of prostitution as the now-defunct WAN site.

Bibliography

Acton, William. *The Function, and Disorders of the Reproductive Organs in Childhood, Youth, Adult Age, and Advanced Life, Considered in their Physiological, Social, and Moral Relations.* London: Churchill Press, 1865.

Prostitution Considered in its Moral, Social, and Sanitary Aspects, in London and Other Large Cities, with Proposals for the Mitigation and Prevention of its Attendant Evils. 1857. New York: Frederick A. Praeger, 1968.

"Actresses at the Armory." Editorial. *Chicago Tribune* 28 February 1870: 3.

Alex. Personal Interview. 5 November 1996, 8 November 1996, 13 November 1996.

Alexander, Priscilla. "Feminism, Sex Workers, and Human Rights." *Whores and Other Feminists.* Ed. Jill Nagle. London: Routledge, 1997. 83–97.

"Prostitution: *Still* a Difficult Issue." *Sex Work: Writings by Women in the Sex Industry.* Eds. Frederique Delacoste and Priscilla Alexander. 2nd edn. Pittsburgh and San Francisco: Cleis Press, 1998. 184–230.

Allen, Robert C. *Horrible Prettiness: Burlesque and American Culture.* Chapel Hill: University of North Carolina Press, 1991.

Amanda. Personal Interview. 5 November 1996, 10 November 1996.

Telephone Interview. 9 November 1996.

"The Amusement Question." Editorial. *The Chicago Times* 21 February 1870: 4.

"Amusements." *The New York Times* 30 August 1868: 4+.

"Amusements." *The New York Times* 31 August 1868: 7.

"Amusements." *The New York Times* 20 September 1868: 4.

"Amusements." *The New York Times* 29 September 1868: 4+.

Anderson, Amanda. *Tainted Souls and Painted Faces: the Rhetoric of Fallenness in Victorian Culture.* Ithaca and London: Cornell University Press, 1993.

Armstrong, Nancy and Leonard Tannenhouse. "Introduction." *The Ideology of Conduct: Essays in Literature and the History of Sexuality.* Eds. Nancy Armstrong and Leonard Tannenhouse. New York and London: Methuen, 1987. 1–24.

Ashlee. Personal Interview. 15 October 1996.

Atchison, Chris, Laura Fraser, and John Lowman. "Men Who Buy Sex: Preliminary Findings of an Exploratory Study." *Prostitution: On Whores, Hustlers, and Johns.* Eds. James E. Elias, Vern L. Bullough, Veronica Elias, and Gwen Brewer. Amherst, NY: Prometheus Books, 1998. 172–203.

Austin, J. L. *How to Do Things with Words*. Cambridge: Harvard University Press, 1962.

Avery, Emmett L. "The Restoration Audience." *Philological Quarterly* 45 (1966): 54–61.

Banner, Lois. *American Beauty*. Chicago: University of Chicago Press, 1984.

Barish, Jonas. *The Anti-Theatrical Prejudice*. Berkeley: University of California Press, 1981.

Barker, Hannah and Elaine Chalus. "Introduction." *Gender in Eighteenth-Century England: Roles, Representations, and Responsibilities*. New York: Addison Wesley Longman, 1997. 1–28.

Barros, Carolyn A. and Johanna M. Smith. *Life-Writings by British Women 1660–1850: an Anthology*. Boston: Northeastern University Press, 2000.

Barrows, Sydney with William Novak. *Mayflower Madam: the Secret Life of Sydney Biddle Barrows*. New York: Arbor House, 1986.

Barry, Kathleen. *Female Sexual Slavery*. New York: New York University Press, 1979.

Barthes, Roland. *The Fashion System*. 1967. New York: Jonathan Cape, 1985.

Baruth, Philip E. "Who is Charlotte Charke?" *Introducing Charlotte Charke: Actress, Author, Enigma*. Urbana and Chicago: University of Illinois Press, 1998. 9–62.

"The Battle of the Blondes." Editorial. *New York Times* 7 June 1869: 5.

Bell, Laurie, ed. *Good Girls/Bad Girls: Feminists and Sex Trade Workers Face to Face*. Toronto: Seal, 1987.

Bell, Shannon. *Reading, Writing, and Rewriting the Prostitute Body*. Bloomington and Indianapolis: Indiana University Press, 1994.

Whore Carnival. Brooklyn: Autonomedia, 1995.

Benedetti, Jean. *Stanislavski: an Introduction*. 1985. New York: Routledge, 1992.

[Berry, Mary.] *Some Account of the Life of Rachel Wriothesley, Lady Russell, Followed by a Series of Letters from Lady Russell to her Husband Lord Russell*. London, 1819.

Betterton, Thomas. *The History of the English Stage from the Restauration* [sic] *to the Present Time, Including the Lives, Characters and Amours of the most Eminent Actors and Actresses*, comp. Edmund Curll and William Oldys. London, 1741.

Bindman, Jo. "An International Perspective on Slavery in the Sex Industry." *Global Sex Workers: Rights, Resistance, and Redefinition*. Eds. Kamala Kempadoo and Jo Doezema. London and New York: Routledge, 1998. 65–68.

Bindman, Jo and Jo Doezema. *Redefining Prostitution as Sex Work on the International Agenda*. London: Anti-Slavery International, 1997.

Blackwell, Elizabeth. *Essays in Medical Sociology*. 1902. New York: Arno, 1972.

Bland, Lucy. *Banishing the Beast: Sexuality and the Early Feminists*. New York: New Press, 1995.

Bloch, Ivan. *Sexual Life in England Past and Present*. 1938. Hertfordshire: Oracle, 1996.

"The Blondes." *Chicago Tribune* 27 February 1870: 6.

Boles, Jacqueline and Kirk Elifson. "Out of CASH: the Rise and Demise of a Male Prostitutes' Rights Organization." *Prostitution: On Whores, Hustlers, and Johns.* Eds. James E. Elias, Vern L. Bullough, Veronica Elias, and Gwen Brewer. Amherst, NY: Prometheus Books, 1998. 267–77.

Bonnie. Telephone Interview. 10 October 1996.

Boyer, Donald. "Male Prostitution and Homosexual Identity." *Journal of Homosexuality* **17**: 151–84.

"British Burlesque Again." Editorial. *New York Times* 9 June 1869: 4.

Bullough, Vern. "Prostitution and Reform in Eighteenth-Century England." *Eighteenth-Century Life.* **9**.3 (1985): 61–74.

Bullough, Vern and Bonnie Bullough. *Women and Prostitution: a Social History.* Buffalo: Prometheus Books, 1987.

"Burlesque Mania." Editorial. *The New York Times* 5 February 1869: 5.

"The Burlesque Mania." Editorial. *The Spirit of the Times* 13 February 1869: 416.

Burn, W. L. *The Age of Equipoise: a Study of the Mid-Victorian Generation.* London: Allen and Unwin, 1964.

Burns, Edward. *Restoration Comedy: Crises of Desire and Identity.* New York: St. Martin's, 1987.

[Butler, George]. "Theatres and Things Theatrical." *The Spirit of the Times.* 8 May 1869: 192.

    "Theatres and Things Theatrical." *The Spirit of the Times* 22 May 1869: 224.

    "Theatres and Things Theatrical." *The Spirit of the Times* 29 May 1869: 240.

    "Theatres and Things Theatrical." *The Spirit of the Times* 5 June 1869: 256.

    "Theatres and Things Theatrical." *The Spirit of the Times* 12 June 1869: 272.

    "Theatres and Things Theatrical." *The Spirit of the Times* 19 June 1869: 288.

    "Theatres and Things Theatrical." *The Spirit of the Times* 7 July 1869: 336.

    "Theatres and Things Theatrical." *The Spirit of the Times* 17 July 1869: 352.

Butler, Judith. *Bodies that Matter: On the Discursive Limits of "Sex."* New York and London: Routledge, 1993.

    Gender Trouble: Feminism and the Subversion of Identity. New York and London: Routledge, 1990.

Cabezas, Amlia Lucía. "Discourses of Prostitution: the Case of Cuba." *Global Sex Workers: Rights, Resistance, and Redefinition.* Eds. Kamala Kempadoo and Jo Doezema. London and New York: Routledge, 1998. 79–86.

Campbell, Rosie. "Invisible Men: Making Visible Male Clients of Female Prostitutes in Merseyside." *Prostitution: On Whores, Hustlers, and Johns.* Eds. James E. Elias, Vern L. Bullough, Veronica Elias, and Gwen Brewer. Amherst, NY: Prometheus Books, 1998. 155–71.

Caputi, Jane. "*Sleeping with the Enemy* as *Pretty Woman*, Part II? Or, What Happened After the Princess Woke up." *Journal of Popular Film & Television.* **19**.1 (1991): 2–8.

Carlo, Ginzburg. "Microhistory. Two or Three Things I Know about It." *Critical Inquiry* **20** (1993): 10–34.

Carlson, Marvin. *Performance: a Critical Introduction.* New York and London: Routledge, 1996.

Carrie. Personal Interview. 17 October 1996, 3 November 1996, 7 November 1996, 21 November 1996.

Carter, Sunny. "A Most Useful Tool." *Sex Work: Writings by Women in the Sex Industry.* 2nd edn. Eds. Priscilla Alexander and Frederique Delacoste. San Francisco: Cleis, 1998. 159–65.

Castle, Terry. *Masquerade and Civilization: the Carnivalesque in Eighteenth-Century English Culture and Fiction.* Stanford: Stanford University Press: 1986.

The Celluloid Closet. Dir. Rob Epstein and Jeffrey Friedman. Home Box Office in association with Channel 4, ZDF/Arte, Brillstein-Grey Entertainment; in association with Hugh M. Hefner, James C. Hormel, Steve Tisch; A Telling Pictures production. 1996.

Certeau, Michel de. *The Practice of Everyday Life.* Trans. Steven Rendall. Berkeley, London: University of California Press, 1984.

 The Writing of History. Trans. Tom Conley. New York: Columbia University Press, 1988.

Chaney, Joseph. "Turning to Men: Genres of Cross-Dressing in Charke's *Narrative* and Shakespeare's *The Merchant of Venice.*" *Introducing Charlotte Charke: Actress, Author, Enigma.* Ed. Philip E. Baruth. Urbana and Chicago: University of Illinois Press, 1998. 200–26.

Chapkis, Wendy. *Live Sex Acts: Women Performing Erotic Labor.* New York: Routledge, 1997.

Chapman, Elizabeth Rachel. *The New Godiva and Other Studies in Social Questions.* London: Unwin, 1885.

Charke, Charlotte. *A Narrative of the Life of Mrs. Charlotte Charke (Youngest Daughter of Colley Cibber, Esq.)* Ed. and with an introduction and notes by Robert Rehder. London: Pickering and Chatto, 1999.

Chatterjee, Partha. *The Nation and its Fragments: Colonial and Postcolonial Histories.* Princeton: Princeton University Press, 1993.

Cherri. Personal Interview. 17 October 1996.

Chetwood, William. *A General History of the Stage.* London, 1749.

Churchill, Sue. " 'I Was What I had Made Myself': Representation and Charlotte Charke." *Biography* 20:1 (1997): 72–94.

Cibber, Colley. *An Apology for the Life of Mr. Colley Cibber, Comedian.* Ed. with an introduction by B. R. S. Fone. Ann Arbor: University of Michigan Press, 1968.

Clapp, Henry Austin. *Reminiscences of a Dramatic Critic with an Essay on the Art of Henry Irving.* Freeport: Books for Libraries, 1972 [1902].

Clark, Anna. "Whores and Gossips: Sexual Reputation in London 1770–1825." *Current Issues in Women's History.* Eds. Arina Angerman, Geerte Binnema, Annamieke Keunen, Vefie Poels, and Jacqueline Zirkzee. New York and London: Routledge, 1989. 231–48.

Cohen, Patricia Cline. *The Murder of Helen Jewett: the Life and Death of a Prostitute in Nineteenth-Century New York.* New York: Vintage Books, 1999.

Coleman, Patrick. "Introduction: Life-writing and the Legitimation of the Modern Self." *Representations of the Self from the Renaissance to Romanticism.* Eds. Patrick Coleman, Jayne Lewis, and Jill Kowalik. Cambridge: Cambridge University Press, 2000. 1–15.

Coleman, Patrick, Jayne Lewis, and Jill Kowalik, eds. *Representations of the Self from the Renaissance to Romanticism.* Cambridge: Cambridge University Press, 2000.

Connelly, Mark Thomas. *The Response to Prostitution in the Progressive Era.* Chapel Hill: University of North Carolina Press, 1980.

Cooks, Leda M., Mark P. Orbe, and Carol S. Bruess. "The Fairy Tale Theme in Popular Culture: a Semiotic Analysis of *Pretty Woman.*" *Women's Studies in Communication* **16.2** (1993): 86–104.

"A Cowardly Assault." *The Chicago Times* 27 February 1869: 6.

Craik, Jennifer. *The Face of Fashion: Cultural Studies in Fashion.* London: Routledge, 1994.

Crouch, Kimberly. "The Public Life of Actresses: Prostitutes or Ladies?" *Gender in Eighteenth-Century England: Roles, Representations, and Responsibilities.* Eds. Hannah Barker and Elaine Chalus. New York: Addison Wesley Longman, 1997. 58–78.

Curry, Ramona. *Too Much of a Good Thing: Mae West as Cultural Icon.* Minneapolis and London: University of Minnesota Press, 1996.

D'Acci, Julie. *Defining Women: Television and the Case of Cagney and Lacey.* Chapel Hill and London: University of North Carolina Press, 1994.

Darrell. Personal Interview. 17 October 1996.

Davidson, Julia O'Connell. *Prostitution, Power, and Freedom.* Ann Arbor: University of Michigan Press, 1998.

Davis, Nanette J. "From Victims to Survivors: Working with Recovering Street Prostitutes." *Sex for Sale: Prostitution, Pornography, and the Sex Industry.* Ed. Ronald Weitzer. London and New York: Routledge, 2000. 139–55.

Prostitution: an International Handbook on Trends, Problems, and Policies. Westport, CT: Greenwood Press, 1993.

Davis, Tracy C. *Actresses as Working Women: Their Social Identity in Victorian Culture.* London and New York: Routledge, 1991.

Dekker, Rudolf M. and Lotte D. van de Pol. *The Tradition of Female Transvestism in Early Modern Europe.* New York: St. Martin's, 1989.

Delacoste, Frederique and Priscilla Alexander, eds. *Sexwork: Writings by Women in the Sex Industy.* Pittsburgh and San Francisco: Cleis Press, 1998.

Denlinger, Elizabeth C. "'A Wink from the Bagnio': Jocular Representations of Prostitutes in Prints in Late Eighteenth-Century London." *Biblion* **9.1–2** (2000): 71–86.

DeRitter, Jones. "'Not the Person she Conceived me': The Public Identities of Charlotte Charke." *Sexual Artifice: Persons, Images, Politics.* [Genders 19]. Eds. Ann Kibbie, Kayann Short, and Abouali Farmanfarmaian. New York and London: New York University Press, 1994. 3–25.

Dixon, Dwight and Joan K. Dixon. "She-Male Prostitutes: Who are they, What do they do, and Why do they do it?" *Prostitution: On Whores, Hustlers, and*

Johns. Eds. James E. Elias, Vern L. Bullough, Veronica Elias, and Gwen Brewer. Amherst, NY: Prometheus Books, 1998. 260–66.

Doherty, Thomas. *Pretty Woman. Cineaste* **16** (1990): 40–41.

Dolan, Jill. *The Feminist Spectator as Critic*. Ann Arbor: University of Michigan Press, 1988.

Donoghue, Emma. *Passions Between Women: British Lesbian Culture 1668–1801*. New York: Harper Collins, 1995 (1993).

Doty, Alexander. *Making Things Perfectly Queer: Interpreting Mass Culture*. Minneapolis and London: University of Minnesota Press, 1993.

Douglas, Susan. *Where the Girls Are: Growing Up Female with the Mass Media*. New York: Random House, 1994.

Downes, John. *Roscius Anglicanus*. Eds. Judith Milhous and Robert D. Hume. London: Society for Theatre Research, 1987.

Dressler, David. "Burlesque as a Cultural Phenomenon." Diss. New York University, 1937.

Dryden, John. *The Conquest of Granada II*. Ed. Mark S. Auburn, London 1981.
  Marriage a la Mode. Ed. Mark S. Auburn, London 1981.
  Secret Love. Ed. Mark S. Auburn, London 1981.

Dumas, Alexandre *fils. La Dame aux Camélias*. Ed. Stephen S. Stanton. New York: Hill and Wang, 1957.

Dunbar, Janet. *Peg Woffington and her World*. Boston: Houghton Mifflin, 1968.

Duneier, Mitchell with Photographs by Ovie Carter. *Sidewalk*. New York: Farrar, Straus and Giroux, 1999.

Dwayne. Personal Interview. 17 October 1996.

Dworkin, Andrea. *Intercourse*. New York: Free Press, 1987.
  Pornography: Men Possessing Women. New York: Perigree Books, 1979.

Dyer, Richard. *Stars*. 1979. London: British Film Institute, 1998.

Elias, James E., Vern L. Bullough, Veronica Elias, and Gwen Brewer, eds. *Prostitution: On Whores, Hustlers, and Johns*. Amherst, NY: Prometheus Books, 1998.

Ells, George and Stanley Musgrove. *Mae West*. London: Robson Books, 1984.

Epstein, Julia and Kristina Straub, eds. *Body Guards: the Cultural Politics of Gender Ambiguity*. New York: Routledge, 1991.

Faber, Doris. *Love and Rivalry: Three Exceptional Pairs of Sisters*. New York: Viking Press, 1983.

Faderman, Lillian. *Surpassing the Love of Men: Romantic Friendship and Love Between Women from the Renaissance to the Present*. New York: William Morrow and Company, 1981.

Ferris, Leslie, ed. *Crossing the Stage: Controversies on Cross-Dressing*. London: Routledge, 1993.

Fields, Polly S. "Charlotte Charke and the Liminality of Bi-Genderings: a Study of her Canonical Works." *Pilgrimage for Love: Essays in Early Modern Literature in Honor of Josephine A. Roberts*. Ed. Sigrid King. Tempe, AZ: Arizona Center for Medieval and Renaissance Studies, 1999. 221–48.

Finkelstein, Joanne. *Fashion: an Introduction.* New York: New York University Press, 1996.

The Fashioned Self. Philadelphia: Temple University Press, 1991.

Fiske, John. *Television Culture.* London and New York: Routledge, 1989. (Methuen 1987).

Folkenflik, Robert. "Charlotte Charke: Images and Afterimages." *Introducing Charlotte Charke: Actress, Author, Enigma.* Ed. Philip E. Baruth. Urbana and Chicago: University of Illinois Press, 1998. 137–61.

Culture of Autobiography: Constructions of Self-Representation. Stanford: Stanford University Press, 1993.

"Gender, Genre, and Theatricality in the Autobiography of Charlotte Charke." *Representations of the Self from the Renaissance to Romanticism.* Eds. Patrick Coleman, Jayne Lewis, and Jill Kowalik. Cambridge: Cambridge University Press, 2000. 97–116.

Foucault, Michel. *The Archaeology of Knowledge and the Discourse on Language.* Trans. A. M. Sheridan Smith. New York: Pantheon Books: 1972.

The History of Sexuality 1: an Introduction. Trans. Robert Hurley. New York: Vintage Books, 1990.

"Nietzsche, Genealogy, History." Trans. Donald F. Bouchard and Sherry Simon. *The Foucault Reader.* Ed. Paul Rabinow. New York: Pantheon, 1984. 76–100.

Friedli, Lynn. " 'Passing Women' – A Study of Gender Boundaries in the Eighteenth Century." *Sexual Underworlds of the Enlightenment.* Eds. G. S. Rousseau and Roy Porter. Chapel Hill: University of North Carolina Press, 1988. 234–60.

Gänzl, Kurt. *Lydia Thompson: Queen of Burlesque.* New York and London: Routledge, 2002.

Garber, Marjorie. *Vested Interests: Cross-Dressing and Cultural Anxiety.* New York: Routledge, 1992.

Gauntlett, David. *Web.Studies: Rewiring Media Studies for the Digital Age.* London: Arnold, 2000.

Gibson, Barrett. *Male Order: Life Stories from Boys Who Sell Sex.* London: Cassell, 1995.

Gilder, Rosamund. *Enter the Actress: the First Women in Theatre.* New York: Theatre Arts Books, 1960.

Gilfoyle, Timothy J. *City of Eros: New York City, Prostitution, and the Commercialization of Sex, 1790–1920.* New York and London: Norton, 1993.

Gill, Pat. *Interpreting Ladies: Women, Wit and Morality in the Restoration Comedy of Manners.* Athens: University of Georgia Press, 1994.

Giroux, Henry. *Disturbing Pleasures: Learning Popular Culture.* New York and London: Routledge, 1994.

Goffman, Erving. *The Presentation of Self in Everyday Life.* Garden City: Doubleday Anchor Books, 1959.

Relations in Public: Microstudies of the Public Order. New York: Basic Books, 1971.

Stigma: Notes on the Management of Spoiled Identity. Middlesex: Penguin, 1968.

Goodson, Teri. "A Prostitute Joins NOW." *Whores and Other Feminists.* Ed. Jill Nagle. New York and London: Routledge, 1997. 248–51.

Gray, Herman. *Watching Race: Television and the Struggle for "Blackness."* Minneapolis and London: University of Minneapolis Press, 1995.

Greenberg, Harvey Roy. "Rescrewed: *Pretty Woman*'s Co-opted Feminism." *Journal of Popular Film and Television* **19**.1 (1991): 9–13.

Greg, William Rathbone. "Prostitution." *Westminster Review* **53** (1850): 448–506.

Grossberg, Lawrence. *Dancing in Spite of Myself: Essays in Popular Culture.* Durham, NC and London: Duke University Press, 1997.

Habermas, Jürgen. *The Structural Transformation of the Public Sphere.* Trans. Thomas Burger with Frederick Lawrence. Cambridge, MA: Massachusetts Institute of Technology Press, 1991.

Hall, Gladys Mary. *Prostitution in the Modern World.* 1936. New York and London: Garland Publishing Inc., 1979.

Hall, Stuart "The Problem of Ideology: Marxism without Guarantees". *Stuart Hall: Critical Dialogues in Cultural Studies.* Eds. David Morley and Kuan-Hsing Chen. London and New York: Routledge, 1996. 25–46.

Haller, John S. and Robin M. Haller. *The Physician and Sexuality in Victorian America.* Urbana: University of Illinois Press, 1974.

Hamilton, Marybeth. "Mae West Live: *Sex, The Drag,* and 1920s Broadway." *TDR* **36**.4 (1992): 82–100.

The Queen of Camp: Mae West, Sex, and Popular Culture. London: Pandora, 1996.

When I'm Bad, I'm Better: Mae West, Sex, and American Entertainment. Los Angeles: University of California Press, 1997.

Harbin, Billy J. "Monty Woolley: the Public and Private Man from Saratoga Springs." *Passing Performances: Queer Readings of Leading Players in American Theater History.* Eds. Robert A. Schanke and Kim Marra. Ann Arbor: University of Michigan Press, 1998. 262–79.

Harris, Barbara. "Marriage, Sixteenth-Century Style: Elizabeth Stafford and the Third Duke of Norfolk." *Journal of Social History* **15** (1981): 371–82.

Henderson, Alexander. Letter. *New York Times* 31 May 1869: 5.

Henderson, Tony. *Disorderly Women in Eighteenth-Century London: Prostitution and Control in the Metropolis, 1730–1830.* London and New York: Longman, 1999.

Highfill, Philip H. Kalman, A. Burnim, and Edward A. Langhans, Eds. *A Biographical Dictionary of Actors, Actresses, Musicians, Dancers, etc. in London, 1660–1800.* Carbondale and Edwardsville: University of Southern Illinois Press, 1973.

Hill, Bridget, ed. and comp. *Eighteenth-Century Women: an Anthology.* London, Boston, Sydney: Allen and Unwin, 1984.

Hill, Marilyn Wood. *Their Sisters' Keepers: Prostitution in New York City, 1830–1870.* Berkeley and Los Angeles: University of California Press, 1993.

Hochschild, Arlie Russell. *The Managed Heart: Commercialization of Human Feeling.* Berkeley: University of California Press, 1983.

Hooker, Isabella Beecher. *Womanhood: Its Sanctitites and Fidelities*. Boston: Lee and Shepard; New York: Lee, Shepard, and Dillingham, 1873(?).

Houlbrooke, Ralph. *English Family Life, 1576–1716: an Anthology from Diaries*. New York: Basil Blackwell, 1988.

Howe, Elizabeth. *The First English Actresses: Women and Drama 1660–1700*. Cambridge: Cambridge University Press, 1992.

Howells, William Dean. "The New Taste in Theatricals." *Atlantic Monthly*. May 1869: 635–644.

Hughes, Derek. *English Drama, 1660–1700*. Oxford: Clarendon Press, 1996.

Hull, Suzanne W. *Chaste, Silent and Obedient: English Books for Women, 1475–1640*. San Marino: Huntington Library, 1982.

Inness, Sherrie A. *Tough Girls: Women Warriors and Wonder Women in Popular Culture*. Philadelphia, University of Pennsylvania Press, 1999.

Review of *Ixion*. *New York Times* 1 October 1868: 6.

Johnson, Merri Lisa, ed. *Jane Sexes It Up: The Truth about Feminist Desire*. Four Walls: Eight Windows Press, 2001.

Jones, Vivien. "Eighteenth-Century Prostitution: Feminist Debates and the Writing of Histories." *Body Matters: Feminism, Textuality, Corporeality*. Eds. Avril Horner and Angela Keane. Manchester and New York: Mancheser University Press, 2000. 127–42.

"Placing Jemima: Women Writers of the 1790s and the Eighteenth-Century Prostitution Narrative." *Women's Writing* **4.2** (1997): 201–20.

Jones, Vivien, ed. *Women and Literature in Britain, 1700–1800*. Cambridge: Cambridge University Press, 2000.

Jones, Vivien, ed. and comp. *Women in the Eighteenth Century: Constructions of Femininity*. New York and London: Routledge, 1990.

Jordan, R. J. "Some Restoration Playgoers." *Theatre Notebook: a Journal of the History and Technique of the British Theatre* 35 (1981): 51–57.

Joyner, William. *The Roman Empress*. London, 1671.

Judge, Henry. *Our Fallen Sisters. The Great Social Evil. Prostitution: Its Cause, Effect, So Called Use, Decided Abuse, and Only Cure or Remedy*. London: Peckham, 1874.

Kahn, Madeline. "Teaching Charlotte Charke: Feminism, Pedagogy, and the Construction of the Self." *Introducing Charlotte Charke: Actress, Author, Enigma*. Ed. Philip E. Baruth. Urbana and Chicago: University of Illinois Press, 1998. 162–79.

Keeble, N. H., ed. and comp. *The Cultural Identity of Seventeenth-Century Woman: A Reader*. London and New York: Routledge, 1994.

Kelley, Karol. "A Modern Cinderella." *Journal of American Culture* **17.1** (1994): 87–92.

Kempadoo, Kamala. "The Migrant Tightrope: Experiences from the Caribbean." *Global Sex Workers: Rights, Resistance, and Redefinition*. Eds. Kamala Kempadoo and Jo Doezema. London and New York: Routledge, 1998. 124–38.

Kendall. "Ways of Looking at *Agnes de Castro* (1695): a Lesbian History Play at WOW Café." *Upstaging Big Daddy: Directing Theatre as if Gender and Race*

Mattered. Eds. Ellen Donkin and Susan Clement. Ann Arbor: University of Michigan Press, 1993.

Kenny, Shirley Strum, ed. *British Theatre and Other Arts, 1660–1800*. Washington: Folger Shakespeare Library; London: Associated University Presses, 1984.

Ketchum, Michael G. "Setting and Self-Presentation in the Restoration and Early Eighteenth Century." *Studies in English Literature 1500–1900* **23**.3 (1989): 399–417.

Kevin. Personal Interview. 15 October 1996, 22 October 1996, 12 November 1996. Telephone Interview. 13 November 1996.

Kincaid, James R. *Child-Loving: the Erotic Child and Victorian Culture*. New York and London: Routledge, 1992.

King, Thomas A. "'As if [She] Were Made on Purpose to Put the Whole World into Good Humour': Reconstructing the First English Actresses." *TDR* **32** (1992): 78–104.

Kirby, Michael. "Acting and Not-Acting." *Acting [Re] Considered: Theories and Practices*. Ed. Phillip Zarrilli. London: Routledge, 1994. 153–69.

Kishtainy, Khalid. *The Prostitute in Progressive Literature*. London and New York: Alison and Busby, 1982.

Knox, Michael P. "Negotiations and Relationships among Male Sex Workers and Clients in Liverpool, Merseyside, United Kingdom." *Prostitution: On Whores, Hustlers, and Johns*. Eds. James E. Elias, Vern L. Bullough, Veronica Elias, and Gwen Brewer. Amherst, NY: Prometheus Books, 1998. 236–59.

Kristeen. Personal Interview. 7 November 1996, 16 November 1996, 29 November 1996.

Kugelmass, Jack. *Masked Culture: the Greenwich Village Halloween Parade*. New York: Columbia University Press, 1994.

Kuhn, Annette. *Women's Pictures: Feminism and Cinema*. London: Routledge and Kegan Paul, 1982.

Lanier, H. W. *The First English Actresses from 1660–1700*. New York: G. S. Scribner and Sons, 1932.

Lapsley, Robert and Michael Westlake. "From *Casablanca* to *Pretty Woman*: the Politics of Romance." *Screen* **33**.1 (1992): 27–49.

Leach, Joseph. *Bright Particular Star: the Life and Times of Charlotte Cushman*. New Haven and London: Yale University Press, 1970.

Leeson, Margaret. *The Memoirs of Mrs Leeson, Madam*. Ed. and introduction Mary Lyons. Dublin: Lilliput Press, 1995.

"The Leg and the Legitimate Drama." Editorial. *Chicago Times* 19 February 1870: 3.

Leibman, Nina C. *Living Room Lectures: The Fifties Family in Film and Television*. Austin: University of Texas Press, 1995.

Leider, Emily Wortis. *Becoming Mae West*. New York: DeCapo Press, 2000.

Leigh, Carol. "The Continuing Saga of Scarlot Harlot I–X." *Sex Work: Writings by Women in the Sex Industry*. Eds. Frederique Delacoste and Priscilla Alexander. Pittsburgh and San Francisco: Cleis Press, 1998. 32–34, 41–42, 59–61, 88–90, 98, 106–107, 123–24, 147, 157, 181–82.

Leonard, Maurice. *Mae West, Empress of Sex.* London: Harper Collins, 1991.

Lesley. Personal Interview. 22 November 1996. 30 November 1996. 3 December 1996.

Lever, Janet and Deanne Dolnick. "Clients and Call Girls: Seeking Sex and Intimacy." *Sex for Sale: Prostitution, Pornography, and the Sex Industry.* Ed. Ronald Weitzer. New York and London: Routledge, 2000. 85–100.

Levi-Strauss, Claude. *The Savage Mind.* 1966. London: Weidenfeld and Nicholson, 1972.

Levine, Laurence. *Highbrow/Lowbrow: the Emergence of Cultural Hierarchy in America.* Cambridge: Harvard University Press, 1988.

Liesenfeld, Vincent J. *The Licensing Act of 1737.* Madison, WI and London: University of Wisconsin Press, 1984.

Lloyd, Richard. *For Money or Love: Boy Prostitution in America.* New York: Vanguard Press, 1976.

Logan, Olive. *Apropos of Women and the Theatre, with a Paper or Two on Parisian Topics.* New York: Carleton Publishers, London: S. Low, Son, and Co. 1869.
Before the Footlights and Behind the Scenes. Philadelphia: Parmalee and Co. 1870.
"The Leg Business." *Galaxy,* 1867: 40+.
"The Nude Woman Question." *Packard's Monthly,* 1869: 193+.

Logan, William. *An Exposure, from Personal Observation, of Female Prostitution in London, Leeds, and Rochdale, and Especially in the City of Glasgow; with Remarks on the Cause, Extent, Results and Remedy of the Evil.* Glasgow: G. Gallie and R. Fleckfield, 1843.
The Great Social Evil: Its Causes, Extent, Results, and Remedies. London: Hodder and Stoughton, 1871.

Lott, Eric. *Love and Theft: Blackface Minstrelsy and the American Working Class.* New York and Oxford: Oxford University Press, 1993.

Lurie, Alison. *The Language of Clothes.* 1981. London: Bloomsbury Press, 1992.

MacCannell, Dean. "Staged Authenticity: Arrangements of Social Space in Tourist Settings." *American Journal of Sociology* **79**.3 (1973): 89–118.

MacFarlane, Alan. *The Family Life of Ralph Josselin; a Seventeenth-Century Clergyman: an Essay in Historical Anthropology.* Cambridge: Cambridge University Press, 1970.
Marriage and Love in England: Modes of Reproduction 1300–1840. London: Basil Blackwell, 1986.

Mackie, Erin. "Desperate Measures: the Narratives of the Life of Mrs. Charlotte Charke." *ELH* **58** (1991): 841–65.

MacKinnon, Catherine. *Feminism Unmodified: Discourses on Life and Law.* Cambridge and London: Harvard University Press, 1987.

Mahood, Linda. *The Magdalenes: Prostitution in the Nineteenth Century.* London and New York: Routledge, 1990.

Mandeville, Bernard. *A Modest Defence of Public Stews: or an Essay upon Whoring, As it is Now Practis'd in these Kingdoms.* London: AMS Publishing, 2001.

Marsden, Jean I. "Charlotte Charke and the Cibbers: Private Life as Public Spectacle." *Introducing Charlotte Charke: Actress, Author, Enigma.* Ed. Philip E. Baruth. Urbana and Chicago: University of Illinois Press, 1998. 65–82.
    "Rewritten Women: Shakespearean Heroines in the Restoration." *The Appropriation of Shakespeare: Post-Renaissance Reconstruction of the Works and the Myth.* Ed. Jean I. Marsden. New York: St. Martin's, 1991. 43–56.
Maus, Katharine Eisaman. " 'Playhouse Flesh and Blood': Sexual Ideology and the Restoration Actress." *English Literary History* **46** (1979): 595–617.
McClintock, Ann. "Screwing the System: Sexwork, Race, and the Law." *Boundary* **2.19** (1992): 70–95.
McKeon, Michael. "Historicizing Patriarchy: the Emergence of Gender Difference in England, 1660–1760." *Eighteenth Century Studies.* **28**: 295–322.
Meisel, Martin. *Shaw and the Nineteenth-Century Theater.* Princeton: Princeton University Press, 1963.
Merrill, Lisa. *When Romeo Was a Woman: Charlotte Cushman and her Circle of Female Spectators.* Ann Arbor: University of Michigan Press, 1999.
Meshella. Personal Interview. 18 November 1996.
Milhous, Judith. "Elizabeth Bowtell and Elizabeth Davenport: Some Puzzles Solved." *Theatre Notebook* **39** (1985): 124– 33.
    Thomas Betterton and the Management of Lincoln's Inn Fields, 1695–1708. Carbondale: Southern Illinois University Press, 1979.
Milhous, Judith and Robert Hume. *Producible Interpretation: Eight English Plays 1675–1707.* Carbondale: Southern Illinois University Press, 1985.
Miller, James. *Prostitution Considered in Relation to its Cause and Cure.* Edinburgh: Sutherland and Knox Press, 1859.
Miner, Madonne. "No Matter what they Say, It's All about Money." *Journal of Popular Film and Television* **20** (1992): 8–14.
"Minor Topics." *New York Times* 1 June 1869: 4.
"Minor Topics." *New York Times* 2 June 1869: 2.
Mittell, Jason. "Invisible Footage: Industry on Parade and Television Historiography." *Film History* **9:2** (1997): 200– 18.
Mizejewski, Linda. *Ziegfeld Girl: Image and Icon in Culture and Cinema.* Durham and London: Duke University Press, 1999.
Montgomery, Heather. "Children, Prostitution, and Identity: a Case Study from a Tourist Resort in Thailand." *Global Sex Workers: Rights, Resistance, and Redefinition.* Eds. Kamala Kempadoo and Jo Doezema. London and New York: Routledge, 1998. 139–50.
Moore, Lisa. " 'She Was Too Fond of her Mistaken Bargain': The Scandalous Relations of Gender and Sexuality in Feminist Theory." *Diacritics* **21**: 2–3 (1991): 89–101.
Morgan, Fidelis. *The Well-Known Troublemaker: a Life of Charlotte Charke.* London: Faber and Faber, 1988.
Morrison, Toni. *Playing in the Dark: Whiteness and the Literary Imagination.* New York: Vintage Books, 1993.
"Mr. Henderson and The British Burlesque System." Editorial. *New York Times* 8 June 1869: 4.

Mullaney, Steven. "Strange Things, Gross Terms, Curious Customs: the Rehearsal of Cultures in the Late Renaissance." *Representations* 1.3 (1983): 40–67.

Murray, Allison. *No Money, No Honey: a Study of Street Traders and Prostitutes in Jakarta.* Singapore: Oxford University Press, 1991.

Nagle, Jill. *Whores and Other Feminists.* New York: Routledge, 1997.

Nead, Linda. *Myths of Sexuality: Representations of Women in Great Britain.* Oxford: Basil Blackwell, 1988.

Nelson, T. G. A. "Women of Pleasure." *Eighteenth-Century Life* 11.1 (1987): 181–98.

Newcastle, Duchess of (Margaret Cavendish). *Poems and Fancies.* 1653. Menston: Scholar Press, 1972.

Nicoll, Allardyce. *History of English Drama I.* Cambridge: Cambridge University Press, 1929.

Norberg, Kathryn. "From Courtesan to Prostitute: Mercenary Sex and Venereal Disease, 1730–1802." *The Secret Malady: Venereal Disease in Eighteenth-Century Britain and France.* Ed. Linda E. Merians. Lexington: University Press of Kentucky, 1996.

Nussbaum, Felicity A. "Afterword: Charke's 'Variety of Wretchedness'." *Introducing Charlotte Charke: Actress, Author, Enigma.* Ed. Philip E. Baruth. Urbana and Chicago: University of Illinois Press, 1998. 227–43.

The Autobiographical Subject: Gender and Ideology in Eighteenth-Century England. Baltimore and London: Johns Hopkins University Press, 1989.

Torrid Zones: Maternity, Sexuality, and Empire in Eighteenth-Century English Narratives. Baltimore and London: Johns Hopkins University Press, 1995.

Parish, James Robert. *Prostitution in Hollywood Films: Plots, Critiques, Casts and Credits for 389 Theatrical and Made-for-Television Releases.* Jefferson, North Carolina and London: McFarland and Company, Inc., 1992.

Parker, Derek. *Nell Gwyn.* Phoenix Mill, Thrupp, Stroud, Gloucestershire: Sutton Publishing Limited, 2000.

Pattullo, Polly. *Last Resorts: the Cost of Tourism in the Caribbean.* London: Cassell, 1996.

Payne, Deborah C. "Reified Object of Emergent Professional? Retheorizing the Restoration Actress." *Cultural Readings of Restoration and Eighteenth-Century English Theater.* Eds. J. Douglas Canfield and Deborah C. Payne. Athens: University of Georgia Press, 1995. 13–38.

Pearson, Jacqueline. *The Prostituted Muse: Images of Women and Women Dramatists, 1642–1737.* New York: St. Martin's, 1988.

Peavy, Charles D. "The Chimerical Career of Charlotte Charke." *Restoration and Eighteenth-Century Theatre Research* 8 (1969): 1–12.

Peiss, Kathy. *Cheap Amusements: Working Women and Leisure in Turn-of-the-Century New York.* Philadelphia: Temple University Press, 1986.

Pepys, Samuel. *The Diary of Samuel Pepys: a New and Complete Transcription.* Eds. Robert Latham and William Matthews. Berkeley: University of California Press, 2000.

Phelan, Peggy. *Mourning Sex: Performing Public Memories.* New York and London: Routledge, 1997.

Unmarked: Politics of Performance. London and New York: Routledge, 1993.

[Pickle, Peregrine]. "The World of Amusement." *The Chicago Tribune* 21 November 1869: 4.

"The World of Amusement." *The Chicago Tribune* 20 February 1870: 3.

Pinero, Arthur Wing. *Iris.* London: William Heinemann, 1902.

Letty. London: William Heinemann, 1899.

The Notorious Mrs. Ebbsmith. London: William Heinemann, 1900.

The Second Mrs. Tanqueray. London: William Heinemann, 1894.

Pollock, Della. "Performing Writing." *The Ends of Performance.* Eds. Peggy Phelan and Jill Lane. New York and London: New York University Press, 1998, 73–103.

Poovey, Mary. *Uneven Developments: the Ideological Work of Gender in Mid-Victorian England.* Chicago: University of Chicago Press, 1988.

Porter, Roy. "Introduction." *Rewriting the Self: Histories from the Renaissance to the Present.* Ed. Roy Porter. London and New York: Routledge, 1997. 1–16.

Poster, Mark. *Cultural History and Postmodernity: Disciplinary Readings and Challenges.* New York: Columbia University Press, 1997.

Press Information. www.salon.com/aboutsalon/index.html. [Accessed On-line 17 February 2001].

Pretty Woman. Dir. Garry Marshall. Touchstone Films, 1990.

Pullen, Kirsten. "Co-Ed Call Girls: Prostitution and the Third Wave." *Jane Sexes it Up: the Truth about Feminist Desire.* Ed. Merri Lisa Johson. Four Walls: Eight Windows Press, 2001. 207–30.

"They Never Raided Minsky's: Popular Memory and the Performance of History." *Performance Research* 7(4): 116–121.

Quaife, G. R. *Wanton Wenches and Wayward Wives: Peasants and Illicit Sex in Early Seventeenth Century England.* New Brunswick: Rutgers University Press, 1979.

Quan, Tracy. "Diary of a Manhattan Call Girl." Salon June 1998–January 2000. http//:www.salon.com/urge.html.

"The Littlest Harlot: Barbie's Career as Role Model." *Whores and Other Feminists.* Ed. Jill Nagle. New York and London: Routledge, 1997. 119–24.

Queen, Carol. *Real Live Nude Girl: Chronicles of Sex-Positive Culture.* San Francisco: Cleis, 1997.

Quinn, James. *The Life of Mr. James Quinn, Comedian.* London: S. Bladon, 1766.

Radner, John B. "The Youthful Harlot's Curse: the Prostitute as Symbol of the City in Eighteenth-Century English Literature." *Eighteenth-Century Life* **2** (1976): 59–64.

"The Raid of the Prostitutes." *The Chicago Times* 26 February 1870: 2.

Roach, Joseph R. *The Player's Passion: Studies in the Science of Acting.* Ann Arbor: University of Michigan Press, 1993.

Roberts, David. *The Ladies: Female Patronage of Restoration Drama 1660–1700.* Oxford: Clarendon, 1989.

Roberts, Nickie. *Frontline: Women in the Sex Industry Speak.* London: Grafton Press, 1986.

Whores in History: Prostitution in Western Society. London: Harper Collins, 1992.

Robertson, Pamela. *Guilty Pleasures: Feminist Camp from Mae West to Madonna.* Durham and London: Duke University Press, 1996.

Rogers, Pat. "Breeches Roles." *Sexuality in Eighteenth-Century Britain.* Ed. Paul Gabriel Bouce. Manchester: Oxford University Press, 1982. 244–58.

Rosen, Ruth. *The Lost Sisterhood: Prostitution in the United States 1900–1918.* Baltimore: Johns Hopkins University Press, 1982.

The Mamie Papers. Radcliffe College, 1977.

Rosenthal, Laura J. "Reading Marks: the Actress and the Spectatrix in Restoration Shakespeare." *Broken Boundaries: Women and Feminism in Restoration Drama.* Ed. Katherine M. Quinsey. Lexington: University of Kentucky Press, 1996. 201–18.

Sanger, William W., MD. *The History of Prostitution: Its Extent, Causes and Effects Throughout the World.* 1859. New York: Eugenics Publishing Company, 1937.

Schanke, Robert A. and Kim Marra, eds. *Passing Performances: Queer Readings of Leading Players in American Theater History.* Ann Arbor: University of Michigan Press. 1998.

Schissel, Lillian. *Three Plays: Sex, The Drag, and The Pleasure Man.* Ed. Lillian Schissel. London: Nick Hern Books, 1997.

Schwoerer, Lois G. "Seventeenth-Century English Women Engraved in Stone?" *Albion* 16 (1994): 389–403.

Scott, George Ryley. *The History of Prostitution.* 1968. London: Senate, 1996.

Scouten, Arthur Hawley. "A Reconsideration of the King's Company Casts in John Downes' *Roscius Anglicanus.*" *Theatre Notebook* 40 (1986): 74–85.

Senelick, Laurence. "Boys and Girls Together: Subcultural Origins of Glamour Drag and Male Impersonation on the Nineteenth-Century Stage." *Crossing the Stage: Controversies on Cross-Dressing.* Ed. Lesley Ferris. London and New York: Routledge, 1993. 80–95.

The Changing Room: Sex, Drag and Theatre. London and New York: Routledge, 2000.

Sharpe, Kevin and Steven Zwicker. "Introduction: Refiguring Revolutions." *Refiguring Revolutions: Aesthetics and Politics from the English Revolution to the Romantic Revolution.* Eds. Kevin Sharpe and Steven Zwicker. Berkeley, Los Angeles, London: University of California Press, 1998. 1–21.

Shershow, Scott Cutter. *Puppets and "Popular" Culture.* Ithaca: Cornell University Press, 1995.

Shaw, George Bernard. *Plays: Man and Superman, Arms and the Man, Mrs. Warren's Profession and Candida.* New York: Signet Classics, 1960.

Sinfield, Alan. *Faultlines: Cultural Materialism and the Politics of Dissident Reading.* Berkeley and Los Angeles: University of California Press, 1992.

Skee, Mickey. "Tricks of the Trade." *Frontiers* 16 (August 22): 43.

Slamah, Khartini. "Transgenders and Sex Work in Malaysia." *Global Sex Workers: Rights, Resistance, and Redefinition.* Eds. Kamala Kempadoo and Jo Doezema. London and New York: Routledge, 1998. 210–14.

Smallwood, Angela J. "Women and the Theatre." *Women and Literature in Britain, 1700–1800*. Ed. Vivien Jones. Cambridge: Cambridge University Press, 2000.

Smith, Sidonie. *A Poetics of Women's Autobiography: Marginality and the Fictions of Self-Representation*. Bloomington and Indianapolis: Indiana University Press, 1987.

Smith-Rosenberg, Carroll. *Disorderly Conduct: Visions of Gender in Victorian America*. New York and Oxford: Oxford University Press, 1985.

Sobel, Bernard. *Burleycue: an Underground History of Burlesque Days*. New York: Farrar and Rhinehart, 1931.

Spacks, Patricia Meyer. *Imagining a Self: Autobiography and Novel in Eighteenth-Century England*. Cambridge and London: Harvard University Press, 1976.

Spongberg, Mary. *Feminizing Venereal Disease: the Body of the Prostitute in Nineteenth-Century Discourse*. New York City: New York University Press, 1997.

St. James, Margo. "The Reclamation of Whores." *Good Girls/Bad Girls. Feminists and Sex Trade Workers Face to Face*. Ed. Laurie Bell. Seattle: Seal Press, 1987, 81–91.

Stallybrass, Peter and Allon White. *The Politics and Poetics of Transgression*. Ithaca: Cornell University Press, 1986.

Stansell, Christine. *City of Women: Sex and Class in New York, 1789–1860*. Urbana and Chicago: University of Illinois Press, 1987.

Stebbins, Emma. *Charlotte Cushman: her Letters and Memories of her Life*. New York: Benjamin Blom Inc., 1972 [1879].

Steele, Valerie. *Fashion and Eroticism: Ideas of Feminine Beauty from the Victorian Age to the Jazz Age*. New York and Oxford: Oxford University Press, 1982.
    Fetish: Fashion, Sex and Power. Oxford and New York: Oxford University Press, 1996.

Stone, Lawrence. *The Family, Sex and Marriage in England 1500–1800*. (Abridged edn.) New York: Harper Colophon Books, 1979.

Stone Jr., George Winchester. "The Making of the Repertory." *The London Theatre World, 1660–1800*. Ed. Robert D. Hume. Carbondale and Edwardsville: Southern Illinois University Press, 1980. 181–209.

Storey, Wilbur. "Blondes in a Nutshell." *Chicago Times* 23 Februaray 1870: 4.
    "A Dramatic Prospect." *Chicago Times* 18 February 1870: 4.

Strand, Ginger. "'My Noble Spartacus': Edwin Forrest and Masculinity on the Nineteenth-Century Stage." *Passing Performances: Queer Readings of Leading Players in American Theatre History*. Eds. Robert A. Schanke and Kim Marra. Ann Arbor: University of Michigan Press, 1998. 19–40.

Strange, Sallie Minter. "Charlotte Charke: Transvestite or Conjurer?" *Restoration and Eighteenth-Century Theatre Research* **15** (1976): 54–59.

Straub, Kristina. *Sexual Suspects: Eighteenth-Century Players and Sexual Ideology*. Princeton: Princeton University Press, 1992.

Styan, J. L. *Restoration Comedy in Performance*. Cambridge: Cambridge University Press, 1986.

Summers, Rosie. "Prostitution." *Sex Work: Writings by Women in the Sex Industry.* 2nd edn. Eds. Priscilla Alexander and Frederique Delacoste. San Francisco: Cleis Press, 1998. 113–18.

"The Theatre – the Force of Example." Editorial. *The Spirit of the Times* 31 October 1868: 128.

"Theatres and Things Theatrical." *The Spirit of the Times* 12 September 1868: 81.

"Theatres and Things Theatrical." *The Spirit of the Times* 26 September 1868: 96.

"Theatres and Things Theatrical." *The Spirit of the Times* 10 October 1868: 112.

"Theatres and Things Theatrical." *The Spirit of the Times* 17 October 1868: 144.

"Theatres and Things Theatrical." *The Spirit of the Times* 24 October 1868: 160.

"Theatres and Things Theatrical." *The Spirit of the Times* 14 November 1868: 208.

"Theatres and Things Theatrical." *The Spirit of the Times* 28 November 1868: 240.

"Theatres and Things Theatrical." *The Spirit of the Times* 5 December 1868: 256.

"Theatres and Things Theatrical." *The Spirit of the Times* 9 December 1868: 262.

"Theatres and Things Theatrical." *The Spirit of the Times* 2 January 1869: 320.

"Theatres and Things Theatrical." *The Spirit of the Times* 16 January 1868: 352.

"Theatres and Things Theatrical." *The Spirit of the Times* 20 February 1869: 16.

"Theatres and Things Theatrical." *The Spirit of the Times* 6 March 1869: 48.

"Theatres and Things Theatrical." *The Spirit of the Times* 27 March 1869: 96.

"Theatres and Things Theatrical." *The Spirit of the Times* 15 May 1869: 208.

Thompson, Lydia. Letter. *The Spirit of the Times* 26 September 1868: 96.

Letter. *New York Times* 8 June 1869: 4.

Trouillot, Michel-Rolph. *Silencing the Past: Power and the Production of History.* New York: Beacon Press, 1995.

Trumbach, Randolph. "London's Sapphists: from Three Sexes to Four Genders in the Making of Modern Culture." *Body Guards: the Cultural Politics of Gender Ambiguity.* Eds. Julia Epstein and Kristina Straub. New York and London: Routledge, 1991. 112–41.

Truong, Thanh-Dam. *Sex, Money, and Morality: the Political Economy of Prostitution and Tourism in South East Asia.* London: Zed Books, 1990.

Sex, Money, and Morality: Prostitution and Tourism in Southeast Asia. New York: Palgrave Macmillan, 1990.

Turley, Hans. " 'A Masculine Turn of Mind': Charlotte Charke and the Periodical Press." *Introducing Charlotte Charke: Actress, Author, Enigma.* Ed. Philip E. Baruth. Urbana and Chicago: University of Illinois Press, 1998. 180–99.

Turner, Cheryl. *Living by the Pen: Women Writers in the Eighteenth Century.* New York and London: Routledge, 1992.

Tuska, Jon. *The Films of Mae West.* Seacaucus, NJ: Citadel, 1973.

van Lennep, William et al. *The History of the London Stage: Part One, 1660–1700.* Carbondale: Southern Illinois University Press, 1963.

"The Vindication of Virtue." Editorial. *Chicago Tribune* 26 February 1870: 3.

Walen, Denise A. " 'Such a Romeo We Never Ventured Hope For': Charlotte Cushman." *Passing Performances: Queer Readings of Leading Players in American Theatre History.* Eds. Robert A. Schanke and Kim Marra. Ann Arbor: University of Michigan Press, 1998. 41–62.

Walkowitz, Judith. *Prostitution and Victorian Society: Women, Class, and the State.* Cambridge and London: Cambridge University Press, 1980.

Wanko, Cheryl. "The Eighteenth-Century Actress and the Construction of Gender: Lavinia Fenton and Charlotte Charke." *Eighteenth-Century Life* **18** (1994): 75–90.

Wardlaw, Cecilia. "Dream Turned Nightmare." *Sex Work: Writings by Women in the Sex Industry.* 2nd edn. Eds. Priscilla Alexander and Frederique Delacoste. San Francisco: Cleis, 1998. 108–12.

Watenabe, Satoko. "From Thailand to Japan: Migrant Sex Workers as Autonomous Subjects." *Global Sex Workers: Rights, Resistance, and Redefinition.* Eds. Kamala Kempadoo and Jo Doezema. London and New York: Routledge, 1998. 114–23.

Weber, Harold. "Carolinean Sexuality and the Restoration Stage: Reconstructing the Royal Phallus in *Sodom.*" *Readings of Restoration and Eighteenth-Century English Theater.* Eds. J. Douglas Canfield and Deborah C. Payne. Athens: University of Georgia Press, 1995. 67–88.

"Charles II, George Pines, and Mr. Dorimant: the Politics of Sexual Power in Restoration England." *Criticism.* **32** (1990): 193–219.

West, D. J. *Homosexual Prostitution.* Binghamton, NY: Hawarth, 1993.

West, Mae. *Goodness Had Nothing to Do with It.* Englewood Cliffs, NJ: Prentice Hall, 1959.

Three Plays: Sex, The Drag, and The Pleasure Man. Ed. Lillian Schissel. London: Nick Hern Books, 1997.

Wiegman, Robyn. *American Anatomies: Theorizing Race and Gender.* Durham and London: Duke University Press, 1995.

Wilkes, George. "The Barbe Bleue of the Blonde Ballet Troupe." Editorial. *The Spirit of the Times* 29 May 1869: 232.

"*The Spirit* and the Naked Drama." Editorial. *The Spirit of the Times.* 5 June 1869: 248.

Wilson, J. H. *All the King's Ladies: Actresses of the Restoration.* Chicago: University of Chicago Press, 1958.

Winter, William. *The Wallet of Time.* New York: Moffat, Yard, and Co., 1913.

Working Girls. Dir. Lizzie Borden. Miramax 1986.

Wycherly, William. *The Country Wife. The Plays of William Wycherly.* Ed. Peter Holland. Cambridge: Cambridge University Press, 1981.

The Plain Dealer. The Plays of William Wycherly. Ed. Peter Holland. Cambridge: Cambridge University Press, 1981.

Wynter, Sarah. "WHISPER: Women Hurt in Systems of Prostitution Engaged in Revolt." *Sex Work: Writings by Women in the Sex Industry.* 2nd edn. Eds. Priscilla Alexander and Frederique Delacoste. San Francisco: Cleis, 1998. 266–270.

Young, William C. *Famous Actors and Actresses on the American Stage.* Vol. 2:2. New York and London: R.R. Bowker, 1975.

Zeidman, Irving. *The American Burlesque Show.* New York: Hawthorn Books, 1967.

Index